Patrick O'Brian's
Bodies at Sea

Patrick O'Brian's Bodies at Sea

Sex, Drugs and the Physical Form in the Aubrey-Maturin Novels

MICHAEL LEIGH SINOWITZ

McFarland & Company, Inc., Publishers
Jefferson, North Carolina

LIBRARY OF CONGRESS CATALOGUING-IN-PUBLICATION DATA

Sinowitz, Michael Leigh, author.
    Patrick O'Brian's Bodies at Sea : Sex, Drugs and the Physical Form in the Aubrey-Maturin Novels / Michael Leigh Sinowitz.
    p. cm.
    Includes bibliographical references and index.

    ISBN 978-0-7864-7555-1 (softcover : acid free paper) ∞
    ISBN 978-1-4766-1484-7 (ebook)

    1. O'Brian, Patrick, 1914–2000. Aubrey/Maturin novels.
2. Human body in literature. 3. Mind and body in literature.
I. Title.
PR6029.B55Z83 2014
823'.914—dc23   2014024052

BRITISH LIBRARY CATALOGUING DATA ARE AVAILABLE

© 2014 Michael Leigh Sinowitz. All rights reserved

No part of this book may be reproduced or transmitted in any form or by any means, electronic or mechanical, including photocopying or recording, or by any information storage and retrieval system, without permission in writing from the publisher.

On the cover: Leonardo da Vinci's 1492 drawing of the *Vitruvian Man* superimposed over the 1795 painting *The Victory Leaving the Channel in 1793* by Monamy Swaine

Printed in the United States of America

McFarland & Company, Inc., Publishers
  Box 611, Jefferson, North Carolina 28640
  www.mcfarlandpub.com

To Robin

Table of Contents

Acknowledgments viii
Introduction: Toes to the Line 1

1. Against Type: The Problem of Bodies and Genre 9
2. Scars, History and Historical Fiction 48
3. "The Virtuous Shrub": The Drug Problem 80
4. Sex at Sea, at Sea with Sex 119
5. The Captain's Bodies: *Desolation Island,* a Case Study 150

Conclusion: Weighing Anchor 184
Chapter Notes 191
Works Cited 193
Index 197

Acknowledgments

This book would simply not have been possible without the support and camaraderie of several fellow travelers in the lands of Patrick O'Brian. I would like to thank, in particular, Wayne Glausser and Marnie McInnes, who both read early sections of the manuscript and have provided advice, support, and friendship. Several colleagues at DePauw University have also contributed to the completion of this book. Harry Brown read through the entire manuscript, offering thoughtful suggestions; any faults that remain are entirely mine. Istvan Csicsery-Ronay offered support and guidance as my manuscript neared completion. Former colleague Srimati Basu has never stopped pushing me. DePauw University provided me with important opportunities to work on this manuscript through a sabbatical and a Faculty Fellowship. In addition, DePauw awarded me several Student-Faculty Summer Research Grants, which gave me the opportunity to do important work towards this project with a group of outstanding students. I am grateful for the assistance and the dedicated work of Vicky Googasian, Sarah Summers, Tyler Hollet, and Robert Schoch; all proved inspiring and extraordinarily helpful.

I would also like to acknowledge the role of my mentors at the University of Miami, particularly Frank Palmeri, Patrick McCarthy, and the late Zack Bowen. I cannot begin to list all that they have taught me.

I would like to thank my family—Allen and Maddie Sinowitz, Judith Krinnes, as well as Louis, Andrea, and Dawn Mendelsohn—for their support over the years of this project (as well as before those years, of course). Most importantly, my unending gratitude goes to Robin Mendelsohn, a fellow O'Brian fan, my first reader, and my best friend. Lastly, my thanks to Harry: this project began before you were born, but I am so glad you will get to see it completed.

Introduction: Toes to the Line

In the days when bookstores flourished, you could walk through the section marked literature and find a kind of muted rainbow palate at the start of the O's. As a graduate student living in Miami, Florida, I would wander through the many large bookstores in the area, looking for books, more and more books. At the time, I read voraciously, and I had a fascination with big, encyclopedic texts. I read *The Brothers Karamazov, War and Peace, Ulysses, Gravity's Rainbow, Midnight's Children, The Tin Drum*, and even poked around in Proust—and about anything that seemed to be some combination of very long and very challenging.

At the very least, the Aubrey-Maturin novels of Patrick O'Brian qualified as long. I remember seeing them many times, all lined up and numbered, on bookstore shelves. I always passed them over in favor of something else. As my list of readings suggest, I wanted to impress people at that time, and, while I knew almost nothing about O'Brian, I feared that the sheer fecundity of his production would lessen my cultural capital if I were seen walking around with them. I had a lot of growing up to do still, but what I suffered from at the time is not unusual in graduate schools.

After I read a review, really a review essay, in *The Atlantic Monthly* of Patrick O'Brian's seventeenth Aubrey-Maturin novel, *The Commodore*, I decided to pick up the first, *Master and Commander*. They started out as something of a guilty pleasure. In the lifecycle of a graduate student, you get to a period in each semester when you do one of two things—grade papers or write your own. Every time I entered that phase, I would read another O'Brian novel.

When I moved to my first—and well, only—job at a small liberal arts college in the Midwest, my new boss told me I would be "simpatico"

Introduction: Toes to the Line

with another professor. One of the first things I discovered about this other professor was that he was an avid reader of O'Brian. So was his wife. So is my wife. I found fans of the series tucked away in other departments, like a classicist who seemed to let himself savor an O'Brian novel periodically like a marooned smoker working his way through his last pack. I learned that one of my Joyce professors had discovered them as well. Fans of the series have not just read their way through the novels; they keep reading their way through. I think I had made my way through twice before I started this project; I have now lost count of how many times I have made the journey. For those who let themselves start the series, the books seem to become lifetime companions. Why?

Part of the origins of this project lay in my own desire to try to answer this question, at least for myself. From that starting point, the project has evolved in a number of directions to become a kind of intellectual ode to the series, a meditation on aspects of reading and interpretation, and an exploration of what I came to see as a singular complexity that ran through the series—namely, the nature of the human body.

To say it plainly, Jack Aubrey, the co-protagonist of the series, is fat. When I began to read *Master and Commander*, that detail struck me immediately. His companion, Stephen Maturin, is short and ugly. To judge these books by their covers—I began reading them in the mid 1990s—with their traditional naval paintings, I expected pretty conventional material, including a tall, dark and handsome Captain. However, this immediate shift in my expectations drew me into the series; the shift in body types made me aware that O'Brian would play with form and genre, and this hooked me. Other details related to bodies also drew my attention. Early on, Stephen's reputation as a surgeon gets made from a combination of amputations and trepannings. As I came to reflect on the series, I realized that the novels show a remarkable attention to and fascination with the human body—its sexual functions, its symbolic or representative functions, its addictions (primarily to drugs), its relation to history and genre. In essence, bodies, both figuratively and literally, receive extraordinary attention in the series. This attention struck me as one of the ways in which O'Brian's work both links to a variety of what we might call genre fictions and simultaneously transcends them.

In this volume, I seek to answer the question of why the novels

Introduction: Toes to the Line

consistently pay attention to multiple aspects of the human body. In answering and complicating this question, I will also investigate questions about how the portrayal of the body affects and relates to several key questions regarding the series, including how we might define the series in terms of genre, what drives the seemingly relentless narrative expansion of the series, why the novels are so particularly interested in sex and drugs (and how the novels treat those subjects), and how the body is linked to the historical elements of these texts. In addition, this book takes on questions of how the novels shape a reader's engagement with text, O'Brian's rhetorical techniques, and considers how and why readers can become invested in such a series to the extent of sticking with it through twenty-odd volumes (an unfinished twenty-first novel was published after O'Brian's death). In all of these discussions, what emerges is the sense of O'Brian's underlying philosophy, a kind of broad generosity to the human, one that sees it as a particularly flawed and animalistic species, but deserving too of a kind of wide-ranging sympathy.

In trying to work through these questions, I have chosen a variety of approaches rather than a more rigid or singular theoretical lens. Although literary theory—what we might call schools of literary interpretation—can often seem to be an either/or proposition, I try to adhere to the notion that theoretical approaches can be equivalent to tools in a toolbox, if I may borrow a phrase various scholars have utilized (see, for instance, *The Theory Toolbox* by Jeffrey Nealon and Susan Searls Giroux). In other words, if we push theories of literary interpretation to their logical conclusions, they can appear to be mutually exclusive because, in essence, they tend to focus on different evidence. If you choose a particular theoretical lens over another, you simply may not pay attention to the same parts of a given text. My approach, though, is to let the evidence that draws my attention lead me to become informed by a given particular approach at that time. A true believer in, say, the psychoanalytical literary approach would likely argue that this approach is always the best way of looking at a given literary text; however, my approach is to use something like psychoanalysis when I encounter a literary text that partakes of certain dreamlike aspects or which seems to operate in a way that defies traditional logic (it's hard to resist, for instance, reading Kafka's "The Country Doctor" with at least some

Introduction: Toes to the Line

thought that Freud's ideas might help a reader make some sense of what appears to be a story that defies sense).

What are the consequences of this approach for the volume in front of you? It means that I have let the subject matter guide me in matters of theory. For instance, in writing about the novels' portrayals of drugs and sex, I have drawn upon historical and literary sources from the time the novels have been set in order to situate O'Brian's approach to these subjects (and to consider whether the attitudes of the novels are more contemporary to the novels' creation or to the novels' setting). In discussing genre, I touch upon a number of scholarly approaches to the issue. In doing so, I have been willing to put an array of very different thinkers—in this case, Stanley Fish, Mikhail Bakhtin, and Patricia Parker—into some conversation. In the closing chapter I have drawn upon both Freud and Michel Foucault. My hope is that these conversations with theorists seem not imposed in any way upon the material but instead to be of a piece with our discussions, as the ideas from the theorists give us a way of thinking about the issues raised in O'Brian's work. In all cases I have diligently tried to avoid jargon—or, if it does arise, find a means of transcending it. Thus, my goal is to use these theorists to make the issues in O'Brian more accessible to his readership, not less.

To this point, I would list three other inspirations for this volume that have little directly to do with O'Brian and figure mostly indirectly in the pages that follow—namely, Wayne C. Booth, Louis Menand, and Gerald Graff. I can trace Booth's place in this volume to a memorial panel dedicated to him at the Modern Language Association Convention held in Philadelphia. I left that panel so impressed that I immediately purchased his classic book *Rhetoric of Fiction* and began reading it. Booth, Graff, and Menand have all served as models to me in their desire to write conversationally and to a broad audience. Although all possess a remarkable intellect, they speak to readers as informed, thoughtful companions. I leave it to the reader to decide if I have done justice to their model, but they have all left a mark on what I try to do in my writing.

In the pages that follow, then, I wish to embark on a longer conversation with you about Patrick O'Brian's novels, about the issues I see arise as I have tried to make sense of them, and to give you some sense of the meaning I have drawn from them. The first chapter begins with a basic question—what kind of books are these? The reason why this

Introduction: Toes to the Line

fascinates me has to do with the very difficulty of answering the question. Trying to answer this question led me both to consider what we mean when we use the term genre and how O'Brian's use of bodies complicates our attempts to label his work. Therefore, in this chapter I investigate the complications of identifying genre in this large, twenty-volume series as they are played out and figured in terms of O'Brian's continuous fascination with bodies. It is this attention to the body that creates generic disruptions and undermines a reader's ability to apply obvious labels to either the series' main characters or to O'Brian's larger project.

The second chapter grows from the first, but here I shift my attention to one particular genre—historical fiction. Because issues regarding history and the novels' relation to the historical novel are quite contested, in both the texts and by O'Brian himself, I have placed that discussion apart from the previous discussion. This second chapter follows the first on genre more broadly and considers how the progress of the body and the representation of the body come to parallel the narrative and historical progress of the novel. O'Brian charts historical change through the progress of his main characters' physical bodies, with the conflicts of the public historical world (here the Napoleonic Wars) becoming literally writ upon the bodies of the individual through scars and disfigurement, so that the physical body comes to be both a record of the personal and public historical spheres, and an embodiment of the struggles between these two. While exploring these issues, I also consider what we mean by historical novel, what we expect of such novels, and what limits any author faces when striving for historical representation. In addition, I consider broader questions here regarding O'Brian's place among historical writers—considering his relation to both traditional historical novelists as well as his contemporaries, the postmodern historical novelists—as well as why O'Brian seemed reluctant to view his work as historical fiction.

From here, I move from genre and the figurative nature of bodies to the more literal use of the body (of course, this requires a brief suspension of disbelief, since all of the bodies in these novels appear to us as figurative or symbolically—in the form of words). In short, we shift from history to drugs. Thus, the third chapter focuses on the extensive use and examination of drug consumption in the series. While the primary locus of discussion here is Stephen Maturin's opium addiction, the chapter also considers the novels' interest in a broad array of substances,

Introduction: Toes to the Line

including caffeine, alcohol, and cocaine. In evaluating O'Brian's approach to and view of drugs in the novels, I consider 18th-century attitudes and practices. The approach here is less informed by theories of genre and historical representation, and more by historical research into practices involving drugs at the time in which the novels are set. This method helps shed light on whether O'Brian seeks to depict Maturin's relationship with drugs in terms of the historical epoch. The larger discussion, however, has more to do with O'Brian's considerations of the needs and desires of the body itself, as well as issues involved in both narrative point of view and long narrative arcs, produced by Stephen's relation to drugs.

A similar approach introduces the discussions of sex and sexuality in this volume's fourth chapter. As in the previous chapter, I attend to the ways in which the depictions of sexuality align with 18th-century attitudes and practices, and how the novel responds to those conceptions of sexuality. In this chapter, the examinations of sexuality range across the novels' depiction of homosexuality, women's sexuality, and the sexuality of their two male protagonists. I seek to raise questions about the narrative roles of sexual practice as well as the complications in the apparent tolerance of a broad range of human sexuality.

Each of the previous chapters explores a single issue across many novels. In the final chapter I take a slightly different approach, focusing on a sort of case study by primarily examining a single novel of the series, *Desolation Island*, though against the backdrop of the entire series itself. Taking a close look at a single text allows me to bring together various aspects of the readings and issues raised in the previous chapters, and also to focus on how the novels play with the trope of the king's two bodies—that a king is both his own literal body and also the figurative body of the nation (and kingship)—one that is perpetual or immortal (or at least hoped to be so). Thus, this chapter examines how the captain, Jack Aubrey, serves as figure for the English king, but also how the ship and the crew become two further figurative extensions of the ship's captain. In developing my reading of what I consider among the most complex novels of the series, I employ two very different theoretical lenses—that of Michel Foucault's ideas about "discipline" (as well as his reading of the trope of the king's two bodies) and a psychological trope developed by Sigmund Freud, who compares the human mind to a house (or, we might say, a ship). I consider, then, how in the novel itself,

Introduction: Toes to the Line

O'Brian uses this complex trope of Jack's body to examine gender constructions, political conceptions, and the complicated psychological desires for controlling what is perhaps uncontrollable—one's unconscious and one's physical self.

As the beginning of this introduction details, I started out reading O'Brian's Aubrey-Maturin novels as a fan. I would be the last to deny that these works can serve as entertainment, as an escape—reading for fun (as my students would say, drawing a sharp line between intellectual stimulation and enjoyment). However, I do not know that O'Brian's work would have produced the kind of passion it has in me and so many others—a passion that would push us not just through the twenty volumes, but one that would make us want to keep returning—without the kind of extraordinary development of character O'Brian has produced. Although I do enjoy the action of these tales (the heroics, the battles, and the chases), many of the joys to be found in the series are, in fact, the small human moments (two characters enjoying a glass of fine wine, some toasted cheese, and a shared love of music). Yet, as I hope this volume will illustrate, there are also extraordinary intellectual joys. Stephen's reflections on human nature provide me with the same thrill and the same comfort as the privilege of gaining George Eliot's insights around the margins of her narrative in *Middlemarch;* you feel that someone very wise, very intelligent and thoughtful has taken some time to let you get a better vision of how the world works. My comparison of O'Brian here to George Eliot perhaps lends itself to the sense that O'Brian's work is of a different age; however, his work has been referenced by two seemingly quite different and much more experimental writers, namely Thomas Pynchon in his own eighteenth-century novel *Mason and Dixon,* as well David Mitchell in *The Thousand Autumns of Jacob de Zoet,* a novel that both cites him as a predecessor but also contains what I take to be an homage—a section of the text set aboard an English ship. I interpret the appreciation of O'Brian from these two highly intellectual and experimental writers as further recognition that O'Brian's work is worthy of study. I hope that this volume will help move that conversation forward.

1

Against Type
The Problem of Bodies and Genre

Genre, Fiction

I really dreaded the opening of *Master and Commander: Far Side of the World*. I knew I had to see it, but I also knew that—like most people—I never liked the film adaptations of books about which I cared greatly. I went to see the film with three other fans of the series. While I liked the movie, I often felt as if it had relatively loose ties to the books themselves—more inspired by than a strict adaptation. Of all the scenes in the film, the one that we all admired featured the Doctor, Stephen Maturin, wandering the Galapagos collecting specimens, live bodies to be studied and dissected at his leisure. Looking back, I realize that one of the reasons why we all praised this scene was that it seemed one of the truest to the novels. For the most part, the film streamlines the elements of the series, producing an exciting, historically-set adventure story; however, this scene shows the essence of the series, which is not at all so narrowly conceived. Perhaps not coincidently, in the film, the Doctor must free his bodies in order to return to the ship in time so that he and the rest of the characters may proceed with the action-adventure plot to which the majority of the movie is dedicated.[1]

Why do most of us feel disappointed by film versions of favorite novels? The most obvious reason is that a filmmaker must give a definite form to that which—with the kind and often generous assistance of the novelist—we have developed into a kind of soft-lined but vaguely substantive image in our own head. Now, if my image of Jack Aubrey in no way resembles Russell Crowe, I am bound to be dismayed when I see Crowe amble around Jack's beloved H.M.S. *Surprise* (and I have to say my image of Stephen Maturin in no way resembles Paul Bettany, who has genetic gifts in height and comeliness that O'Brian never bestowed upon Stephen). Also, of course, along these same lines of how we imagine characters comes my—and any reader's—sense of mood, decorum, vision, sense of place, or, to put it simply, just how this all should look. However, none of us arrive at any novel or text as a blank slate either; instead, we use what we have read and seen in building our own world in relation to the novel we are reading. Likewise, our expectations and understanding of genre—its conventions, its plots, its motifs—figure prominently in how we respond to and understand what we read and view. If I am expecting a comedy, I am likely going to be aghast when the director instead gives me a horror movie, or even more aghast if she begins by giving me—in terms of conventions, character, plot—the romantic comedy I am expecting and then, perhaps, mid-way through, begins to deliver all the conventions, plots, and characterizations I might expect from a horror film. We might also consider how we come to associate certain types of bodies with certain types of characters, and how such expectations help us to discern what kind of text we are encountering. We do not, to use a relevant example, expect our action hero to border upon the obese. We would not expect to find Chris Farley as the star of *Die Hard* (or any of its myriad sequels); at best, an obese actor might feature as comic relief. Upon reflection, these views of the role genre plays in our reading process may seem common sense; however, as we will discuss, there is a great deal of debate even about some of the assumptions I have described above.

Nevertheless, as we begin to think through Patrick O'Brian's Aubrey-Maturin series here, we may begin by asking exactly what kind of novels we are reading. Though they are not the unhappy marriage of romantic comedy and horror film I have described above, we cannot so easily answer this question of what genre or label it is best to apply to O'Brian's twenty-volume series. In this chapter I will explore how the complications of genre in the series—viewed here as both individual volumes and, inevitably, as moments in a larger, accumulating text—become played out and figured in terms of O'Brian's continuous fascination with bodies. It is this fascination with the body that creates generic disruptions—hybrids, uncertain combinations, sometimes fractured vessels—and undermines a reader's ability to apply obvious labels to either the characters or the larger project. While exploring these issues, I also will consider the ways in which attention to bodies figures in the narrative

1. Against Type

technique of the series, such as how O'Brian creates narrative momentum, how O'Brian continues to produce one novel after another, and the related dilation and expansion of time, history, narrative, and plot required to accomplish this feat.

In the course of this series, bodies are everywhere—in the ships filled with men, in the physical ails of the sailors, in the site where sailors are to be punished and disciplined in a panoptic display, in the references to the surgeon's ability to "whip the leg off a man," in the lusts and desires of the crew, in the dead of the enemies and the allies strewn across the decks of the ships. The assessment of a person's worth inevitably begins with a close analysis of his or her physical characteristics. Consider this brief example from *The Far Side of the World* (1984) when Captain Jack Aubrey is attempting to find a new Master for his mission: "As [Jack] spoke, he looked intently at Allen, a tall, upright, middle-aged man with a fine strong face, wearing the plain uniform of a master in the Royal navy, and as he took off his hat to a superior officer, a lieutenant of barely twenty, Jack saw that his hair was grey. 'I like the look of him,' he said" (64). This is but one example; however, this process repeats itself many times throughout the series: Jack reads the signs on the body of the person he encounters and subsequently interprets and makes judgments based upon those signs.

Thus, bodies—that of the sea, of the ship, of the captain, of the state—figure as a complex system of tropes and meaning-producers comparable to what Pierre Bourdieu observes in a somewhat different context: "The sign-bearing, sign-wearing body is also a producer of signs which are physically marked by the relationship to the body" (192). Bodies, then, are both signified and signifier; they represent and produce meaning, they can be adorned with signs, and they can create signs that speak back or represent the body itself. Such a complicated notion of how bodies figure in these texts helps us to envision why the bodies so central to O'Brian's tale produce both meaning and seeming contradiction, acting as sites of narrative "inscription"—places upon which stories can be read—and catalysts for narrative expansion.

O'Brian's interest in bodies does not, however, make him unique. In his book *Body Work*, Peter Brooks argues, "In imaginative literature the body has always been an object of fascination, at once the distinct other of the signifying project—which, as an exercise of mind and will on the world, takes a stand outside materiality—and in some sense its vehicle (this living hand that writes), perhaps even its place of inscription" (1). Brooks recalls here how bodies are produced in texts, how bodies produce texts, and how getting to know the body through its signs is akin to finding meaning in a book through its inscriptions. In doing so, Brooks reminds us of one of the central roles such inscriptions play in our earliest literature, when Odysseus' true identity is revealed in *The Odyssey* by way of a "mark on the body itself," and thus "the sign imprints the body, making it part of the signifying process" (3). Brooks' project is not mine. He is particularly interested in the relationship between erotic desire, bodies, and narrative, and focuses largely on the novel of the eighteenth and nineteenth century. Nevertheless, Brooks' discussion of the ways in which bodies may stand in like a text, with signs that we seek to read like texts in the hopes of finding answers, of getting at a larger truth, of, in his phrase, making bodies mean, has relevance to my notion of the way O'Brian's treatment of bodies operates in this series. As I examine the detailing of bodies and the concomitant relation of those bodies to genre—and later in this book to history, sexuality, and drugs—I will also seek to unpack the ways in which O'Brian's project reveals how the body can be a site of narrative, a place where meaning can be inscribed and produced, while also suggesting ways in which the body in and of itself fails to offer a fullness of explanation, but instead outlines the limits of that knowledge.

    Before moving into the specifics of the characters and the novels, I wish to take a few moments to discuss the complications of the term genre. This phrase—especially in discussion of the arts—is so commonplace that I think most people, even professional literary scholars, tend to take it for granted. However, any casual survey through academic discussions of the term—its meaning, its usefulness, its ability to aid in critical analysis—reveals just how highly a contested term "genre" actually is. In Rene Welleck's and Austin Warren's now classic study *Theory of Literature,* they take a chapter to discuss this term, and while this text has been superseded by post-structuralist approaches to literature, these authors still offer us a clear path into the issues at stake in how we understand and apply the term genre. They begin by comparing the notion of "the literary kind" to "an institution," claiming, "One can work through, express oneself through, existing institutions, create new ones, or get on, so far as possible, without sharing in politics or rituals; one can also join, but then reshape, institutions" (226). In this analogy they get at a

1. Against Type

central conception about the notion of genre: they may certainly exist before the writer begins, but they may not remain the same once the writer finishes. Thus, for Welleck and Warren, "With the addition of new works, our categories shift" (227). In *Reason and the Nature of Texts,* a more contemporary discussion of literature, theory, and genre, James L. Battersby borrows the terms of T. S. Eliot and sees the contest as between the individual talent (the author) and the tradition (the preexisting genres or the conventions of preexisting genres). Of course, these discussions of genre are quite ancient in origin, dating back at least as far as Aristotle, Plato, and Horace, and to a time where genres seemed fixed and no one had imagined the modern novel. I will not rehearse here for you the history of genre and its uses, but I will simply say that the basis for how we distinguish one genre from another has shifted a great deal over time. For Battersby, it can be seen in some ways as a factor not only in the distinction between various literary kinds, but between literature and non-literature (although he dismisses the notion that genre conventions actually allow for, or are, the basis for this differentiation—another point of some debate).

Welleck and Warren note that the division of literary kinds or genres takes place on two distinct levels. We have the "ultimate categories," which include "poetry, fiction, and drama," and then we have the "subdivisions," which might begin by distinguishing, say, "in the eighteenth century" or "the novel and the romance," but which ultimately signal the proliferation of various generic labels for the novel, for example (229). For the most part, a great deal of criticism of genre in the eighteenth century attended to "purity of kind" and "hierarchy of kinds," which Welleck and Warren call "hedonistic calculus" (230). Nevertheless, those divisions of genre, the praising of some and dismissing of others, continues to inform the way we think about various texts (and has given way to even further academic debates, such as those between John Guillory and Barbara Hernstein Smith, on the question of literary value). Ultimately, Welleck and Warren call upon critics and readers to "lean to the formalistic side" when dividing literary texts rather than "subject-matter classifications" (233)—tragedy, say, rather than sea stories. For them, "genre represents, so to speak, a sum of aesthetic devices at hand, available to the writer and already intelligible to the reader. The good writer partly conforms to the genre as it exists, partly stretches it" (235).

These claims seem sound, but they beg a question—namely, which of these "aesthetic devices" is integral to the identification of a given genre? This is where problems begin to arise. As outlined in "Family Resemblances and Generalizations Concerning the Arts," by Maurice Mandelbaum in 1965, there had been attempts to categorize types of art based on the examples of Wittgenstein's analogy of "family resemblances," allowing us to, for example, identify things as various as tennis and solitaire as both being games; but such groupings inevitably have become challenged by our difficulty in determining a defining criteria. In fact, Battersby argues that the same problems arise when we simply wish to identify what qualifies as literature (130). Instead of suggesting a defining characteristic of the literary, Battersby explains that "particular works are like particular uses of water, functional constructs of justified constituents. Literature, then, is a protean entity that alters as its alteration finds in the observer (that is, in the interests and categories of the observer)" (132). We change the definition of what constitutes literature on a seemingly continuous basis and to meet our own ends. Does genre, in dividing and categorizing literature, function in the same way? Battersby's discussions of literature and genre seem tied to those discussions sparked by Stanley Fish's "How to Recognize a Poem When You See One," an essay which begins with a story about how Fish's class "made" a poem out of a list of names based on the students' shared sense of a particular type of poem and its conventions, a shared knowledge, that Fish generalized could be known as "interpretive communities." Some of those who sought to counter Fish's claims, such as Reed Way Dasenbrock in his essay "Do We Write the Text We Read?" suggested that Fish's students essentially constructed a *temporary* "theory" that allowed them to make sense of the names in terms of a poem. Battersby feels that we all do this every time we read: "We must learn a new practice with the reading of each new work, depending as we go on our prior familiarity with a rich stock of mastered practices and on our imaginative capacity for improvising and understanding new possibilities" (138). Battersby goes on to claim that "even when the end of a particular genre can be clearly stated ... it is clear that every production not a mere copy of something already existing embodies artistic choices that culminate in a unique realization of the ends specified for the genre" (144). For example, even if we claim that O'Brian intends to write a sea story, and even if we claim that sea stories possess particular characteristics—in

1. Against Type

milieu, character, and plot—O'Brian will still produce something different from what has preceded his work (let's put aside questions of what Fredric Jameson calls pastiche until Chapter 2). Thus, there are clearly limits to what identifying a text by a genre or multiple genres can tell us, and there are not necessarily rules that cannot be reformulated or improvised, as each text produces something different, and, going back to Welleck and Warren, every new text forces an adjustment of our previous conception of these categories. For Battersby, then, genre "cannot determine the 'specific content' of any writing whatsoever" (145). I wish to grant Battersby these claims and objections about the uses of genre, but we also need to acknowledge, as he does when he asserts how we read, that our prior knowledge—which includes expectations shaped by genre based upon our knowledge of genres and their conventions—does factor into how we interpret, respond to, and simply make sense of what we read.

In short, genre, as a concept, can still do some work for us. Therefore, the tasks I am setting before you include not only considering the ways in which O'Brian recasts genre, but also the ways in which his texts ask us to "improvise and understand new possibilities," to borrow Battersby's phrasing. As Dean King's biography, *Patrick O'Brian: A Life*, makes clear, O'Brian's novels' relation to genre posed problems from the very outset—even in the sense that his earliest reviewers felt hidebound to place his books in relation to Horatio Hornblower (207)—and that O'Brian had trouble finding an audience because of the very uncertainty publishers and marketers faced in saying just what these texts were. For King, the issue had to do primarily with the inconsistencies between O'Brian's literary style and his intended audience, and the ways in which his work did not fit in terms of adventure stories (written for young adults usually) or historical fiction (not literary enough) (308). I propose that these questions and problems are more complicated than those King describes, and that the complications can be found in the very bodies of O'Brian's characters.

The Captain's Body

I will begin my discussion of genre in the series itself with Captain Jack Aubrey, whose body and character provides the main source of narrative in the series. On a very superficial level, it is easy to view the naval captain, Aubrey, as a traditional hero of the sea, larger-than-life in both physique and in skills. As such, we are likely to see him as a figure of the naval or high seas adventure story, perhaps as a figure in certain types of historical novels, and perhaps a kind of swashbuckling figure of romance—a warrior on a quest of some sort. All of these are genres that tend to center on a heroic, elevated figure, someone cast close to the mold of an epic hero, one possibly summed up in a heroic epitaph. An obvious example of the type would be C. S. Forester's protagonist, Horatio Hornblower. Jack's monikers—though not referenced frequently—include Lucky Jack Aubrey and Goldilocks. Not exactly swift-footed Achilles, true, but they do at least suggest a kind of status outside the norm (compared, say, with one of Jack's frequent crewmembers, Awkward Davies). On some level we might say that Jack's heroism is beyond question—no one could likely accuse him of physical cowardice, for instance. However, we might also wonder if we—desiring perhaps to fit his actions into the frame of texts we have encountered before—are mistaking great professional competence, though it involves a clear risk of death, for outsized heroism. At least from the point of view of Jack's seagoing companion, Stephen Maturin, Jack has every claim—at least in those moments related to war—to an elevated status. Praising Jack's heroism in trying to get the grounded *Surprise* off the shoal in a letter to Diane in *The Far Side of the World*, Stephen confides, "If you had watched him this last fortnight I believe you would allow him a certain heroic quality, a certain greatness of soul." During the proceedings, "we were perpetually aware of that impassive, determined and authoritative eye; we felt it upon us in all our comings and goings, and we were as meek as schoolboys" (170–171). In moments of decision or danger, Jack appears to not simply "rise to the occasion," but to "swell" to it. Consider the following description—again from the perspective of his close friend and ship's surgeon, Stephen Maturin—from the third novel in the series, *H.M.S. Surprise*. As French ships approach for battle, Stephen says of Jack: "'On these occasions ... my valuable friend appears to swell, actually to increase in physical as well as his spiritual dimensions: is it in an optical illusion? How I should like to measure him. The penetrating intelligence in the eye, however, is not capable of measurement. He becomes a stranger: I, too, should hesitate to address him'" (289). Such moments are not confined merely to the early novels, as this

1. Against Type

passage from the much later book *The Wine-Dark Sea* illustrates: "When Jack Aubrey was strongly moved he seemed to grow taller and broader-shouldered, while without the slightest affectation or morosity his ordinarily good-humoured expression became remote" (158). We also see Jack's size expand into the space of the ship and intimidate, as it does in this conversation between Jack and an upstart lieutenant in *The Letter of Marque:* "But the sight of Jack's bulk towering there, filling the meager space and all the more massive since he had to crouch under the lower deckhead, his grim face and the natural authority that emanated from him, overcame young Dixon's resolution" (42). We also witness Jack, like an outsized great hero, casually demonstrate his profound strength in that same novel: "He heaved Stephen and then Martin up on to the platform, and once again Stephen wondered at his strength: Stephen's bare nine stone was perhaps natural enough, but Martin was more stoutly built. For all that he was swung up with a lift as effortless as though he had a moderate dog, held by the nape—swung right up through the hole and set down on his feet" (56). In moments like these, Jack seems no ordinary man.

Part of what marks this difference can be directly connected to his body itself. From the very start of the series, O'Brian insists we, as readers, take note of Jack as a physical entity, as O'Brian directs our attention to Jack's size, noting how his "big form overflowed his seat" (*Master and Commander* 7). The ambiguity of this description is indicative of the role Jack's size plays throughout the series. On one level the narrator makes us aware that Jack is larger than the average individual of his era (and he is certainly taller than most), but we do not know if this means that he is larger than life (a giant among men) or profoundly obese. Nevertheless, at the least he has been set apart. I would like to reflect on both the significance of Jack's size and the ambiguity of how that size is represented in the text.

One way to consider the issue would be to contemplate whether a correlation exists between Jack's size and his place in the naval hierarchy. In his sociological and theoretical study, *Distinction*, Pierre Bourdieu discusses how one of the ways in which members of a society mark or sign their social position and their "taste" is through their own bodies, and considers, too, how those signs are received by others. He proceeds to observe that "the 'great' are perceived as physically greater than they are," because "authority of whatever sort contains the power of seduction" (192). And, of course, we may tend to confuse figurative, or at least intangible, power with physical power (hence size, stature, presence). Besides these more cultural or sociological elements, we may also note that there are realistic reasons why Jack would gain weight in seeming proportion to his gaining more authority. As Jack rises to captain, there are simply more and more limits placed on his ability to be active. On most occasions it is his crew that takes on that role, and his role on the ship instead limits him to walking back and forth on the quarterdeck, as we are told many times. He conducts this walk so often, in fact, that he creates a shine on the bulkhead from his foot turning upon it. Attention to factors like these on O'Brian's part recalls Brooks' identification of the attention to bodies coinciding with the rise of realism—"that species of literature for which the careful registering of the external world counts most" (3).

Although, following Bourdieu's theory, our sense of Jack's size may be connected to his power in the context of naval life, I would contend that Jack is not simply larger-than-life; Jack seems to expand at an alarming rate—beyond contemporary standards that would simply suggest prosperity—so that Stephen, as a physician and friend, feels obligated to constantly monitor Jack's weight. Again, early in the first novel, *Master and Commander*, the narrator notes that "like so many sailors he was rather fat, and he sweated easily on shore" (80). After some victories at sea and the capturing of a French cook, Jack "was putting on weight like a prize ox" (229). Later he is described as a "healthy well-fed fattish man" (239). Such attentions to Jack's weight are ubiquitous in the series. In *Treason's Harbor*, much later in the series, we are told that the Bedouins have lent Jack the horse of "the heaviest man in the northern wilderness." To which Jack can only respond, "Well ... there is nothing like candour" (151). In *Far Side of the World*, the narrator informs us that "turning, he [Stephen] saw Jack's great bulk filling the gangway—like many big powerful portly men, Jack was very light on his feet" (205). Thus, even Jack's skills at movement become measured against his bulk.

We can begin to see that Jack's size can be read not so much in terms of his outsized heroism but simply in terms of being out-sized. Maturin, the physician, seems almost obsessed with charting these fluctuations in Jack's weight, and his concerns often lead to comical undermining of what would otherwise be heroic moments. For example, as Jack and the Master of the H.M.S. *Sophie*, a homosexual who clearly

1. Against Type

admires the captain, plan a cutting out party that they estimate will proceed in ten minutes, Stephen offers the following commentary, wonderfully undercutting Jack's plans for attacking the battery:

> "Allow twenty if you please," said Stephen. "You portly men of sanguine complexion often die suddenly, from considered exertion in the heat. Apoplexy—congestion."
> "I wish, I wish you would not say things like that, Doctor," said Jack in a low tone: they all looked at Stephen with some reproach and Jack added, "Besides, I am not portly."
> "The captain has an uncommon genteel figgar," said [the master] Mr. Marshall [*Master and Commander* 219].

In this sequence we can see several elements at work—the process by which the body and attention to its expansion ironically deflate the aspirations of the narrative to a heroic, more epic order; the surgeon's role as literally and figuratively a deflator (opening up bodies and letting air in); and the duality of Jack's body as both attractive and suspect. Stephen—in his role as friend and physician—steps outside the figurative body of the naval hierarchy and brings the Captain down to a more human level. Comments like these are not isolated.

While the extended example above was taken from the first novel in the series, we can find countless reminders of Stephen's warnings to Jack about his size. In *The Wine-Dark Sea*, for example, the sixteenth novel in the series, Jack expresses worries that he has "put on half a stone," in part because "he wished to hear no more remarks about letting out his waistcoats, no grave professional warnings about the price big heavy men of sanguine temperament had so often to pay for taking too little exercise, too much food and too much drink: apoplexy, softening of the brain, impotence" (65). For the most part, these comments and views on Jack's size, particularly those about him being obese, either come directly from Stephen or from the narrator giving us an inside view of Stephen's opinions (or, as in the case above, Jack hearing Stephen's words in his own mind). This technique aligns with one of Stephen's roles in the novels. Although eventually he becomes a naval surgeon, Stephen never fully becomes assimilated into the navy, and he remains often in a position outside the traditional hierarchy of the navy, in his various roles as the Captain's guest or the Captain's "particular friend" (and because of Jack's willingness to make allowances for Stephen's failures to adhere to the hierarchy, since he always considers

Stephen a landsman). Even when Stephen does become a naval surgeon, that appointment places him in an odd position, as he is the one crew member who could declare the captain unfit, and he has unusual access, in the daily run of his profession, to a full range of the crew. As I will discuss at greater length in later chapters, Stephen fills a particular role in the novels, one derived from his position as both physician and scientist. He becomes a kind of window through which readers get to see and understand how humans viewed their world at this time. Thus, O'Brian exploits Stephen's position to let us see Jack as we could not necessarily see him otherwise. Stephen, through his probing attention to Jack's body, becomes instrumental—pun conceded—in calling into question Jack's status and position, and bringing him back to something closer to a middling position. Therefore, in such scenes as this one, we also see what Bourdieu points to as necessary for contesting authority figures, a kind of "caricature" that suggests "a distortion of the bodily image intended to break the charm" of the powerful (192). However, even in this extended scene from the first novel we see the difficulty in making such attempts—manifested here in Jack's attempts to quell such comments, and the "charmed" Master's denial of Jack's "portliness."

In these instances, Jack's size provides humor and also indicates his weaknesses in terms of his lack of self-control, an inability to control physical desires, his essential humanity. These failures to control himself undermine his status because they beg the question of whether he can control a body of men if his own body remains undisciplined. His inability to control desires tied to the physical body extends to his proclivity for eating vast quantities of food as well as imbibing extraordinary amounts of alcohol; in addition, he is prey to what the Doctor calls his "animal spirits," a phrase reminiscent of Jane Austen's description of the improper Lydia Bennet. In the second novel we see Jack become aroused by a painting, and, according to Stephen, "celibacy will never do for him" (462). Throughout the course of the series, Jack has several affairs, contemplates having several others, suffers from an apparent lack of mutual sexual desire in his marriage, and can generally be seen to suffer various forms of mental distemper if he has been too long without sexual relations. I will expand upon the issues related to sexuality and the body more fully in Chapter 4.

While Stephen is frequently forgiving of Jack's—and just about anyone else's—need for sexual pleasure, he is far less accepting of Jack's propensity to eat far beyond what a normal individual would need to consume in any one sitting. Thus, reporting to Jack's future wife Sophie on how Jack is doing, Stephen notes, "He still eats for six," and, "He is far too fat" (*Post-Captain* 189). While I could recount an inordinate number of Jack's culinary indulgences—there is little surprise that a cookbook has been produced based on the meals in the series—I will just offer this example of Jack's dining habits from *H.M.S. Surprise,* which also comes in the common form of Jack receiving a reprimand for his behavior from Stephen: "I was sorry to see you help yourself to him [the duck] a fourth time: duck is a melancholy meat. In any case the rich sauce in which it bathed was not all the thing for a subject of your corpulence. Apoplexy lurks in dishes of that kind. I signaled to you, but you did not attend" (278). Like Jack's failure to exercise regularly, his culinary indulgences are at least partially the consequence of his position on the ship. As Captain, he must regularly entertain and be entertained, and, in either case, he must attend to proper decorum throughout these often rather elaborate affairs. While we might scoff, as modern readers, at Stephen's worries about Jack's humors—and see this as a part of the novel's purposeful comedy—his attention to the relation of body and mind here and elsewhere should certainly not be dismissed as anachronistic (even if part of Stephen's general concern about Jack's health is also tied to his having a "sanguine temperament").

Jack Aubrey, Satire and the Epic Tradition

The novels' attention to Jack's "corpulence" and "animal" urges seems to align itself quite clearly with the techniques of satire and with the tradition observed by Bakhtin in his discussions of Rabelais. In other words, Jack's appearance and body lend themselves both to his being the central figure in a heroic adventure story and a comedy, or perhaps even a satire or a parody of the adventure tale. This concentration on, in Bakhtin's term, the "material bodily lower stratum" suggests that these novels are satiric in nature (qtd. in Palmeri 10). In discussing the process of material leveling in his book *Satire in Narrative,* Frank Palmeri says, "Epic and tragic decorum elide the processes of ingestion, elimination, and sexual activity" (10). For O'Brian, then, the novels' recurring preoccupation with bodies, bodily functions, and the function of its central body, Jack Aubrey's, serves to "weigh" the novels down so that they do not rise to the level of epic or tragedy. In his article "The Diegetic Achievement of Patrick O'Brian," Thomas J. Farrell, in the course of discussing a concept he calls diegetic supplement (and specifically an allusion to James Joyce's *Ulysses* in *Post-Captain*), sees O'Brian as "carnivalizing both his sources and his own novels by rooting them firmly in what Bahktin would call the lower body strata." Farrell sees this as a means by which "his characters can contribute to" the ways in which O'Brian's vision of his world extends beyond that of Jane Austen (a figure to which O'Brian has been compared, primarily by James R. Simmons). Like Farrell, I see O'Brian's interest in "the material lower body stratum," though my interest lies more fully in terms of issues of genre (and later in the very workings of the body itself).

I will elaborate upon Bakhtin's insightful demarcation of the novel and the epic in a moment, but in expanding upon these ideas, we can see that implications of the epic—texts focused upon, in Bakhtin's phrase, the absolute past, and figures so heroic and mythic as to be almost beyond the human—was a concern for O'Brian from the very start. In the author's note to the first novel, O'Brian discusses how the fiction writer need not embellish the heroism and exploits of the officers and men of this period, "for so very often the improbable reality outruns fiction."[2] The implications here, though, are that the facts are such that the author—even attempting to rely upon realistic depiction—may spin a tale that will inevitably seem unrealistic and almost exaggerated in its depiction of heroism. In his landmark essay "Epic and Novel," Bakhtin says the epic recounts "a world of 'beginnings' and 'peak times' in the national history, a world of fathers and of founders of families, a world of 'firsts' and 'bests'" (13). We can thus see that though O'Brian's novels are not an origin story, they do concentrate on a time when the British Navy was at its "best" and where, as O'Brian implies in his author's note, members of the British Navy appear to have been among the "best." The inclination, then, tilts toward the epic. However, it becomes clear, though, that O'Brian wishes to pull his project back from an attempt at some kind of modern epic. In an author's note to the tenth novel, *Far Side of the World*, O'Brian makes his methods even more plain, proclaiming that "the reader will meet no basilisks that destroy with their eyes, no Hottentots without religion, polity, or articulate language, no Chinese perfectly polite and completely skilled in all sciences, no wholly

1. Against Type

virtuous, ever-victorious or necessarily immortal heroes; and should any crocodiles appear, [the author] undertakes that they shall devour their prey without tears." It is perhaps no mere coincidence that O'Brian, in declaring that if you have come to his work looking for unrealistic adventure tales and unreasonably elevated mythic heroes, of tales of history writ large into the pattern of epic, you have chosen badly, employs irony and sarcasm—the tools used by the satirist to deflate—in making his points.

In addition to these statements suggesting O'Brian's firm intentions to avoid inflating his subject matter, O'Brian directs the reader to observe the remarkably stoic manner by which these exploits were typically recorded by the participants. In doing so, O'Brian suggests that the subjects upon whom his works are based did not wish to elevate their own exploits or to see them in a kind of mythic or epic light. Periodically, O'Brian offers samples of these logs to underscore his point; in *Mauritius Command,* the narrator notes that the account was not complete until Jack had "stripped [it] of all humanity" (158). Thus, these logs actually stand in contrast to the novels themselves, since the novels are about recovering that humanity, and thus we get the sense that the official record is also insufficient to tell their story. To flesh out but not embellish that record, though, is to try to work a delicate balance between avoiding unrealistic or unwanted elevation—a dehumanizing of another kind—and too little vision of the people, the real, living bodies once tied to these moments.

Therefore, in avoiding both grandeur and stoicism, the novels do not go to the other extreme entirely, for rarely do they give themselves over to broadly satiric episodes or outright caricature (in the manner of Swift, Rabelais, or even contemporary authors such as Pynchon or Barth), but they also resist giving themselves over fully to the many other genres of which they partake, including the action-adventure tale, the spy thriller, and the novel of ideas. The novels certainly feature satiric and parodic elements, however. Perhaps these parodic elements are another way in which O'Brian seeks to distance his novel from the epic, for, as Bakhtin argues, the novel "parodies other genres ... ; it exposes the conventionality of their forms and their language; it squeezes out some genres and incorporates others into its own peculiar structure, reformulating and re-accentuating them" ("Epic and Novel" 5). The novels' drawing on, and incorporation of, multiple genres adds to the essential *heteroglossia* of O'Brian's project, one of the characteristics Bakhtin has argued helps mark the novel (and, for him, is clearly one of its most evocative traits); that is, the text becomes, in essence, filled with many voices. Farrell, also drawing upon Bakhtin, suggests that O'Brian achieves this condition by also including "less literal dialogues imagined by Bakhtin between the action occurring in his novels and a wide range of other texts" (154). In other words, O'Brian's dialogic structure includes both the incorporation of multiple voices within the text and intratextual allusion to a wide range of other texts. In just the most overt way, we can confirm this multi-vocaled quality of O'Brian's work, which typically tells its story by way of third-person limited omniscience from both Stephen and Jack's point of view, but also through Stephen's personal notebook and letters, and Jack's official correspondence and his serial missives to his wife, Sophie.

Satire also plays its role in this multiplying of voices. The word satire, we should recall here, comes from ancient phrases for mixture. As we begin to think through the roles played by these multiple genres and the satiric techniques O'Brian employs, we may think of the series as a wavering between epic tendencies and constant vigilance to retreat from this pull toward the elevated, the finished, the absolute. In other words, the heroism involved in the historical events that O'Brian recounts, and the vast scope and size of the series, in some way increase the danger of the series rising to epic; the focus on bodies and perhaps the production of laughter—which Bakhtin says "destroys the epic" (23)—prevents this inflation from occurring.

The variety of generic kinds, the multiple points of view, and the sense that either of our main characters cannot be simply reduced to a singular role helps provide a kind of multiplicity or *heteroglossia*, then, that pushes this series away from the epic and back towards Bakhtin's ideal of the novel. At the very least, at the heart of this series are two figures who, despite being the best of friends, are essentially quite different—in bodies and in minds. Thus, the underlying exchange of the texts—so often mimicked by their many musical duets (with Jack on the violin and Stephen on the cello)—is dialogue. Contrast this with Bakhtin's characterization of the epic world as one that "knows only one single and unified world view, obligatory and indubitably true for heroes as well as authors and audiences" (35). If O'Brian is to avoid such situations, he must include multiple voices—and multiple forms that suggest

1. Against Type

varying perspectives and varying experiences of the world—and he must include laughter (here we may see this as not only the outright comic, but also irony), for, as Bakhtin argues, "laughter destroyed epic distance" (35). In other words, "laughter" allows the reader to approach a character as a human being because our ability to "laugh" with or at the character and, or her situations brings our experience together as it humanizes the character.

The laughter that pervades O'Brian's series marks it in stark contrast to its one clear literary predecessor, C. S. Forester's Horatio Hornblower novels, written some forty-odd years previous to those of O'Brian, but set during the same war and centered on a naval officer. To be blunt, Hornblower is a humorless prig, and the novels seem to follow Hornblower in avoiding all humor. It is likely pushing too far to say that O'Brian's novels seek to broadly parody Forester's—there is nothing like an Austin Powers and James Bond parodic relationship here—nor would it seem likely that O'Brian has sought to satirize Forester's novels in particular. O'Brian's work only holds a passing resembles to something like the *Flashman* series. Yet, the overall effect of O'Brian's series and how it has been constructed is that, through the inclusion of satiric and parodic elements, it can come to be read as something of a corrective to Forester's tales.

The contrasts between Hornblower and Aubrey are numerous, but perhaps the most singular distinction between the two men is that Aubrey lacks Hornblower's almost pathologic self-consciousness. When we meet Hornblower for the first time—that is, in the novel *Beat to Quarters*—he is a captain like Aubrey. We learn that Hornblower, like Aubrey, is rather tall, but we also learn that "down there where his ribs ended there was no denying the presence of a rounded belly, just beginning to protrude beyond the line of his ribs and iliac bones" (10). This passage tells us that Forester's novels also place a certain attention to the body, and some weight gain may seem inevitable for a captain, even a young one. However, ultimately, this protrusion seems more to resemble a kind of symbolic humanity that seeks to find its way out and must be repressed, for "Hornblower hated the thought of growing fat with an intensity rare for his generation; he hated to think of his slender smooth-skinned body being disfigured by an unsightly bulge in the middle" (11). This is not a man who laughs at himself. Unlike Jack Aubrey, who possesses a kind of unselfconscious authority, Hornblower spends a considerable amount of time courting his own authority. Throughout this first novel we are told how Hornblower had made the mistake of being too much himself, of sharing too much with his officers, and thus "he wanted still more to appear in the eyes of his officers and crew to be a man of complete self-confidence and imperturbability" (14). The narrator, from this inside view, goes on to tell us that "this was only partially to gratify himself," and that he was doing this all for his ship. We may concede some logic in this, and undoubtedly there are countless passages in the O'Brian series where we see Jack struggling with the difficulties of command and the need to appear strong and decisive, and Jack clearly finds comfort in having someone on board ship with whom to confide. However, there seems to be something almost ridiculous in Hornblower's artifice, perhaps best exemplified in this early passage: "He was not in the least hungry, but the desire to appear a hero in the eyes of his steward overrode his excited lack of appetite" (22). This passage makes Hornblower resemble a surgeon I once knew who would only allow himself sugar packets in front of his residents.

Because Hornblower lacks a companion or friend—excluding his eventual love interest in the novel—the mode of this novel is monologue, and from that position Forester has created a difficult situation in making Hornblower a particularly likable figure. Therefore, he paints figures on the outside who again and again are shown to admire Hornblower. Thus, one of Hornblower's officers, Bush, "blinked at him as at a miracle worker" (29). Yet, these moments of admiration come compete with the reader's knowledge that Hornblower cultivates such responses. Consider that "his heart was leaping with joy" because "it would appear like a miracle to his officers that he should conjure rum and tobacco from this volcano-riddled coast" (52). His achievements, too, seem to cast him—despite his flaws—as a figure of epic success. Here, in a moment of self-deprecation on Hornblower's part, we are told that "he had no time to rejoice in the knowledge that his frigate last night, in capturing a two decker without losing a man, had accomplished a feat without precedence in the long annals of British naval history" (70). Hornblower may have little time to spare for elevating his own success, but clearly Forester feels some burden to lift Hornblower and his accomplishments to a plane that O'Brian quite resists and consciously works against.

If Hornblower has two selves, it is because one is false. This is not the case with Jack Aubrey. In the O'Brian novels, sometimes the pres-

1. Against Type

entation of multiple selves can appear relatively gentle, such as in this sense of Jack's two selves in *Far Side of the World*: "the readily-pleased, conversable Jack Aubrey" and "the tall, imposing, splendidly-uniformed Captain Aubrey, his face moulded by years of absolute authority" (199). Then there is this sense of Jack being more than or different than his exterior when Stephen informs Jack's lawyer, Lawrence, in *Reverse of the Medal*: "From his jolly, rosy-gilled, well-fed appearance you would scarcely think so, but he is in fact something of a stoic" (238). However, sometimes the contrast becomes more dramatic. For example, shifting outside of the perspective of Stephen to that of his mate and friend, Martin, we see the kind of respect Jack commands in *Letter of Marque*, as Martin gives even more of an outsider's perspective on Jack than is available to Stephen:

> Perhaps you are so used to your friend that you no longer see what a great man he is to the sailors. If he can leap and bound at night in the pouring rain, defying the elements, they would be ashamed not to do the same, though I have seen some weep at the second assault, or when they are desired to go through the cutlass exercise once more. I doubt they would so much for anyone else. It is a quality some men possess [158].

In *The Thirteen Gun Salute*, the officers of the *Surprise* are worried when Jack is to leave because "they knew very well how much easier it was to command a fierce, turbulent crew when there was a legendary figure aboard—legendary for courage, success, and good fortune" (83). Thus, in these passages we have Jack Aubrey as a figure above and beyond others, even a "legend."

These moments, then, require an antidote, the laughter that Bakhtin describes. Bakhtin calls this an "uncrowning, that is, the removal of an object from a distanced plane, the destruction of epic distance, an assault on and destruction of the distanced plane in general. In the plane (the plane of laughter) one can disrespectfully walk around whole objects; therefore, the back and rear portion of an object (and also its innards, not normally acceptable for viewing) assume a general importance" (23). In other words, part of the "assault" on the exalted or elevated, what we might here also call the sense of the "legendary figure," is to see him whole, to see him from behind, to see him materially leveled and subject to the same workings of the lower body as us all. Thus, in *Nutmeg of Consolation* we find that Jack, having complained of various discomforts, has been given his dose by Stephen. O'Brian, however, makes sure that we learn the results. Killick, Jack's servant and steward, reports, "Which [Jack] has taken a ninety-year lease of the quarter-gallery: all you can hear is groaning and gushing. He ain't been out since you was there" (234). This window into the privy has all the hallmarks of satire, and this satire provides balance. We may think of O'Brian's commitment to this way of depicting Jack as being expressed fairly late in the series, through Jack's own perspective: "He was, after all, a professional man of war, not a hero" (*The Wine-Dark Sea* 112).

Thus, in the space of Jack's body, we see this inevitable hybridity (or multiplicity) performed, for Jack's girth does not simply translate him from a hero to a clown.[3] Although Jack's weight undermines and, to a certain degree, satirizes his stature as a traditional hero of the epic, the Romance, or even an action adventure tale, Jack is still known for his bodily prowess and physical strength. Late in the series Jack still can be seen climbing masts, rescuing the drowning, and generally accomplishing the physical tasks his occupation requires of him, despite his own increasing fears of oncoming age. His reputation as a tremendous "fighting captain" seems to progressively grow. Perhaps this is why Stephen—and, to a more limited degree, Jack—are concerned that Jack maintain a certain physical size.

Literary Fat Men and Narrative Dilation

In this next section I would like to take up the question of Jack's body from a perspective apart from the tilt between satire and epic. Let us return to the problem of Jack's weight. A few brief passages from the second novel in the series, *Post Captain*, will help to elaborate on the problem of the fluctuations in Jack's size. After receiving a commission for the *Polychrest*, Jack seems "to fill his uniform again" to Stephen's approval (204). Shortly after this, however, Stephen reports, "I am glad to say he does not eat at all well. I used to tell him over and over again … that he was digging his grave with his teeth" (247). Later in this very same novel, though, it appears this weight reduction may go too far, as Stephen tells Jack, "You are thin, grey—costive, no doubt. You have lost another couple of stone: the skin under your eyes is a disagreeable yellow" (338). In a similar vein—reflecting the need to not expand beyond all usefulness—the narrator reflects that "he was growing fat again, but

1. Against Type

in any case he had no intention of getting out of the way of running up and down the rigging, as some heavy captains did" (*H.M.S. Surprise* 31). Frequently, in moments of inactivity or stasis, Jack's weight declines, almost an inversion of typical notions of activity producing weight reduction (here I am thinking of activity in terms of a mission rather than the limiting of activity that seems to parallel the rise in Jack's position in the navy). Later in the series Jack has the disheartening assignment of commanding a ship in the Toulon blockade, and Maturin and his friend, Captain Heneage Dundas, both note that he appears to have dropped a stone.

This sense that somehow Jack's size must be maintained, that he cannot get too fat, that he cannot expand beyond functional bounds, but that he cannot shrink away, led me to further thoughts on the relation between his size and the extraordinary length of this series—inverting Michel De Certeau's formulation that "books are only metaphors for the body" (140), as Jack's body becomes a metaphor for the series. In other words, there becomes a sense that if O'Brian is to be able to continue to produce books, deploy plots and put Jack's body into action, then that body must remain serviceable. Considering the role of my literary fat captain brought to mind the arguments made by Patricia Parker concerning "literary fat ladies." In the chapter "Literary Fat Ladies and the Generation of the Text" from *Literary Fat Ladies: Rhetoric, Gender, Property*, Parker identifies a pattern in Renaissance literature first associated with the Romance—namely, the role of women as figures of delay and dilation, and the forestalling of narrative closure, what she calls a "history of linkages between female copia, of body and of word, and the copiousness of texts" (8). In building her case, she notes that "'dilate' comes to us from the same Latin root as Derrida's '*différance*' and involves ... that term's curious combination of difference and deferral, dilation, expansion, or dispersal in space but also the postponement in time" (9). Clearly, these associations have resonance for a series of texts that seem to expand and continue despite the seeming historical limitations of such expansion—and I will come back to this idea more fully in the chapter on history and the body—and in the seeming propensity for avoiding full narrative closure.

Parker, after concluding her survey of various figures of Renaissance texts (including two male figures—Hamlet and Falstaff), argues that the dilation and control of copiousness figured as female might at the highest level of generalization be seen as the gendered counterpart of what Steven Mulraney and other recent interpreters of representation in the Renaissance have characterized as a "rehearsal"—an allowed expansion or proliferation of the alien, multi-form, and multilingual in order to dramatize the very process of its containment, the limiting of structures of authority and control [31].

In other words, Parker suggests that the issues she sketches out about these figures who foster delay, who threaten the main action of the text—and hence some principle of the society—might be depicted in part so as to show the possibilities of overcoming them. Parker goes on to successfully note the perpetuation of this pattern, technique and imagery into contemporary literature, including James Joyce's *Ulysses*. The question then becomes, can Parker's theory help us make sense of how and why the narrative expands in the manner that it does and whether such expansion is tied to Jack's girth.

For the most part, I find that the correlations do not hold, but we can learn something of what O'Brian is doing by sketching out the divergences. Let's start with the obvious. Of course, Jack is not a "lady," but he does not even resemble the kind of feminized figure that Parker discusses. While Falstaff dresses as a lady in *Merry Wives of Windsor*, Jack pretends to be a bear in *Post Captain*. While Parker argues that "Falstaff's fat is repeatedly associated with the copiousness or 'dilation of discourse'" (21), Jack is marked by his ability in action and his inability to control language. In other words, the men that take on the roles of "literary fat women" for Parker are in various ways feminized—through transvestitism, through the conforming to the misogynist stereotype of favoring words over action, or by becoming figures who can be seen as obstacles for closure—usually by delaying a male hero (such as Prince Hal), though, arguably, Hamlet can be read as taking on both roles.

The closest Jack comes to resembling Falstaff might be some of his misadventures on land, but even these are not in any way derived from the kind of masked cowardice of Falstaff's misadventures. In terms of Jack's resemblance to a figure like Hamlet, one who might be said to be the feminized figure of delay as well as the male hero figure, this may only apply here if we see the narrative arc of the series in terms of Jack's rise from Master and Commander through Admiral. However, again, while Jack may sometimes be an impediment to his own progress, these are not typically because of the kind of stereotyped or misogynistic

1. Against Type

conceptions of gendered behaviors outlined by Parker. Early in the series Jack hurts his reputation with Admiral Harte because he has an affair with Harte's wife. When confronted by his superiors, though, Jack is inevitably silent in the face of "dressing downs." The only exception of note is when Jack alienates himself from an Admiral late in the series by refusing to back the enclosure of the lands near Jack's estates. However, this one example in twenty volumes seems relatively insignificant. In addition, since we know O'Brian was writing a twenty-first novel when he died in which Jack was an Admiral, even the claim that the series can find closure in Jack becoming an Admiral seems suspect.

Parker's theory of the feminized male figure who delays often gets grounded in figures known for their felicity with language or almost paralyzing interiority. Besides the fact that Jack is the protagonist of the novels—thus an unlikely figure to play the role of both delayer and mover of action—Jack has none of Falstaff's eloquence (and little of Hamlet's habit of vacillation). A character remarks how, for instance, Jack "derives a greater pleasure from a smaller stream of wit than any man I have ever known" (*Master and Commander* 297); and, in the mode of the traditional, masculine hero, Jack is often at his most intimidating when he is at his least verbose, or when he chooses action over conversation, such as when he simply stops talking to the French revolutionary Dutourd in *The Wine-Dark Sea*: "Dutourd opened his mouth to speak, but it was too late. Jack, throwing off his coat, sped from the cabin, making the deck tremble as he went" (34). Rather than wit or word play, we are more likely to see passages like this one from *Far Side of the World*, in which Jack attempts to explain a situation to Stephen:

> "It was the strangest experience: there he was, telling me things to my face as though he were invisible, while I could see him as plain as ..."
> "The ace of spades?"
> "No. Not quite that. As plain as a ... God damn it. As plain as the palm of my hand? A turnpike?"
> "As Salisbury sphere? As a red herring?"
> "Perhaps so. At all events the *Defenders* gave to understand they were unhappy" [106].

Passages likes these contribute more to the satiric elements of the text—as I discussed in the previous section—than to delays (other than Jack's failure to close the joke or bromide itself).

Despite his absent powers of linguistic control, we may, nevertheless, think further about the issues of closure and Jack's size. Here, Parker's theory may be more to the point. Parker elaborates on how *Bartholomew Fair* can only be brought to a close once "the fat lady in question is brought under control," and that movement of the play coincides "explicitly with the shrinking of Ursula's body size" (25). We might then consider that there is an implied correlation in the maintenance of Jack's size and the continued suspension of closure necessary for the series to progress through its twenty volumes. The linkage between maintaining Aubrey's weight within a reasonable range corresponds to the dilation of the series itself. If Jack "shrinks" away, we have no figure that can propel these narratives forward; if he becomes too large, he becomes cast too much in a comical role and can no longer also participate—except in a broadly parodic way—in the adventure-oriented generic elements of the novels (boarding ships, fighting in the gangways, commanding a large body of men because of their respect for the captain's courage and bravery).

I suppose that what ultimately reconfigures the template that Parker lays out is that in some ways those narratives about which she talks all seek—ultimately—a closure; however, we may question whether O'Brian seeks only perpetuation and renewal of his narrative. We should also consider that closure bears directly on the problems of genre, since how texts close frequently conform to generic conventions. For instance, we know we have read or watched a tragedy when the protagonist dies in the end, a comedy when the protagonist marries. What do we know, though, when we read a series that never comes to a close? This reluctance to end may not have been there from the start. The opening of the series reads as something of a trilogy, as the first three books contain several clear narrative arcs—including Jack finding a wife and establishing his reputation, Stephen losing his love interest, and Jack rising from Master and Commander to the much more secure position of Post-Captain. However, once the series moved beyond that arc, the problem becomes how to continue to spill out these plots in the seemingly narrow historical window of the late Napoleonic wars (since the series begins not at their outset, but well after the heyday of Nelson, Jack's idol and former commanding officer). The answer comes in O'Brian's explanation of the need to seemingly fold in years within years. In addition to carving new layers in time, various storylines must also find renewal if the series

1. Against Type

is to avoid closure. Consider Stephen's role in the genre of romance quest, his pursuit of his beloved Diana. After meeting her and nearly losing her to Jack in the second volume, he seeks her out in India in the third volume. In the fifth novel of the series, Stephen spends a great deal of time with a woman who both resembles Diana and who is her friend—and thus keeps Diana on both Stephen's and our minds. In the sixth novel he rescues Diana. He finally marries her in the seventh novel of the series, *The Surgeon's Mate*. This seeming closure, though, does not settle matters. Instead, as I discuss more fully in Chapter 3 in relation to Stephen's drug use, he proceeds to lose her and regain her companionship twice more. Then he loses her once more—this time permanently—when she dies. O'Brian, then, gives Stephen a new love interest, who also turns down his initial marriage proposal, and yet who we find he is still pursuing in the unfinished—and untitled—twenty-first novel. Thus, in a series that wants perpetual renewal, closure is itself a kind of delay or obstacle. And what kind of romance plot is it that never finds closure or seemingly renews in a never-ending fashion, a Sisyphus rolling his rock?

The Nine-Stone Surgeon

Although, as I've contended so far in this chapter, Jack Aubrey's is the central body of the text, that which stands at the center of the action and around which the narrative most often circulates, the body of his "particular" friend and companion, Stephen Maturin, also holds a very prominent role in the novel(s). Thus, in the following section, I will further explore the significance of Stephen—and his body—in some of the issues I have begun to sketch out here regarding body and genre. In many ways Stephen and Jack form a classic pair of opposites—in both body and personality. If Jack is typically noted (especially early in the series) for a degree of rugged handsomeness, flowing blonde hair, and ruddy complexion that rises to outright redness, Stephen, in contrast, appears immediately to Jack as an "ill looking son of a bitch" (*Master and Commander* 8) with a "dead-white face" (15). Stephen even says of himself that he is "a little ugly small man, with no name and no fortune" (*Post Captain* 330). In *The Wine-Dark Sea* and elsewhere we are informed that "Jack Aubrey weighed sixteen or seventeen stone, Stephen barely nine" (61).[4] Jack's flowing blonde hair contrasts quite distinctly with Stephen's, which he wears closely cropped when not masked by his unkempt and raggedy wig (a sign of his profession). The contrasts between the two also extend beyond the body. Jack is an English Tory from a landed family and an Anglican; Stephen is a "natural son" of Irish and Catalan ancestry, and a Catholic. Jack has little learning beyond nautical matters because he was sent to sea so young (though he proves to be something of a math prodigy); Stephen is a physician—not, importantly, *just* a naval surgeon—and a natural philosopher with a membership in the Royal Society. Stephen possesses the wit and command of language that continuously escapes Jack, as I have hinted at earlier. The problems of language and wit are replayed throughout the series, but here is a typical example of their dialogue, which not only highlights Jack's poor wit but Stephen's felicitous tongue. In this exchange from *Desolation Island* we find Jack, as ever, seeking a clever turn and Stephen's deflation of the attempt:

> "You cannot make an omelette without breaking some eggs," said Jack quickly, before the chance should be lost for ever. "Ha, ha, Stephen, what do you say to that?"
> "I might say something about pearls before swine—the pearls being these priceless eggs, if you follow me—were I to attempt a repartee in the same order of magnitude" [293].

These kinds of exchanges highlight and reflect their other differences. Jack's size seems to lack subtlety, while Stephen's requires it: their control of language reflects the same parameters and requirements (commands, for example, need to be blunt and plain). Jack's skills lie in his ability to work in a public sphere and on a large scale, whereas Stephen specializes in surgical precision—as a physician and as an intelligence officer.

Although Jack's larger body is tied to perhaps the most prominent genres that compete for space in this extensive series—namely, the historical novel, the adventure tale, the sea story—Stephen's body also finds itself a part of and a contesting point between multiple genres. However, Stephen has a limited ability to participate in a central way in the primary genres associated with Jack. During battle, Stephen inevitably retreats to his surgical station below decks, he has no—and never gains—mastery of ship life, and he is by physique and temperament highly unsuited for adventure and romance (in a traditional sense, and despite the fact that, as I have already noted, he features in the version of romance that the

1. Against Type

novels embrace). Despite these limitations, it is also worth noting that, to a certain extent, Stephen becomes increasingly integral to the development and proliferation of plots as the series continues and expands. He begins his sea travel as a guest of Jack's before being enlisted officially as a ship's surgeon (and later as an intelligence officer). In this role, Stephen's body figures importantly in two ways. As a surgeon, he continuously finds himself awash in the bodies of others: sewing them back together, opening them up to remove intruding shrapnel or splinters, or, in the case where a part of the body must be sacrificed for the whole to survive, his ability to amputate a limb (an ability most prized). In *The Wine-Dark Sea*, he even finds himself performing an amputation upon himself following frostbite, having "removed the peccant members" rather unsentimentally "with a chisel" (225) (this, of course, is not nearly as impressive as the work that Sylvester Stallone's Rambo performs on himself). As an essentially non–Naval member of the crew, Stephen's other bodily role—though this is for O'Brian rather than the ship—seems to be constantly displaying his physical incompetence aboard ship. Thus, he seems to highlight Jack's own place in those adventure narratives by his own inability to participate in them. Similarly, Jack is as ill-suited to Stephen's primary genres—the novel of ideas and the spy novel—as Stephen is to Jack's, since Jack finds spying distasteful and has none of the subtlety necessary for it, and eschews the kind of philosophical meditation that often envelops Stephen's mind (though Jack does practice deception in naval encounters on a regular basis).

This duality is established early in the series, but it never dissipates, even after Stephen's long exposure to a nautical life. Jack's initial invitation to Stephen allows him to re-enter the more physical aspects of the medical life. In preparation, Stephen plans to attend a surgery at the local hospital of Port Mahon, and the narrator notes his excitement for surgery: "'It is a great while since I felt the grind of bone under my saw,' he added smiling with anticipation" (*Master and Commander* 68). His skills with the knife are contrasted a few pages later with Jack's struggles to carve a ham (109–110). In this first novel, Stephen makes his reputation by trepanning the gunner—opening up his skull in front of the crew, and fitting it back together with a metal plate. Jack's faith in Stephen's medical skills, his power over the ailments of physical bodies, is nearly limitless as early as the second novel, *Post Captain*. Consider how Jack, contemplating an injured sailor, believes, "'Stephen will soon set him right,' he thought: it was known that Stephen could raise the dead so long as the tide had not changed" (180). Later, in that same novel, Jack writes a letter to the parents of his midshipman, William Babbington, describing the boy's injuries: "His arm is so badly broken, that I fear it must suffer amputation" (385), but Stephen "wishes me to say, that the arm may very well be saved. But, I may add, he is the best hand in the Fleet with a saw, if it comes to that; which I am sure will be a comfort to you and Mrs. Babbington" (386). Strangely, for Jack, Stephen's skills as a healer are signified by his ability to remove limbs more than Stephen's ability to bring the body back together, such as when Stephen sewed up "Lakey's private parts so neat" (*Master and Commander* 140). Of course, amputating Babbington's arm would make him resemble Jack's hero, Nelson.

In the emphasis on dismemberment, Stephen's physical skills become commensurate with Jack's: they both are marked in terms of taking bodies apart (even if, in Stephen's case, they are ultimately to the benefit of allies, as opposed to the destruction of an enemy, as in Jack's case). However, these kinds of physical feats are not the kind typically highlighted and celebrated in adventure stories. We get a further glimpse of this interplay between the two figures, highlighting these contrasts, during a second trepanning, this time of Joe Plaice in *The Far Side of the World*. As Stephen performs a trepanning on Plaice, we find that it leaves Jack "pale," but he finds it nonetheless "extremely gratifying" for the "blood running down Joe's neck regardless—brains clearly to be seen—something not to be missed—instructive, too—and they [Jack, Bonden, and the rest of the crew] made the most of it" (194). It is as if only the taking apart of bodies—despite the unease it produces, especially when the more private world of surgery enters the deck and the more public sphere of the ship—conveys the true measure of Stephen's abilities. We also witness the strange converse doubling of the taking apart of bodies that leads to death—namely, the onboard violence of a naval ship at war, the kind much more common to the adventure story. This is made most plain in *The Thirteen Gun Salute*, in which, after Jack asks after "your patient," the narrator tells us that "Stephen had several patients, two with syphilitic gummata who were near their ends and some serious pulmonary cases, but he knew that to a naval mind only an amputation really counted" (140).

Nevertheless, as seemingly incompatible as these two figures and

1. Against Type

the stories to which they are both suited seem to be, Stephen does aid in many ways in the prolongation of Jack's narratives (and so contributes to genres to which he appears alien), and Jack similarly contributes to Stephen's. Consider how Stephen's casual remark to Sophie in *Post Captain*—"I sew his ears on from time to time, sure" (190)—suggests that, in part, one of Stephen's roles in the series is keeping the Captain together, specifically by repairing his damaged body after battle (in keeping with his lack of attention to the subtleties of bodies, including his own, Jack is often ignorant of his having been wounded, or, at the least, ignorant of the extent of his injuries—and he receives at least some injury with great frequency). As Stephen tells Clarissa Oakes in *The Truelove*, "I should scarcely like to number the wounds I have sewn up and dressed, or the musket and pistol balls I have extracted" (186).

As I have earlier suggested, as physician and friend, Stephen is also remarkably attuned to the fluctuations in Jack's corpulence. However, we should not underestimate the role Jack, conversely, has in keeping Stephen alive and his body intact. For all of Stephen's abilities in the field of medicine, he is often extraordinarily incompetent aboard ship. After Stephen wakes for the first time aboard ship, he promptly smacks his head on the beam above him (*Master and Commander* 89). From this moment forward, Stephen continuously takes pratfalls as he attempts to board ships or simply maneuver his way about them. Just as frequently, Jack—or various other members of the crew—must come to his rescue, plucking him from the sea or grabbing him as he nearly falls to his death from a masthead. We might consider that such moments serve two purposes for the novels. First, they act in a manner akin to the satirical emphasis on Jack's size and bodily functions, humanizing and often literally bringing Stephen down to earth after his more exalted triumphs in medicine. (In *H.M.S. Surprise*, for example, Jack says of sailing in Stephen's company, "tis a great comfort to me to have you aboard: it is like sailing with a piece of the True Cross" [119].) Second, these moments provide another example of the kind of balance of types O'Brian constructs through Jack and Stephen: on some basic level, their skills and weaknesses require the presence of the other in order to compensate for lacks and to highlight strengths. Perhaps the most symbolic example of this balance can be found in *The Far Side of the World* in a scene in which Stephen falls out of the Captain's cabin while attempting to catch some of the "immense population of phosphorescent marine organisms" floating by (260). After Jack realizes that Stephen has fallen through the window, he plunges after him, and eventually, as they float in the sea, Jack asks Stephen to "put your arms round my neck" and essentially keeps Stephen alive by letting him hang onto his neck and back (263).

As we see in this example—which moves from the comic to the nearly tragic—just as there seems to be some kind of real danger (at least to the narrative momentum) in Jack's weight, Stephen truly is at risk for his life (well, his imaginary life, that is—of course, to passionate fans of the novels, Jack and Stephen likely stop seeming imaginary if they stick with the series). At almost any moment, Stephen seems vulnerable, much more vulnerable than any but the youngest or most incompetent individuals aboard ship. These are not isolated incidents we are talking about. Consider this sequence from the fourth book of the series, *The Mauritius Command,* which I will discuss in greater detail in Chapter 5. During a hurricane, Dr. Maturin, "having pitched down two ladders, found himself lying on the ship's side. Presently, she righted and he slid down; but on her taking a most furious lee-lurch on wearing round, he shot across the deck, through all his remaining stock of Venice treacle, to land on hands and knees upon the other side, clinging to a suspended locker in the darkness, puzzled" (194). Later, when trying to get aboard a ship,

> they let [Stephen] drop between the boat and the ship's side. In his fall he struck his head and back on the gunwale, cracking two ribs and sinking stunned down through the warm clear water: the frigate was under way, and although she heaved to at once not a man aboard did anything more valuable than run about shouting for some minutes, and by the time she had dropped her stern-boat Stephen would have been dead if one of the bale-carrying black men had not dived in and fetched him out" [240].

Later, Stephen again falls: "A slack slabline at once took a turn about his dangling legs and jerked him into a maze of cordage that he could neither name nor disentangle.... Stephen therefore swung in a sickening downward curve to strike the frigate's side a little below the waterline" (308). And the passage goes on at length. It is difficult to say how one should read these elaborate descriptions. On one hand, since we know Stephen survives, they can be read comically: his incompetence serving to highlight the profound competence of the others or to stand in marked contrast to his remarkable abilities in his specific fields of expertise, as I have suggested. Yet, in each of these descriptions, O'Brian makes it fairly

1. Against Type

clear that Stephen truly could have died: that the price for physical clumsiness can be mortal. After witnessing yet another similar sequence to this, Jack wonders to himself, "but how [Stephen] has survived so long at sea I cannot tell" (*The Truelove* 118). On some level, the answer, of course, is simply he must.

While there are countless examples of these incidents, including one that leads to Stephen being nearly trepanned himself in *The Far Side of the World*—only to escape possible death at the hand of a well-intended friend by miraculously awakening—his work in intelligence also puts him at a great deal of risk. He lost his toes escaping from Peru after a failed bit of covert action, and early in the series he is tortured to such a degree that his hands never fully recover. As in the incident in which Stephen falls out of the ship, Jack, though, rescues him from his torturers before more than just his hands become truly endangered.

It should be noted that the dichotomy between Stephen's physical abilities and his failings closely corresponds to those of Jack. Like Jack, whose body corresponds to or modulates between multiple genres, Stephen too has his connection to various generic strands in the series. While Stephen begins the series largely as a companion to Jack—and in this way more of an aid to plot development rather than a central catalyst of it—he gradually becomes involved in intelligence work, work that often provides commissions for Jack, for "intelligence and action complemented one another" (*The Truelove* 67). As the novels progress, the genre most closely associated with this field—namely, the thriller or the spy thriller—increasingly becomes one of the central genres at play in the larger generic mix of the novels, though again ones that largely leave Jack on the margins of the story. As the series progresses, we find several novels that have, at the least, prolonged sequences involving Stephen's work in intelligence, including *Fortune of War* (which I will discuss in a moment) *Treason's Harbor*, and *The Wine-Dark Sea*. In fact, the long sequence of the late middle part of the series involving Jack's dismissal from the Navy and his attempts to gain reinstatement is intimately tied up in a similarly long sequence in which Stephen attempts to overcome the covert French agents operating in British intelligence and government, which includes Wray, an agent who hates Jack.

Stephen also most fully participates in another genre: the novel of ideas, the novel of philosophical contemplation or scientific investigation—a book about the world of the mind, in contrast to, say, the novel of action. Not only is Stephen an accomplished and fully educated physician, but he is also a natural philosopher. Again, though, Jack's stories and narratives tend to do as much to interrupt these genres as they do to allow them to take shape. Stephen's intelligence work gets further tied to natural philosophy in the series because the head of naval intelligence, Sir Joseph Blaine, is also a natural philosopher, preoccupied primarily with the study of beetles. The connections between Stephen's relation to the novel of ideas and his body are complex. They follow his preoccupations with bodies other than his own. He spends a great deal of time collecting specimens from all over the world; we find him harboring specimens in all kinds of absurd locales (a liver in his pocket, badgers in cupboards, for example); and we hear him lament the exorbitant price of cadavers and offering advice on the best types for dissection, as in *Desolation Island*, where "he observed that it was shocking how corpses had risen: he had been cheapening one that very morning, and the villains had had the face to ask him four guineas—the London price for a provincial cadaver!" (16). His treatment of bodies—of specimens, of the dead—in this impersonal manner also carries over to his views of his patients. As he informs Louisa Wogan in *Desolation Island*, "When I am called in to a lady, I see a female body, more or less deranged in its functions. You will say that it is inhabited by a mind that may partake of its distress, and I grant your position entirely. Yet for me the patient is not a woman, in the common sense. Gallantry would be out of place, and what is worse, unscientific" (243). These shifts in genre can sometimes be abrupt, even jarring. Perhaps one of the most spectacular examples of such a shift occurs in *The Thirteen Gun Salute*, which centers a great deal on Stephen—both his intelligence work and his work as a naturalist. Thus, after he successfully eliminates the French spies, Ledward and Wray, he brings them to his friend, Van Buren, a rather well-connected naturalist who had earlier complained that "it is very difficult to get a really prime cadaver in this country: nothing but the occasional adulterer" (189).

These interests in bodies also connect very clearly with Stephen's desire to repress the urges and desires of his often incompetent, rebellious, or unattractive body in favor of a situation in which the mind rules the body. I will discuss these issues at greater length in the subsequent chapter on addiction and drug use, but, because of the relevance of drug use and genre, please allow me to briefly sketch out this issue

1. Against Type

in the series. Stephen's attempts to wrest control of his body lead him, ironically, to become an opium addict—in his preferred form, the tincture of laudanum—and later a consumer of coca leaves (which Stephen, somewhat obtusely, fails to connect with his former opium addiction). His attraction to these substances is quite clear: they give him at least the impression of mental control over bodily frailties and desires. Examples of his rationale for its use permeate the series, but one example can be found in *Desolation Island*. At this point, Stephen has once again tried to stop using it—when logical reasons show its role in his life—but here he openly wonders, in the convoluted logic of an addict, if he owes it to his role as intelligence officer to take opium so as to control his attraction to an American spy, Louisa Wogan. I will take up the issues of both Stephen's drug use and his sexuality—as well as *Desolation Island*—in the final three chapters.

As the novels in the series develop, Stephen's desire to concentrate on the outside world and his passions of the mind consistently collide with the ambitions—and genres—connected to Aubrey. On several occasions throughout the series, fellow lovers of natural phenomena express their envy of Stephen's position—as a natural philosopher who has the opportunity to travel all over the world, often to places unfamiliar or unknown to his fellow scientists. However, Stephen's reply is almost always the same: his position is not to be envied, for, in fact, it is essentially torturous. His desires for intellectual pursuits are always placed in abeyance to the greater needs of Jack in his role as naval captain. The depiction of adventure, historical events, and battles, these all win out over the investigations Stephen so desires; the historical novel or adventure tale wins out over the novel of ideas. Such is the case in the fourteenth novel of the series, *The Nutmeg of Consolation*, where Stephen's "great hopes of seeing Amsterdam Island, a remote and uninhabited speck untouched by any naturalist, its flora, fauna, and geology wholly undescribed," are sunk as usual, as he "saw it indeed, but only far to windward, and the ship carried on under a press of sail for Java Head" (189). He is similarly incensed when he accuses Jack of "hurrying past inestimable pearls, bent solely on destruction, neglecting all discovery" (*The Far Side of the World* 248). Only in rare moments can Jack offer Stephen these opportunities, and they often occur when the ship has been brought to shore in need of repairs, as when the eponymous Desolation Island becomes something of a paradise for Stephen while the rest of remaining crew try to make the *Leopard* seaworthy. (Perhaps not coincidentally, the spy genre also features in the conclusion, as it is the narrative that comes closest to closure at that novel's end.) It is almost as if the novel of ideas is given moments to bloom only when the historically-driven sea stories are delayed by forces beyond the control of the bodies most attached to those adventures.

As in the case I described involving Stephen's killing of and dissecting the French spies in *The Thirteen Gun Salute,* the spy story or thriller forms an unusual companion to the novel of ideas in the series. First, it is important to note that Stephen almost always considers his work intelligence rather than spying—although the distinction might be one of semantics—and he prides himself on making his services to England voluntary. O'Brian's use of Stephen's body in relation to this genre resembles his use of Jack's body in its more heroic undertakings. Although Stephen may be more likely to fall into the ocean than successfully climb aboard a ship on any particular occasion, he is quite capable of extreme physical skill and, when called upon, devastating violence. In other words, just as Jack is both powerful and even athletic while being decidedly fat, Stephen harbors both great physical awkwardness and a vast array of physical skills. I would emphasize, however, that in Stephen's case they are largely skills, techniques and movements one can master and practice rather than a kind of "natural" or fluid athleticism. These kinds of skills correspond to those required for expert surgical work. There may be a basic hand-eye coordination required for excelling, but practice and attention to fine detail can allow for eventual mastery. Perhaps not coincidentally, these skills are put on display in *The Fortune of War,* in which Stephen dispatches two French spies by employing a surgical tool as one of his weapons. Early in the novel he explains his choice of weapon to Jack: "'I have borrowed this from Mr. Choates' instrument-cabinet.' He unwrapped his handkerchief and showed a catling with a heavy handle and a short double-edged blade. 'We use these for amputations,' he observed." Jack responds that "It looks precious small." In contrast, Stephen notes, "Bless you, Jack, an inch of steel in the right place will do wonders. Man is a pitiably frail machine" (228). Later, after several near escapes from his French enemies, "Stephen strode forward and as the Frenchman turned he brought the massive obsidian down on his head, breaking both. Pontet-Canet was on the floor, limp, but breathing. Stephen bent over him, catling in hand,

1. Against Type

felt for the still beating common carotid, severed it, and stood back from the jet of blood" (248). This passage represents a perfect—or, depending upon your point of view, monstrous—commingling of several threads connected through Stephen's body, and the associations with bodies and Stephen, reiterated over the course of the series: Stephen's success as surgeon and intelligence officer lies in part in his ability to separate himself from responses to bodies—both his own and the fate of another's—and his skills reveal their duality as well. Again we see him as master of both healing, as suggested by his knowledge of anatomy, and dismemberment, revealed in the literal severing of the "still beating carotid."

The relation of Jack and Stephen individually to violence complements those genres which seem to narrate these acts. On the one hand, Stephen is the most consistent voice against violence throughout the series: he declines to participate in battles or raids (with one exception); he speaks out against corporeal punishment; and he finds slavery abhorrent, to name but three examples. Jack, while not necessarily of a violent temperament, clearly enjoys combat in ways Stephen does not, and he is clearly less moved by things like floggings than Stephen (although he is remarkably indisposed to punishment unless it is absolutely called for). O'Brian states the contrast plainly in *Thirteen Gun Salute*. We are told that Jack

> had boarded many and many an enemy and it was at these times he felt most wholly alive. Ordinarily he was not at all aggressive—a cheerful, sanguine, friendly, good-natured creature, severe only in the event of bad seamanship—but when he was on a Frenchmen's deck, sword in hand, he felt a wild and savage joy, a fullness of being, like no other; and he remembered every detail of blows given or received, every detail of the whole engagement, with the most vivid clarity [8].

In contrast, there is Maturin, "who disliked violence and who took no pleasure in any battle whatsoever. When he was obliged to fight he did so with cold efficiency, but never without apprehension that had continually mastered, disliking both the occasion and the recollection of it" (8). Jack's manner in combat perfectly coincides with his character's flirtation with the overly heroic, epic, or tragic figure: Jack experiences battle "in an extraordinarily vivid state of mind, a kind of fierce exaltation, an intense living in the most immediate present," which is almost inevitably followed by a kind of deflation and depression (*The Nutmeg of Consolation* 44). While in these moments Jack appears most fully alive, Stephen's moments of violence—almost always more private and more intimate—are marked by the expression first witnessed by Jack as Stephen prepared for a duel: he finds "something disagreeable, and somehow reptilian, about the cold contained way Stephen took up his stance..." (*Post Captain* 303). Throughout the series, O'Brian comes back to the adjective "reptilian" to describe Stephen in these moments, emphasizing how his violence is achieved by a kind of dehumanization, a distancing of himself from the actions of his body (and the commonplace figure suggests "cold-blooded"). If Jack's intensity lends itself to the epic or tragic, Stephen's coldness suggests the kind of dispassionate and sinister violence associated with the world of intrigue found in thrillers and spy narratives.

As I have noted, the effectiveness of Stephen's skills in these moments gets at least balanced again and again by his ubiquitous moments of clumsiness—of being a poor lubber, as the crew might say. However, his body in and of itself also works to both make him more effective as an intelligence agent and to stand in stark contrast to the kind of heroic—almost James Bond–like—figure his actions would seem to suggest. In *The Surgeon's Mate,* after Stephen has come to report his successes against the French agents he encountered in Boston, the intelligence officer, Beck, "found that he was most illogically disappointed by the meager, shabby, undistinguished man who sat on the other side of the desk, slowly undoing a sailcloth parcel. Against all reason Beck had expected a more heroic figure: certainly not one who wore blue spectacles against the sun" (21). Stephen simply does not look the part. Before either Jack or Stephen's future wife, Diana, realize that Stephen is an intelligence officer, they fairly explode with laughter when others suspect Stephen's covert profession.

Later in *The Surgeon's Mate* we find a moment in which O'Brian brings these various connections and uses of Stephen's body together, and a moment in which we see the kind of contestation of genres—as they are represented, narrated and figured through the body—present throughout the series. Stephen is offered an opportunity to present a paper in Paris delineating his research on the solitaire, a bird related to the dodo. Before his address, Stephen looks in the mirror: "He did so, and a grim reflection peered back at him, a small round close-cropped head, its sparse hair standing straight up like the bristles on an old worn-out scrubbing-brush. 'Jesus, Mary, and Joseph,' he said in a low inward

1. Against Type

tone, 'I have forgot my wig. What shall I do?'" (152). Here, we again witness Stephen scrambling to keep himself together, his wig—as a sign of his profession—seemingly essential to forming his whole person (usually members of crew, such as Jack's steward, Killick, perform the role of making Stephen presentable). Stephen's decision to sport green spectacles disturbs Diana and reveals his nervousness: he believes that the glasses "give me countenance" (154), while also masking his opium use and "pale eyes." First, Stephen begins in a "voice so loud and aggressive that its returning echo shocked him extremely—shocked him almost fatally." However, after this astonishing beginning, "Most of the rest of his discourse was delivered in a low mumble" (155). His terrible speech puts off thoughts among Bonaparte's agents that he "has anything to do with intelligence" (156). Instead, a spy says of Stephen: "Madame Dangeau is sure he is a paederast, and I think she is right. He is a friend of La Mothe's" (157).

This scene marks a moment in which Stephen's intellectual pursuits might have taken over the larger plots of the novel and essentially stalled Jack's naval pursuits. Had this presentation garnered him fame, he might have been encouraged to make these pursuits the center of his preoccupations. Instead, O'Brian crafts this scene so that Stephen earns the respect of those who were particularly interested in the subject—they crowd in to hear it—while the more general audience is instead left first with the impression of physical awkwardness rather than his intellectual adeptness, and then they simply abandon him and return to their own conversations. Meanwhile, not only does this performance undermine any aspirations to the novel of ideas—or put those ideas into a comic (perhaps even satiric) light—it also emphasizes Stephen's failure to physically embody more typical notions of what a masterful intelligence officer might appear to look like. Lastly, if Jack's conduct often links him to a more epic order, Stephen's, particularly in his long pursuit of the maddeningly beautiful and elusive Diana, could be connected to the romance. As a final deflation, the scorn of the French agents also underscores how paltry a figure for that role Stephen—especially in his physical stature and visage—appears to be.

Stephen's body may be thought of as functioning in this series in much the same way that satire pairs with the epic or tragic: he provides a balance and a counter, drawing the narrative focus back again and again to places where they each meet. I have suggested that Stephen's body undermines, among its various generic connections, the romance, the quest whose object becomes often embodied in an elusive woman. However, as I sketched out earlier, Stephen does fashion a connection to Diana: they do marry and—however unusual the arrangements and tenuous the relationships—they do have a child. Diana dies before the series stops (we cannot really say it concludes). Nevertheless, following the path I traced previously, this romance quest is one that never so much concludes as is perpetually renewed.

The one romance, the one connection that keeps getting pursued to the very end, though, is that between Jack and Stephen. However, this is not a quest; this is a relationship that persists, develops, and thrives. It fluctuates, but it follows no neat—or even rough—narrative arc. Perhaps this constant interplay between these characters represents the similar exchange and interrogation of bodies and genres throughout the series. O'Brian does not use the central bodies of Aubrey and Maturin to make any kind of simple or direct one-to-one correspondence between the body—its shape, its strengths, its weaknesses—and either a genre of narrative or corresponding meanings associated with or commonly produced by such genres. As I have argued, Jack, for example, is not simply a figure of adventure or even epic because of his size or his strength, and neither is he solely a comic figure, let alone a clown, because of his weight or failings at wit. Instead, these bodies, while full of signification, also draw our attention to the limits and complexities of such meanings. In other words, yes, Jack's oversized body becomes a kind of trope that figures these seemingly ever-expanding narratives of the Royal Navy, but it also brings in to play a number of other diverse narratives. Following again the ideas of Bakhtin regarding the power of the novel to encompass and almost ingest other genres for the purpose of evaluating and critiquing them, we may then consider that O'Brian ultimately employs the complications of the body as a way of bringing the many genres evoked in the series both into play but also under heel. However, he also creates a series without end—one that only meets its end with O'Brian's death. We might consider some of the conversations in *The Nutmeg of Consolation* between Stephen, Martin, and Martin's friend, an aspiring novelist. Stephen underscores the importance of novels: "I look upon them—I look upon good novels—as a very valuable part of literature, conveying more exact and finely-distinguished knowledge of the human heart and mind than almost any other, with greater

1. Against Type

breadth and depth and fewer restraints" (253). Here we see him prioritize character and, importantly, the lack of "restraints" on the presentation of humanity. This view corresponds also with Stephen's take on endings—a problem, not coincidently, haunting the aspiring writer: "The conventional ending, with virtue rewarded and loose ends tied up is often sadly chilling; and its platitude and falsity tend to infect what has gone before, however excellent" (256). In this series we find that O'Brian arrives at a solution to this problem: never to end, never to conclude, but to simply stop. In this, life seems renewed perpetually in the continuous perpetuation of narrative.

2

Scars, History and Historical Fiction

"Deep-Dish Costume Dramas"

As I alluded to in the introduction, my own interest—okay, let's call it an obsession if we can do so without images of stalkers and selling off one's property in order to acquire Patrick O'Brian memorabilia floating into your consciousness—began in 1995, after the completion of my graduate coursework, when I came across a review of Patrick O'Brian's *The Commodore*, by Katherine A. Powers, in a 1995 issue of the *Atlantic Monthly*. The review, to which I will return shortly, sent me to a local bookstore and down to a shelf—well, *shelves* actually—where the span of O'Brian's late-life project spilled from one plank to the next. These editions, notably those by Norton produced before Peter Weir's film and the subsequent alteration of the artwork, all appear in various muted colors—the first, *Master and Commander,* a faded powder blue, almost turquoise. Upon each novel's spine appears a number. This is enough to stop the curious. As a friend who had contemplated picking up the books recently said to me, "If I start, I need to read them all, right?" Even back in 1995 I was asking myself something like the same question as I panned down the spines, seeing that the numbers reached seventeen. Pulling *Master and Commander* from the bookstore shelf, I gazed upon a painting by Geoff Hunt of—no surprise here—a Napoleonic-era naval vessel lying at anchor. The painting itself seems to be from a bygone age. The cover provides a quote from Sir Francis Chichester proclaiming this "the best sea-story I have ever read." I don't know that I would have been terribly impressed even if I knew that Sir Francis Chichester held the world record for quickest voyage, sailing around the world via the clipper route (there was no *Wikipedia* to clue me in at that time, not to mention no iPhone

2. Scars, History and Historical Fiction

to allow me to look it up). I had never been terribly impressed with sea stories anyway. However, when I flipped the book over, I noted a blurb that appears upon all of the Aubrey-Maturin series, one from Richard Snow proclaiming these "The best historical novels ever written." This leads us back to a consideration of genre and the series, but from an altogether different lens than my initial exploration of that question.

It is not my goal in this chapter to question the validity of Snow's endorsement, but it is worth considering the whole notion of whether these are to be considered historical novels. Let's then return briefly to Powers' review, which includes some interviews and biographical sketches of O'Brian, in addition to some commentary on *The Commodore*. She, too, begins with an imaginary potential reader, but in this portrayal she calls into some doubt the assumptions of Snow's comment (okay, I wasn't imaginary and that was a true story, but the suspense of whether I would, in fact, take the leap and buy one of these novels seems to have died a natural death many pages earlier in this volume). After highlighting the "booming industry" that the O'Brian novels had become, she notes that there remain "cautious readers who would not consider taking up one of these volumes, believing them to be no more than deep-dish costume dramas" (92). I am as puzzled as you about how these novels might be said to resemble an indulgent pizza or pie, but the basic premise here is that some potential readers might view these novels as closer to historical romances found somewhere between your cat's litter and the frozen foods than to Leo Tolstoy's *War and Peace*. In fact, when pressed by Powers, O'Brian concedes that

> What I hadn't understood when I began these things ... was what a depraved genre it is in the general mind. It had never occurred to me that to shift the scene of a novel to another age ... and to cast it in an English in some degrees pleasanter than the current, put me in a disreputable genre. I met some very astonishing statements—such as that I was a writer of adventure stories [92].

O'Brian's statement is confusing for a few reasons. On the one hand, it is not entirely clear what genre he means in light of Powers' set-up of the quote referring to costume drama. Is the disreputable genre historical fiction, its false-shallow cousin, "costume drama," or its debased cousin once-removed, "adventure stories," the dreaded realm of adolescent reading? O'Brian's comments that he was "astonished" to find folks calling him a writer of adventure could indicate the answer, but we can also recall the fact that Dean King, in his biography of O'Brian, says that the "'historical novel' ... was a term that to him had little validity" (207). Only to complicate the problems of interpretation further, Powers quickly asserts that "these books are, in fact, extraordinarily exciting, with adventure very much on the page," and then goes on to label O'Brian the heir to the obscure Victorian novelist Captain Marryat, author of *Midshipman Easy*, "another witty and intelligent author who has been tarred with the genre brush." While I could wish that Powers had refrained from using language seemingly derived from the history of race and racism, she does point to the problems in considering what these novels actually are, as well as the potential danger to how we read them cast by a sense that they are one genre or another—because, as I explored in my first chapter, to read them with the expectations of adventure story inevitably has some power to shape what we see, based on what we expect. Snow's blurb and Chicester's blurb, then, seemingly work at cross-purposes and open up these questions before one even finds the diagram of "the sails of a square-rigged ship, hung out to dry in a calm" that precedes even the "Author's Note."

The previous chapter focused primarily on the problem of genre in the series, and particularly the relationship between human bodies and this problem. In doing so, I have put off the question of one noteworthy genre—namely, the historical novel. That topic now moves to the center of this chapter's focus, in which I will explore three main inter-related issues. The first will be thinking through what we mean by calling a novel a historical novel—what we expect it to do, what questions and issues we expect it to entertain, and the related question of whether we should take Snow's assumptions about O'Brian's novel at face value. From here, I will explore more directly how the novel depicts history, and what role history and historiography play in the novels—as related to, but not exclusive of, the concerns of postmodern historical fiction and traditional historical fiction. Lastly, I will explore the role of the body in the treatment and representation of history in the novels. It will be my contention that bodies of both the author—in terms of its aging and mortality—as well as the similar concerns regarding the novels' more figurative bodies (in particular those of Aubrey and Maturin, and perhaps even the novels themselves as an extension of O'Brian, his "body of work"), both help construct and shape the way in which the novels interact with and represent history.

2. Scars, History and Historical Fiction

Do We Know Historical Fiction When We Read It?

Let us abide a bit longer with Powers' review before we depart for other places and theorists. Early in her review, after raising this question of "disreputable genre," Powers offers a relatively familiar list of generic ingredients that comprise the Aubrey-Maturin series. These include "comedy of manners, moral tales, and stories of naval domesticity, technology and war" (admittedly, the last troika seem a bit obscure) (92). This mix of genres does, however, reinforce the point I developed in the first chapter that, following Bakhtin's ideas about how the novel differs from the epic, O'Brian seeks to attain a "novelistic" quality to his work through, in part, the *heterglossia*—a mixture of many voices—that Bakhtin sees as characteristic of the novel. This is not to say that O'Brian sought to follow a prescription, but that Bahktin's description seems accurate when examined in light of O'Brian's work (a point upon which other critics of O'Brian, like Thomas J. Farrell, agree). Powers, however, does not build from this initial claim. In fact, later in the essay she operates as if it had not been a subject of some consternation, particularly for O'Brian, that the series are, of course, historical novels. Powers reveals this assumption by beginning the second section of her essay with the phrase, "The best historical novelists have bridged the gap of time and made a bygone reality accessible by bringing, without obvious anachronism, the insights of the present to bear on the past" (93). Thus, not only is she assuming the obviousness of the answer of whether these novels should be considered historical novels, she also assumes that the historical past is accessible and reproducible for the reader if the author has skill and control in his or her writing. Perhaps the first is not such a leap; the second ignores a rather loaded cauldron of simmering postmodern critiques of history and historiography. Thomas J. Farrell's essay "The Diegetic Achievement of Patrick O'Brian" seeks to challenge one of the underlying assumptions of Powers' comments (and those of most other previous commentators on O'Brian) that the novels are governed primarily by mimetic concerns—that is, reproducing the world of the novels as they were. O'Brian himself holds some responsibility for this belief in his acknowledgment of historical sources for his narratives, such as *The Reverse of the Medal*. Dean King describes the variety of sources O'Brian regularly drew upon, including letters and memoirs of the likes of Admiral Cuthbert Collingwood, Admiral James Saumarez, and Admiral Byam Martin. For data on the Pacific, he turned to the writings of Charles Darwin, Samuel Wallis, James Cook, and Joseph Banks. He also consulted Richard Henry Dana, Jr.'s *Two Years Before the Mast*, which contained a superb account of sailing around the Horn. For ship, armory, and fortification vocabulary, as well as sailor's slang, he had *Sailor's Word Book*, compiled by Admiral William Henry Smyth, president of the Royal Geography Society from 1849 to 1851 [236].

In addition, King goes on to claim that O'Brian "liked to read the print that Aubrey and Maturin might have seen and to smell the binding" (237). Such accounts make O'Brian seem almost like a method-actor who must live the part in order to perform it; they also help to mystify O'Brian's relation to his historical sources. To counter this notion, Farrell, instead, provides a great deal of evidence that storytelling and narrative (technically, "diegetic") concerns frequently come into play in O'Brian's work (he cites in particular some anachronisms at which O'Brian nods, intertextual allusion, anachronistic allusion—to works like *Heart of Darkness* and *The Waste Land*—as well as O'Brian's employment of free indirect discourse). While from a certain point of view, I have a difficult time imagining that O'Brian would not concern himself with storytelling over and against historical reportage, Farrell does useful work in charting out some of the ways in which O'Brian's concerns surface, however subtle the techniques may be.

In contrast, Powers concerns herself with O'Brian's attention to the details of Aubrey's and Maturin's world for somewhat different reasons. Later in her essay, after establishing O'Brian's preoccupations with "eighteenth-century literature," a preoccupation that led him to read "a considerable run of *The Gentleman's Magazine*, an eighteenth century journal once edited by Dr. Johnson," Powers reverses course to say (seeming to now anticipate Farrell's arguments) that the novels are "not primarily a historical project." To substantiate that claim, she reports enquiring whether O'Brian "has any of the aims of the historian." His response—and perhaps Powers' claim—seems to rest on something of a false dichotomy, for he says, "'No.' ... He is ... an artist 'first, last, and all time'" (94). She concludes this paragraph with a somewhat confusing final comment on O'Brian: "In this way, he can be distinguished from the growing ranks of academic and intellectual dabblers in historical fiction such as Susan Sontag and the historian Simon Schama" (94). He's

2. Scars, History and Historical Fiction

not a "dabbler" because he's an "artist?" Real artists write or create art and not historical fiction? It seems that Powers wishes to rescue O'Brian from the fate of that "disreputable genre" once more by constructing some kind of puzzling hierarchy of art and literary genres. Of course, what seems to raise O'Brian up in her estimation is what O'Brian believes about himself more than what he actually writes. In addition, it seems to me that the whole premise from which this discussion began—and I'm tempted to blame Powers more for the question than O'Brian for his answer—is that there is the historian and history on one side, and then there is the artist and presumably art on the other. In King's biography's various discussions of the problems of marketing O'Brian's work, this problem gets reinforced by the sense that O'Brian's work is "too well written, too nuance laden, and too challenging to be classified as 'adventure-genre stories'" (308), but these judgments sometimes seem to also speak to the problem of being labeled historical rather than artistic. First of all, at the very least, we need to consider the kinds of critiques of this reasoning developed by historiographers and thinkers like Hayden White. It has been White's contention from nearly as far back as the publication of the first Aubrey-Maturin novel that literature and history have far more in common than historians—and seemingly novelists—wish to admit. It was one of the central premises of White's "The Historical Text as Literary Artifact" that historians rely on literary genres to convey, write, and interpret the chronological events from which we construct history. In other words, to employ Farrell's terminology, even historians have diegetic concerns. All of this also leaves us with questions about whether O'Brian is then, in fact, writing historical fiction, and what exactly do we mean by that phrase in the first place.

Before we go any further, we need to try to work through some kind of definition of historical fiction. Writing around the publication of *Master and Commander*, and at a time that Hayden White was also beginning to publish on historiography, Avrom Fleishman takes up the subject of historical fiction in his classic study of the genre, *The English Historical Novel* (1971). Fleischman begins his discussion in "Towards a Theory of Historical Fiction" by describing historical novels as others are wont to describe pornography, with something of the concession that everyone seems to know a historical novel when they read one, and perhaps this "is why few have volunteered to define it in print" (3). When we consider some of Fleischman's most generalizing criteria for defining a historical novel, there may at first seem little doubt that O'Brian's series fits. However, it is beneficial to explore these criteria and their implications in relation to the novels. Fleischman suggests such novels must offer the reader "the feeling of how it was to be alive in another age." Just a bit further in this chapter he argues that a defining characteristic of the historical novel is the appearance of real historical figures; thus, "when the novel's characters live in the same world with historical persons, we have a historical novel" (4). Perhaps more significant to our discussion is Fleischman's acknowledgment that "the genre is unashamedly a hybrid," and that "the historical novelist uses the universals of literature—such categories of esthetic experience as romance and satire, tragedy and comedy—to interpret the course of historical man's career [we might add 'historical woman' here too]" (8). In truth, Fleischman finds himself drawing on historiographers like RG Collingwood—just as White does—which leads him seemingly further away from distinguishing between historians and historical novelists than his intention of showing their dissimilarities. Some of Fleischman's other criteria for the historical novel include that it be set in the past, which he says can be defined by "an arbitrary number of years, say 40–60." In addition, "The plot of the novel must include a number of 'historical events,'" and, while it must have "real personages" out of history (3), the main characters ought not to be "world-historical figures" like Napoleon. While wrestling with some of Collingwood's theories, which turn a bit too much on things like "degree" of "imagination" involved, Fleischman asserts that "the better historical novels fill in the threads [which 'fill the gaps in the received data'] where there is room for alternative hypotheses, but not where the gaps are so wide as to allow any hypothesis" (6). It seems that Fleischman feels that it simply isn't playing fair to write historical fiction that focuses on overly large blind spots in our historical past. If there are not restraints like those elaborated by Brian McHale in *Postmodernist Fiction,* then the texts really fail in the ways Fleishman describes regarding what it is that historical fiction should achieve. To interrupt our course for a moment, we might note that McHale suggests these limits or "constraints" upon the historical novelist:

1. persons, events, specific objects and so on ... can only be introduced on condition that the properties and actions attributed to them in the text do not actually contradict the official record;

2. Scars, History and Historical Fiction

2. the constraint on contradictions of the "official record" extends beyond specific realemes (persons, events) to the entire system;

3. the logic and physics of the fictional world must be compatible with those of reality if historical realemes are transferred from one realm to the other [87–88].

Of course, Fleishman highlights the lack of constraints as almost unfair game—as if to say, where is the challenge to the historical novelist in writing too much in the blanks of history?—and McHale is noting the restraints in order to set up their violation (more on this later). Nevertheless, it would seem that Fleishman would certainly admit the validity of the rules McHale sketches out (even if he might find the repetition of "realemes" a bit too much).

Lastly, to return more fully to Fleishman's definition, I would highlight Fleishman's notions regarding the aim of historical fiction. He sees an essential boomerang in the movements of the historical novelist, as he or she goes back into the past as a means of also coming back to the present; thus, "the esthetic function of historical fiction is to lift the contemplation of the past above both the present and the past, to see it in its universal character, freed of the urgency of historical engagement" (14). Of course, the problematic and now highly contested assumption at work here is that there is universal experience. Why the historical novel should ultimately seek to distill that from this engagement between the contemporary world and the past is left somewhat ambiguous here. However, if we put aside the more abstract of Fleishman's criteria in favor of the more concrete, we can quickly deduce that on these grounds alone, the Aubrey-Maturin series are clearly, in part at least, historical novels. They are set during the Napoleonic Wars, feature several well known battles, and occasionally feature figures directly out of history, such as admirals in the English navy (for example, Sir James Saumarez makes a brief appearance in *The Surgeon's Mate*) or what we may call historical cameos, like the comic, but brief appearance of Moses Maimonides in *Treason's Harbor*. They don't have much truck, however, with "world-historical figures"; in fact, Napoleon does not even make a cameo anywhere in the twenty volumes, and Nelson appears only by way of Jack's occasional stories about his time serving under his command.

However, as Fleischman would no doubt concede, what is most important about historical fiction is that the features that ground it in history are not simply pageantry intended to cloak the story in some kind of exotic locale. That instead, as Georg Lukács argues in *The Historical Novel*, the "derivation of the individuality of historical characters [come] from the historical peculiarity of their age" (19). Without that attention to the "historical peculiarity of their age," we find ourselves, no doubt, back in Powers' "deep dish costume dramas." We can have little worry that O'Brian has constructed his characters and essentially his fictional world out of the peculiarities of the era in which it is set. The precision—whatever deviations from accuracy or purposeful anachronisms may be evident to a very trained eye—by which O'Brian reconstructs life at sea during roughly the turn of the 18th century into the 19th suggests that he in no way sees it as window dressing on his story; in many ways, giving us a picture of that life, especially the human component of that life—the way in which a ship becomes a kind of microcosm of the larger society, but one that, for periods of time, becomes isolated almost like a science project—figures quite substantially in his work. It is also worth noting that in selecting the Napoleonic wars as his setting for his novels (although there appears to be a way in which the setting chose itself), O'Brian has sought out a time that Lukács argues was an era "which for the first time made history a mass experience, and moreover on a European scale" (23).

While I have just credited O'Brian with a strong adherence to and interest in representing the historical past in which his novels are situated, we might consider that this does not as neatly tie up the question of whether we should view these as historical novels in the classic sense. To return briefly to Powers' review, she asks a pertinent question: "Is this art or is it a piece of ventriloquism?" (94). As you recall, Powers went to some pains to show how embedded O'Brian was in the eighteenth century—and as she points out, O'Brian, following various academic trends, tends to see the first quarter of the 19th century proper as, in fact, a part of the "long" eighteenth century—but she just as quickly tries to suggest that, while his voice may appear to be imitating those of the eighteenth-century prose stylists he admired, he is not: "His language transcends pastiche, even style—O'Brian himself employs the expression 'prose rhythm' to describe it" (94). To keep in mind the kind of language that captures the possibility of pastiche, I offer just this small snippet of dialogue from *The Hundred Days*. After Stephen introduces himself to the scholar James Wright by announcing his name, Wright

2. Scars, History and Historical Fiction

says, "It might just as well be Beelzebub.... Not a brass farthing will you firk out of me before the end of the month, as I told that pragmatical bastard, your chief." Stephen responds that "I have ventured to call upon you as a fellow member of a learned society, not, upon my soul and honour, as a dun: bad luck to them all" (77). This is certainly language that, on its face, calls attention to its distinctiveness in both rhythm and vocabulary. Such moments raise this question of pastiche. The fact that I chose the above passage essentially by randomly opening up one of his novels underscores their frequency. Let's both keep such passages in mind when we consider the matter of pastiche and put aside the question Powers raises of whether one can "transcend" style, and instead consider the dangerousness of the phrase "pastiche." Later she will say, "O'Brian's choice of words is pure eighteenth-century, but the actual note he hits is uniquely his own" (95).

Why does Powers perform rhetorical gymnastics in order to suggest that O'Brian is not using pastiche but is also giving us something authentically eighteenth century (let's ignore, if we can, how loaded that adjective is)? The most obvious answer is that Powers wants to be sure to attest that O'Brian is not the anachronism for which you might take him—to put it directly, he is not essentially an eighteenth-century author writing in the twentieth century (not that undertakings which have taken on this kind of task—perhaps John Barth's *The Sot-Weed Factor* or Thomas Pynchon's *Mason & Dixon*—do not require remarkable skill to pull off). In a similar vein, Powers will assert that O'Brian's "writing is joyous" seemingly to distinguish it from the drudgery of eighteenth century prose (I'll concede Richardson, but Swift, Sterne, Fielding?). However, there is a more complicated issue involved in the question of pastiche, and this is its centrality in the thesis of Fredric Jameson concerning historical representation in postmodern art. In his essay "Postmodernism and Consumer Society," first published in 1983, Jameson argues that one of the markers for the transition from modernism to postmodernism is the pervasiveness of pastiche. He sees its outgrowth as a response to modernism and "its explosion into a host of distinct private styles and mannerisms" (25). Jameson implies that, stylistically, modernism left its successors no place to go. We might note, then, that Powers seems to arguing for the distinctiveness of O'Brian's style rather than seeing it as pastiche, which Jameson defines as

> the imitation of a peculiar or unique style, the wearing of a stylistic mask, speech in a dead language: but it is a neutral practice of such mimicry [unlike parody], without parody's ulterior motive, with the satirical impulse, without laughter, without that still latent feeling that there exists something normal compared to which what is being imitated is rather comic [25].

For Jameson, then, pastiche occurs when an artist rehearses the styles and forms of an earlier artist or time, but without any attempt to criticize or make jest of that source material. It simply recurs without a wink or nod. Following this conception of pastiche, then, it appears that Powers is arguing that if O'Brian is an anachronism, it is a modernist one (to be fair, she never invokes Jameson in the essay, but by 1995 it is hard to imagine how the mention of pastiche was not at least alluding to his ideas or his critiques).

Jameson's definition is in itself problematic, of course. To recognize pastiche or parody, we must locate the hazy line between them in terms of "latent feeling" as well as intention, and, of course, the very notion he offers here seems to suggest a kind of emptiness and bottoming out of culture by way of pastiche (the familiar pattern of decrying living in a fallen world seems to echo from the utopian Marxist in much of his writing on postmodernism). It seems to me that one might not be quite so apocalyptic about pastiche as Jameson appears to be, and that there may be many examples in which seeing the difference between parody and what he calls "blank parody" is heavily linked to one's perspective. Nevertheless, for Jameson, the rise of pastiche in art is tied up rather heavily in historical representation. He sees postmodern art as "going to be about art itself" (26) and not, one supposes, the real world. To make his point, Jameson discusses what he calls the nostalgia film and distinguishes it from the historical film. He cites examples like *Chinatown* and *Body Heat,* in which the film can be seen "as a narrative set in some indefinable nostalgic past, an eternal '30s, say, beyond history" (28). In talking about the projects of the novelist E. L. Doctorow, I think Jameson gets to the heart of his fears by saying, "His narratives do not represent our historical past so much as they represent our ideas or cultural stereotypes about the past" (28). I take Jameson to mean that we have nothing but a kind of endless cycle of representations, and, in the words of another theorist and critic of postmodernism, Jean Baudrillard, the real has dropped away, and we have only simulacra.

Before we tackle questions about whether we should even consider

2. Scars, History and Historical Fiction

O'Brian a postmodernist, a label he would certainly not append to himself, I do want to deal with the implications of Jameson's critique here and its relation to attempts to define historical fiction. Jameson fears that "we seem condemned to seek the historical past through our own pop images and stereotypes about that past, which itself remains forever out of reach" (29). Well, what is it that Jameson is exactly afraid of? It seems as if he fears that if we seek the past only in representations of the past, we may risk a violation of the very real human suffering of lived experience that is a part of the record—or should be a part of the record—of human experience (a blunt hypothetical example might be our notions of the Holocaust deriving primarily or solely from, say, *Schindler's List*). The real/virtual dichotomy at work here is something that Derrida, among others, might object to as false, but we cannot digress further on that dichotomy or false dichotomy. Here, however, is my own pertinent concern with Jameson's case. Underlying Jameson's argument—and Baudrillard's and perhaps even Fleishman's—is a kind of nostalgia itself. Jameson seems to hanker for a time when historical fiction *really* represented the *real* past. Was there ever such a time? Is fiction's ability to represent some kind of objective, non-representational notion of history a faulty premise? Is there history that does not provide some kind of representational shape through narrative? In *Founding Brothers*, historian Joseph J. Ellis notes that John Adams essentially arrived at this insight—"that all seamless historical narratives are latter day constructions"—at the tale end of the eighteenth century (216). It is, as Ellis notes, today "at the center of all postmodern critiques of historical explanations" (216).

Whether O'Brian can be seen as a postmodernist (or, for that matter, whether someone can write in this period but remain untouched by the arguments, trends, and concerns of this period) is something I will take up again a bit later in this chapter. However, it seems to me that Powers' concerns with pastiche lead us to consider the ways in which a kind of either/or dichotomy develops around O'Brian's use of the past—where he either is a unique stylist who transcends the sources and styles he relies on, or he is a "ventriloquist," a weaver of pastiche. (I suppose the third option would be that which Farrell contests, namely that O'Brian's goal is historical reproduction above all else—whether that can be separated from pastiche is also another matter.) Is O'Brian using his writing to show us a real past, or is he imitating representations of the past in the manner of *Chinatown?* Powers wants to rescue him from the pejorative labels that have become associated with debased or empty shells of history in Jameson's view, a kind of postmodern version of the "costume drama deep-dish." On some level she has every right to such a rescue project, but we might also wonder if that project is tied to idealized notions of what historical writing can be and ever was.

How O'Brian Represents the Past

Before I develop my arguments regarding the role of the body and history, I want to elaborate more fully on the methods O'Brian uses to represent the past. This discussion will help set the stage for that later argument. Perhaps, for the purposes of this discussion or historical representation, the question might become: what exactly is O'Brian's approach to representing the Napoleonic Wars, and, perhaps even more to the point, is he particularly interested in representing those wars? The Aubrey-Maturin series is largely guided by the career of its main protagonist, Captain Jack Aubrey, and to a lesser extent that of his close friend and ship's surgeon, Stephen Maturin, who is also an intelligence officer. While Jack's story allows O'Brian to elaborate extensively on particular components of the wars, such as specific battles and, more generally, some of the various power plays around the globe conducted through the long reach of assorted navies, the very nature of a navy captain's life—especially one with a ship—precludes O'Brian from going extensively into the kinds of larger political activities of the time and simply does not give him much access (or certainly not regular access) to historical figures who were more decidedly landlocked. As I mentioned previously, we never even get a remote glimpse of Napoleon at any point in the series. Jack himself does not reflect a great deal upon why he is fighting Napoleon, but simply that he is fighting an enemy, and the successes of his career rest largely on his ability to consistently defeat and preferably capture enemy ships (not because capture is the game per se, but because captured ships became translated into funds; they were "prizes"). As Stephen says of Jack in *Post Captain,* "Jack is not an analytical thinker, except aboard a ship in action: but light creeps in, from time to time" (329).

So, one will not gain insight into the failure of the French Revolu-

2. Scars, History and Historical Fiction

tion, say, in Jack's journal-like letters home. In fact, the broad sweeps of history and, more specifically, the war tend to be tackled on the periphery of the novels. A typical example can be found in the opening of *H.M.S. Surprise.* In a technique employed throughout the series, O'Brian has a character's ignorance stand in for ours (usually this is Stephen, who remains mystified by the workings of ships and the Navy for more or less the entire run of the novels). At the start of this particular novel we find Stephen Maturin alone with Jack's fiancée, Sophie, who begins by saying that she has "been meaning to draw you aside ever since you came.... It is dreadful to be so ignorant, and I would not have Captain Aubrey know it for all the world" (19). Stephen thinks that the young and future bride wishes to ask him about sex, since he is a "physician," but really what she wants to understand is exactly who is fighting whom in this war that has been "going on for ever." She's rather confused about who, besides the French, are now England's enemies, and "it would be very shocking—treason no doubt—to put the wrong people in my prayers" (19). Stephen then offers Sophie a lecture on the "present state of the world" that appears almost parodic:

> Well now, for the moment it is plain enough. On our side we have Austria, Russia, Sweden and Naples, which is the same as your Two Sicilies; and on his [Napoleon's] he has a whole cloud of little states, and Bavaria and Holland and Spain. Not that these alliances are of much consequence one side or the other: The Russians were with us, and then against us until they strangled the Czar, and now with us; and I dare say they will change again [20].

So far, so good. The tone of the passage suggests O'Brian is saying something like "yes, I will nod to what is going on at the time of these books, I'll even show you that I have a thorough knowledge of the major players, but let's not get all that caught up in what is essentially a confusing situation" (not to mention the failure to really get at why the situation is so fluid and confusing—though, to be fair, even reading a substantial history of this period, such as Tim Blanning's *Pursuit of Glory,* is not likely to make most vacationers in the eighteenth century any more in control of the facts, motives, and complexities of the internecine politics of Europe at that time). Thus, Stephen then turns to what a reader of these novels should find more pertinent historical knowledge: "What matters to us is Holland and Spain, for they have navies." The real importance, Stephen asserts, is what happens at sea, for "if ever this war is to be won, it must be won at sea" (Blanning asserts that British Naval superiority was quite substantial, so Stephen may not be exaggerating due to bias) (20). Then Stephen takes us to the truly relevant—how this all affects our main characters:

> Bonaparte has forty-five ships of the line, and we have eighty-odd, which sounds well enough. But ours are scattered all over the world and his are not. Then again the Spaniards have twenty-seven, to say nothing of the Dutch; so it is essential to prevent them from combining, for if Bonaparte can assemble a superior force in the Channel, even for a little while, then his invasion army can come across, God forbid. That is why Jack and Lord Nelson are beating up and down off Toulon [20].

The emphasis at long last comes down upon the individual living through history. Nevertheless, I think it may be fair to consider what role this information serves. Is it giving us a window onto the era depicted within? Is it setting up the context for an adventure novel (with its tallies of ships like a key moment in the games *Battleship* or *Risk*)? The information seems more background and context, to be perfectly fair, and the nearly parodic tone suggests that O'Brian has self-awareness of the absurdity of the information being packaged in this manner (though this may also arise from Stephen's attitude toward his audience). The narrowing down of the information to its relevance to the main characters also suggests that the novels will not take interest in the complex political machinations of the war, except as they might bear on the missions and lives of the protagonists. Nevertheless, the information allows the reader to know where Jack is at the moment and why he's doing what he's doing (in an admittedly superficial sense), and also to give us, at least early on in the series, a firm foothold as to where in this war—at what moment in history—the novels have arrived.

Although spoken by Stephen, the above passage reflects in many ways on Jack, and for him, those bare bone explanations and numbers are really all that matter. He's a sailor fighting a war. Rationales for that war matter little in terms of his duty and actions. In fact, peace is his real enemy, since his career depends upon the war (and, as I will touch on later in this chapter, peace becomes a kind of enemy to the perpetuation of the series). Perhaps the most notable exception to this pattern of the historical circumstances providing context would be the late novel *The Yellow Admiral*, the eighteenth of the series. That novel, one of the few set extensively on land, finds Jack dealing with enclosure (in fact, the situation I have described above gets inverted in this novel, with

2. Scars, History and Historical Fiction

Stephen asking another character—Jack, in fact—to explain what the practice entailed).

However, the scenario from *The Yellow Admiral* stands out as unusual (though it can be seen in relation to a kind of reversion history in the series, a point to which I will return). In contrast to the role history or the historical situation more generally plays in the life and mind of Jack for the author, Stephen Maturin does give O'Brian a means to contemplate more of the historical questions at play, both because of his work as an intelligence officer and because he is simply a much more reflective individual. It is for Stephen, for example, to give us insight into what someone like Jack goes through by engaging in the kind of hand to hand warfare necessitated by a boarding action: "He is a romantic creature: after this affair [Stephen's rescue] he tossed his sword into the sea, though I know the value he had for it. Then again, he loves to make war—no man more eager in the article of battle; but afterwards it is as though he did not feel that war consisted of killing your opponents. There is a contradiction here" (80). Stephen himself is something of a romantic, as least as far as political causes go. He has a true hatred for Napoleon (at one point in *Mauritius Command*, for example, Stephen reflects upon his hatred and declares Napoleon to be not properly French [221])—but also a love for French culture. In short, Stephen has been associated with Republican causes. When, in the same novel, Stephen declares his hatred of slavery as well (56), it comes as no surprise.

Stephen's political views, at least nominally grounded in the "peculiarities of the age," surface many times in the series. In *The Thirteen Gun Salute*, for instance, after the Envoy Fox makes a sarcastic comment about the crew, the narrator describes Stephen's response: "Remarks of that kind always irritated Stephen, a revolutionary in his youth, above all when they were applied to the lower deck, whose qualities he knew better than most men" (166). Occasionally, Stephen's political opinions will rather clearly be ones that can transcend their own time, such as in *The Truelove*, where Stephen declares, "I am in favour of leaving people alone, however imperfectly their polity may seem. It appears to me that you must not tell other nations how to set their house in order; nor must you compel them to be happy" (148). Politics certainly come up frequently in relation to Stephen over the course of the series. In part, this results from his views, and in part it relates to Stephen's work as a voluntary intelligence agent, which also puts the plots into relation with some kind of political intrigue.

These reflections, however practical or based in narrative need, also help embed the novels in their historical milieu. Thus, because of Stephen's turn of mind, O'Brian investigates many of the practices of the time, such as corporal punishment aboard ships or slavery. For instance, in the novel *Fortune of War*, which finds both Jack and Stephen in America, the novel gives us a window onto the practices of slavery, particularly through Stephen's eyes. Mr. Johnson, Diana's "keeper" at this time, is identified negatively by his large number of slaves (172). Later we learn that "Johnson has dozens like that—he breeds the house-slaves for size" (188). When a slave drops something, Stephen watches as the slave "stared in naked terror, her arms down by her sides" (190). Diana discusses the range of slaves—all reflecting Johnson in one way or another—on his plantation (210). Stephen later stumbles into segregation when he tries to get a black man to enter a bar with him for a drink, and they are turned away (238–239). Thus, the characters run against the complexities and troubles of their historical world, particularly early on in the series, but again towards the end, when slavery, particularly in *The Commodore*, becomes a central thread. Although that particular novel focuses a surprisingly large amount of time on homosexuality, we also have direct encounters with slavery, such as when O'Brian details Stephen's horror at the "unbreathable fetor" onboard the slave ship (190).

Besides his sensitivity to such political issues, Stephen is also a renowned natural philosopher, and so his work also allows O'Brian to both investigate the work in this field during this age (see Wayne Glausser's article for a substantive discussion of Maturin's relation to other thinkers of his age) and to offer some brief depictions of other significant natural philosophers from this period. These moments clearly offer O'Brian the opportunity to show us his characters "living in the peculiarities of their age" while contemplating issues of that age that can continue to speak to a contemporary audience (we are far from having done with the ethical dilemma of corporal punishment, for example, in its most extreme cases; and while slavery has passed us by, clearly its aftermath and even the logic that rationalized the practice continues to haunt our world). In all of these texts and particular moments, the primary interests of the novels are not necessarily on these large intractable and highly charged issues like the slave trade, but, for the most part, the novels do bring us into contact with those issues and problems, and give us, however briefly, a sense of how they affected the novels' protagonists.

The Classical Model

I would venture to say that if O'Brian has a model of historical novel upon which he seems to draw, it most overtly appears to be that which Lukács identifies as the "classical form." For Lukács, the ultimate exemplar of this form appears to be Sir Walter Scott; Fleishman, I should add, concentrates a good deal on Scott as well. Lukács suggests that Scott is the novelist who seems most to evoke a sense of the epic (35), and we can at least grant O'Brian's series as having reached for an epic scope, if not other characteristics of that form, as I have discussed in the previous chapter. In particular, however, it seems that one can see elements of Scott's methodologies being employed by O'Brian (it does not, however, seem as if O'Brian has the kind of ambitions to chart out a course of history in, say, the manner of Scott's *Waverly* novels—O'Brian favors a narrower scope, though partially out of necessity). Typically, Scott's heroes were not the central figures of the historical events he describes. As Lukács asserts:

> The "hero" of Scott's novel is always a more or less mediocre, average English gentleman. He generally possesses a certain, though never outstanding, degree of practical intelligence, a certain moral fortitude and decency which even rises to a capacity for self-sacrifice, but which never grows into a sweeping human passion, is never the enraptured devotion to a great cause [33].

In short, the Scott heroes always stand at a certain remove from the figures who appear to shape their own times. In assessing whether O'Brian's characters fit this mold, you might hesitate, for it is unlikely—especially if you are a fan of the series—to consider either Aubrey or Maturin mediocre figures. After all, Lucky Jack Aubrey is a remarkably adept sea captain who has had a long series of successes as a naval captain. Stephen Maturin is clearly praised and admired as a surgeon (noted for his skill at amputation, among other things), for his intelligence work by those who are aware of it, and for his work in natural philosophy. And, for readers, they seem largely to be at the center of novels' world, if not the major historical events of the novels' times. Before we examine this judgment further, I would also add that Lukács' view is not an unusual one. In fact, Fleishman largely agrees with Lukács' position that the protagonist of the historical novel must be a "typical man of an age ... whose life is shaped by world-historical figures and other influences that epitomizes the processes of change going forward in the society as a whole," but goes a step further in saying that "the relation of the representative hero to the society of his time is not one of statistically-determined typicality but that of symbolic universality" (11). As I've implied earlier, this seems a slightly problematic criteria, but Jack—and, to a lesser extent, Stephen—certainly seem to experience many of the very common, if not universal, struggles of a man of a certain power and rank in his society. One might, however, also argue that each character possesses a number of serious flaws in each of their make-ups (see my outlining of the issue of drug addiction in the following chapter). However, putting aside the ways in which O'Brian insists upon his audience witnessing his characters' various flaws for a moment, we should also note that O'Brian is also very careful to keep his heroes in positions of only relative power. Although Stephen is, for example, considered for the position of Surgeon for the Navy, he declines. After a fairly steady rise in the first two novels, Aubrey's career pace slows down considerably, and he does not realize his dream of becoming an admiral until the very end of the series (these restrictions have much to do with the extension of the novels beyond their initial conception, as well as keeping the protagonists in this middle sphere).

For O'Brian (as for Scott), keeping the hero in a position between the highest and lowest orders of power allows for a greater movement between these worlds, and ways to reveal the complexities of the society, that focusing on figures like Napoleon alone simply do not offer. If we consider the Royal Navy as something of a microcosm of society—a trope reinforced many times throughout the series—then between the perspectives of Aubrey and Maturin, the reader is able to see into the decision making of the Admiralty and Naval Intelligence, the life of a captain and an officer aboard a "post ship," and the life of the average seaman through their interactions with these figures (as a naval surgeon, Maturin simply must interact with all the members of the crew on a regular basis, as his response to Envoy Fox, cited earlier, underscores). Although we find examples in the novels of the ways in which the Royal

2. Scars, History and Historical Fiction

Navy, as opposed to a great deal of British society at that time, can be understood as a meritocracy—that is, individuals can rise based on their aptitude—it's also clear that children of the wealthy are more likely to be found in positions of power. Jack's aristocratic father helped him find his initial place, for example. Stephen comes late to the navy, but has something of a mixed class background, being the illegitimate child of an aristocrat. In some ways Jack's time in the Royal Navy has given him a fuller appreciation of individuals from a wide swath of backgrounds. Not to mention that both his and Stephen's time on shore also involves interacting with many different levels and registers of society.

Perhaps the O'Brian novel that most overtly draws upon a Scott-like methodology for representing historical events is *The Fortune of War* (1979), the sixth in the series. Throughout the series, as I mentioned earlier by documenting King's account of O'Brian's research, O'Brian clearly draws upon documented historical events to supply the plots of his novels. Let me offer another bit of evidence on this account. In the collected papers held at the Lilly Library at Indiana University, for example, I found clear evidence of O'Brian's research, which included notes from *The Croker Papers: The Correspondence and Diaries of the Late Right Honourable John Wilson Croker, Secretary to the Admiralty from 1809 to 1830* (1885). Thus, O'Brian undoubtedly drew inspiration from the historical record. The question then becomes: how does O'Brian position his work in relation to that record? In discussing the constraints—which I outlined above—typically placed upon historical novelists, Brian McHale suggests that "freedom to improvise actions and properties of historical figures is limited to the 'dark areas' of history, that is, those aspects about which the 'official' record has nothing to report" (87); while, as you recall, Fleishman suggested that these areas should not be too dark or too broad. What of O'Brian? In a typical plot, O'Brian varies this formulation in that he sometimes draws very heavily from "official records," such as those drawn from the career of Lord Cochran (and often concedes as much or identifies his sources in his Author Notes to many of his novels); however, if the event, although official, is somewhat obscure, he is likely to insert Aubrey into the position of a historical personage (such as in the *Mauritius Command*) or call upon a somewhat obscure event within which he can improvise.

In *Fortune of War*, or in other texts where Aubrey and Maturin encounter more well known historical events, Aubrey and Maturin move much more fully into a position seen in Scott's novels: they can participate in the scene, but often their main role is to bear witness to the event and allow the author to depict it from nearly inside the scene without really violating the "official record" by, for example, giving a fictional hero a role more significant than a historical figure known to have such a role. The central events described in this novel involve early naval battles between the British and Americans as a part of the War of 1812. Clearly, in part, O'Brian seeks to show the debilitating effects on the morale of the British navy created by a succession of early defeats, and the revitalizing effects of Captain Broke's victory outside Boston Harbor. After a series of somewhat contrived, if often harrowing, events take Jack and Stephen from Australia to near the coast of Brazil, they find themselves aboard the H.M.S. *Java* shortly before it encounters the U.S.S. *Constitution*. Although Jack participates in this battle, he does so as essentially an outsider to the events, as he is not an official member of the Java's crew and so takes no "official" responsibility for the events. However, Jack does suffer significantly in the battle. As the narrator describes, "Jack had taken three strides aft when he fell—it was nothing, he found, scrambling up and slipping again in Broughton's blood—a musket ball had grazed his head" (116). Later, Jack finds himself shot, and that his "right arm would not obey him, that it was hanging at an unnatural angle" (121). Following these events, Stephen comments, "Now I know what Jack Aubrey will look like when he is sixty-five" (130). O'Brian thus utilizes Jack to symbolize the consequences of this battle on the navy. This passage signals one of the moments in which O'Brian depicts the way history becomes written upon the body, a subject I will return to more fully momentarily. Following this battle, Jack is imprisoned in Boston, although, because of his injuries, he is actually interred in a hospital. While in Boston, other captured officers visit Jack, and as he, seemingly rendered impotent by his injured arm, hears their accounts of other British defeats, he becomes depressed. Upon being told of several Royal Navy defeats, even Maturin, who has also been taken to Boston, finds himself affected: "'Oh,' said Stephen. There was a curious stab at his heart: he had not known how much he felt for the Navy" (154).

Later, O'Brian will also represent the revival through Jack, as the captain slowly gains strength, leads a rescue of Maturin, and eventually escapes to the H.M.S. *Shannon,* which is blockading Boston Harbor.

2. Scars, History and Historical Fiction

Here again, Aubrey moves to a position of access to power, but not one that violates the rules commonly adhered to by historical novelists. At a late moment in the novel, the captain of the *Shannon*, Broke, an actual historical figure and subject of more than one published account, is revealed to be Aubrey's cousin. Therefore, through this connection, we are led to understand why Broke would be so forthcoming with Aubrey. For example, Broke discusses his plans with Jack and shows him the letter he wrote to challenge Lawrence, the American captain (301). Again, like earlier in the novel, as the battle commences, Jack participates, but the reader does not witness Jack alter the events in any significant way, and, following the "official" record, Broke receives what will prove a fatal wound during the battle. In essence, this presentation of historical events closely mirrors the ways in which Scott would depict battles in his Waverly novels, such as *Old Mortality*, or the way Scott's disciple, James Fenimore Cooper, depicts the French and Indian War. We might consider this approach to have much to do with perspective, and the ways to offer as much of a reliable or comprehensive view on such an event.

In fact, O'Brian takes up this very question early in the last novel of the series, *Blue at the Mizzen*. Jack raises the matter when he learns his neighbor at dinner had been at the Battle of Waterloo. "Was you able to see much?" Jack asks him, before explaining, "In the few fleet actions I have known, apart from the Nile, I could make out precious little, because of the smoke; and afterwards most people gave quite different accounts" (13). Through Jack's comments here, we may have a window onto O'Brian's own hesitations about the very problem of the historical record—"quite different accounts"—and his own concerns about capturing historical events in his work. Colonel Roche's response offers the kind of solution O'Brian found in *Fortune of War*, and Scott found in much of his work: "I had the honour of being one of the Duke's aides-de-camp, and he nearly always took up a position from which he—and of course we underlings—could see a great stretch of country" (13). While O'Brian does not typically take us to this kind of bird's eye view when his protagonists are the focal point of the action, he does follow something akin to this approach with the more notable events, such as the battle with the U.S.S. *Constitution*. One could be tempted, however, to read a moment like this as almost a confession: if I were to tackle big historical moments like Waterloo, here's how I would have gone about it (in fact, the next few pages of *Blue at the Mizzen* consist largely of Roche's account of the battle).

O'Brian's adherence to the constraints of "official" record, as I've implied, lines him up most clearly as a writer of classical historical fiction, whose heyday was almost two hundred years before O'Brian began creating a series that carried on for roughly the last thirty years of his life. In suggesting that he adheres to the record, I am not contending that O'Brian has done so slavishly; instead, I am suggesting that he has not altered notable events or had notable historical figures act or speak in ways that run counter to what we know of them. O'Brian wrote the first novel in the series, *Master and Commander*, in 1970. In his "Author's Note" to that novel, O'Brian comments on how the fiction writer need not embellish the heroism and exploits of the officers and men of this period, but also acknowledges the fairly deadpan way in which these exploits had been recorded in the official record. Essentially, then, his project becomes one of shading in the details surrounding the "official" record while feeling no need to fictionalize the events themselves.

O'Brian and the Postmodern

At roughly the same time, or a few years before, O'Brian begins his series, John Barth pens *The Sot-Weed Factor* (1967), Thomas Berger composes *Little Big Man* (1964), and Gore Vidal produces *Burr* (1973). These texts rather clearly resemble postmodern historical novels as defined by Brian McHale, as they "revise ... the content of the historical record, reinterpreting the historical record, often demystifying or debunking the orthodox version of the past," and also "revise ... the conventions and norms of historical fiction itself" (90). Barth shows John Smith in ludicrous circumstances involving an eggplant; Berger's novel provides, among many other things, a satirical portrait of George Custer (and about all our traditional notions of the settlement of the American West); and Vidal's novel seeks to undermine the mythologizing of several of America's founding fathers. You might say that all of these examples come from America, a country challenged at the time by the Vietnam War, and you would be right; however, I could also point to novels like John Fowles' *The French Lieutenant's Woman* (1969), Salman Rushdie's *Midnight's Children* (1981) or Gunter Grass' *The Tin*

2. Scars, History and Historical Fiction

Drum (1959) as examples of earlier and later European novels that speak to the same revision of the classic historical novel as the American texts (Rushdie composed his novel in England). When one juxtaposes O'Brian with these more overtly postmodern texts, it appears that, in regards to historical representation, O'Brian is an anachronism—unless, perhaps, you consider his adherence to the classical model to be in the form of the pastiche (in contrast to Powers' claim, one, as I've outlined, not particularly well-defended). King suggests that by comparison to work like I've described, O'Brian's can seem "quaint, even antediluvian," suggesting that this may have tempered the immediate reception of O'Brian's work, particularly in the United States (207). As with the earlier discussion of Powers' essay, this sense of O'Brian working outside of time is a charge frequently directed at him, and there is no doubt—wherever one stands on these debates—that his works, be it from imitation or inspiration, can often feel like those of another era. (I should add, however, that many traditional historical works have, of course, been published before and after O'Brian began working on his series and not been influenced by the emergence of postmodern literary techniques. One such writer, Mary Renault, became an early supporter and champion of O'Brian's [King 203]. However, certainly the more overtly literary versions of historical fiction at the very time O'Brian began did engage more with what has come to be termed postmodernism.)

However, in this penultimate section of this chapter, I would like to contend that, in representing the relation between private, individual history and public (or perhaps more "official" or "orthodox") history, especially in how it is figured upon the body itself, O'Brian does speak directly to concerns often taken up in postmodern historical fiction. In his essay, Farrell takes on this question to some extent via his claims that O'Brian's novels contain metafictional elements, but he also acknowledges that these elements seem muted in comparison to more postmodern historical fiction, like Umberto Eco's *The Name of the Rose* or A. S. Byatt's *Possession*. I would see the connections between O'Brian and the postmodern in terms perhaps more of theme than technique. The question of metafiction appears in this debate due to Linda Hutcheon's arguments that postmodern historical representation, rather than being empty or, even worse, willfully ignorant and dangerous (to extrapolate Jameson's concerns), should be read as what she calls "historiographical metafiction" (Hutcheon discusses these ideas extensively in *A Poetics of Postmodernism* and *The Politics of Postmodernism*). What does Hutcheon mean by this phrase? Well, she suggests that postmodern historical novels include a great deal of self-reflexivity—a kind of acknowledgment of their own status as fictions—and an interest not so much in accurate historical representation but instead the processes by which we record and know history. In O'Brian's novels, no narrator interrupts the action to explain Freytag's pyramid, as happens in John Barth's famous metafictional story "Lost in the Funhouse" or anything like that. Therefore, the relative subtlety of the metafictional components of O'Brian's work has tended to keep it from being thought of in these terms (in fact, I would venture to say that this question never came up before Farrell introduced it). Considering some of the ways that I have outlined the novels' depiction of historical events and moments of reflection on historical knowledge, as I sketched out in the example from *Blue at the Mizzen*, I would say that a case could be made for a historiographic element in O'Brian's work, but one that seems almost as subtle as the metafiction to which Farrell alludes.

I would argue, though, that further connections to postmodern concerns can be found in O'Brian's work. To this point in the chapter I have not yet returned to how extensively these novels focus their attention on bodies. As I have discussed at great length elsewhere in this book, these novels seethe with images of bodies, attention to their inner workings, and a pervasive sense that bodies can be read like texts, or symbols, or complex pieces of figurative language. In particular, we get extensive details regarding the bodies of the main characters, Aubrey and Maturin. While Jack's seemingly ever-expanding girth, and Stephen's seeming inability to make his way around the ship without falling through a hole or dropping off the ladder, can lead to generic confusion and satiric complication, as I have discussed in the first chapter of this work, we might consider here how the progress and the representation of the body come to parallel the narrative and historical progress of the novel, something that may connect O'Brian's work to more of his contemporaries than metafictional or historiographic elements do.

Like other contemporary and postmodern historical works—even from as seemingly diverse narratives as Toni Morrison's *Beloved* or Salman Rushdie's *Midnight's Children*—the Aubrey-Maturin series records or narrates the historical through the progress of its main characters' physical bodies, with the conflicts of the public historical world

2. Scars, History and Historical Fiction

(here the Napoleonic Wars) becoming literally writ upon the bodies of the individual through scars and disfigurement, so that the physical body comes to be both a record of the personal and public historical spheres, as well as an embodiment of the struggles between these two. The novels themselves display the violence of battle quite explicitly. In the first novel alone, we observe how Jack's ear is hit and "pouring with blood" (134). Later, Jack's "scalp and face were hideously seared and bruised" (225). These injuries give Jack "a wicked, degenerate, inverted look" (228). Stephen confirms that Jack is "hideous," and Jack is compared to a Mandrill (269). Jack eventually is stabbed and loses part of his ear (332). In almost every battle in every novel, Jack suffers some kind of injury. These scars reinforce the role of Jack's body as signifier, as something of a meaning-producing machine, for the narrative of his intersection with public history has been inscribed upon him. Early in *Post Captain,* several of his neighbors on shore hear of Jack's exploits, but when Jack actually appears and they witness his "fine open battle-scarred countenance" (33), the tales take on a new life—the history to which he has been a part is conveyed clearly to the witnesses through the signifying scars on his face. Similarly, in the fifth novel, *Desolation Island,* Stephen discusses the difference between Jack and his officer, Grant:

> He has seen no action, as I understand, whereas Jack's body is pierced and criss-crossed with evidence of battle: Macpherson pointed this out when Jack was stripped for his swim, the young gentleman gazing with awe, and Grant cried in a passion, "'twas all luck, all luck—no man was wounded from choice—a man might have all the courage and conduct in the world, and no wound to show for it" [129].

In moments like these, Jack need not say anything, but his body—put on full display for his crew—speaks of his encounters with public history and his own place in those conflicts. About mid-way through the series, when Jack has been unfairly struck from the navy, his body's power to testify for him becomes crucial in the plans of Joseph Blaine, head of Naval Intelligence, and Maturin to get Jack reinstated in *Letter of Marque.* In a battle against the *Spartan,* Jack receives a series of injuries: "A musket dashed Jack's sword from his hand: a pike-thrust furrowed the side of his neck and a short thick heavy man butted him under the chin, knocking him back on to a corpse" (104). In all, the battle proves gruesome, in Jack's recounting "as bloody a little engagement as ever I saw—the gundecks were aswim with blood.... It was most shocking butchery"

(106). Even later in the same novel, Jack receives further injury by a French soldier in the attack, who, "slashing upwards with his saber, [caught] Jack's leg above the knee.... Jack parried, but a trifle late and the point ploughed up his forearm" (196). The accumulation of injuries and further scars, then, can speak for Jack in ways that his own verbal defenses have failed him. Blaine wishes to use Jack's injuries to help get him reinstated, noting "a pale hero is far more interesting than a red-faced one," while describing his plans to present Jack at a party to folks with political power (210). At the party, the narrator says Jack appeared "pale and severe," partially due to "extreme hunger," but also concedes that "his wounds had their effect upon his colour too, while almost the whole of his severity was an armour against the least hint of disrespect" (213). During this meal, in order to help make Jack's case, some of the guests recount his battle record; but clearly the key to that narrative lies in the way Jack's body can attest to the encounters with the large-scale, public historical conflict in a way that transcends words (the fragility of words is underscored in the scene by Jack's tenuous handling of a story he tries to tell).

While perhaps more attention gets paid to Jack's body (which more obviously comes to resemble a kind of historical compendium), O'Brian also returns repeatedly to the marks on Maturin's body, especially the damage done to his hands as the result of having been tortured by French agents in the third novel of the series, *H.M.S. Surprise.* Perhaps because Stephen spends so much of his time focusing on bodies and in contemplating the character of his friend, he also becomes a reader of Jack's body, as evidenced by the following exchange between Clarissa Oakes, who had stowed away aboard ship in the novel *The Truelove,* and Stephen. Observing Jack, Clarissa asks Stephen, "Captain Aubrey would be considered a fine figure of a man even in Ireland, would he not?... But surely he has been most dreadfully cut about?" (185). Stephen's replies, "I should scarcely like to number the wounds I have sewn up and dressed, or the musket and pistol balls I have extracted.... You are to observe, ma'am, that they are all honourably in front; except for those that are behind" (186). One cannot, in O'Brian's novels, pass through neutrally the historical events shaping those times. Those active in the time become inscribed by those times (but in the perversity of naval life, such inscriptions, like the common tattoos of sailor myth, are sought out and prized).

In *The Practice of Everyday Life,* French theorist Michel De Certeau suggests that "in the obscurity of their unlimitedness, bodies can be distinguished only where the 'contacts' of amorous or hostile struggles are inscribed on them" (127). These scars mark, in De Certeau's formulation, the space where Aubrey's and Maturin's bodies have encountered the frontier, and, here specifically, these scars then signify where their private historical selves have met the frontier of the larger, public historical world. Hence, the body does become something of a book: history can be read across Jack's countenance—sometimes to the extent of it in the form of bullets, becoming embedded in his flesh. Of course, following De Certeau's notion, Aubrey's or Maturin's very identity—as marked by the places of contact—cannot be derived without these encounters. Throughout the series, the tracing of history moves from the public historical view and the seeming objectivity of the "natural history" recorded by Stephen to more personal history.

History, however, is not only marked here by its physical inscriptions on Jack's body, but in Jack's and also Stephen's markings upon others. In fact, in different ways, the progress and success of both Stephen's and Jack's careers can be measured through their success in taking bodies apart, as well as the changes and alterations to their own bodies. Jack's role as naval captain, of course, involves his ability to disrupt and destroy the figurative body of a ship or the opposing navy, as well as, quite frequently, the literal bodies of Britain's enemies (a process readers of the series encounter again and again). Hence, for O'Brian, bodies become part of a larger figurative and generic system, a place where meaning is produced, where meaning is received, and where his own larger project is represented—both in terms of history and genre. Ultimately, O'Brian's series seems to most closely follow the model of the classic historical novel, but, as I have suggested, this tracing of history through its inscription on the body does align itself with much more contemporary texts. His emphasis on the individual highlights his emphasis on reading history both through the individual's experience of it and through the impact the historical forces have on the life of the individual.

Trying to Escape History and the Compulsion to Repeat

I have spent much of this chapter discussing the nature of historical fiction and the way history functions in the Aubrey-Maturin novels.

However, to this point in the chapter I feel that I have concealed a kind of secret, only hinting at it once. Namely, that as the series progresses, one may wonder if O'Brian truly has lost some of his initial interest in representing the historical events of the Napoleonic Wars. There seem to be less and less of the kinds of moments I have described in *Fortune of War*, and instead, O'Brian seems to have a growing interest in following Aubrey through the "dark passages" of history, of encounters in remote spaces such as in the Pacific Ocean or against Turkish rebels near the Turkish peninsula. In fact, Powers, in reviewing the late novel *The Commodore*, observes that Jack and Stephen's "precise whereabouts in history remain obscure" (92). To help make this point, let me briefly note the moment when I believe this turn begins to occur, and how some of the later novels directly indicate this movement into historical "obscurity." We may tie these interests to those of the body, I think, as perhaps O'Brian grows more and more inclined to follow the path of private history and so tries to find space in this historical realm where that private history need not run up against the public historical world with the same force. After all, as O'Brian writes in his "Author's Note" to the twelfth novel of the series, *Far Side of the World*, he may be forced to take certain liberties in order to keep his series going and so "may be led to make use of hypothetical years, rather like those hypothetical moons used in the calculation of Easter: an 1812a as it were or even an 1812b." Here he makes reference to the kind of smaller scale historical precedents he has used alongside the larger kinds of battles covered in *Fortune of War*, and suggests, "Historical time has not yet run out of these tales." Here, history, more than anything else, seems to be O'Brian's muse.

Yet, we should also note that this confession at the start of *Far Side of the World* really does mark a turn in the series, and not just because of a necessity to slice time in such a way as to allow for more plots to happen in—if this can be translated this way—a logical fashion. In fact, I would argue that a number of factors are at work here—a desire to let Jack take action, a desire to keep Jack "alive," and a desire to keep narrative moving. I believe that Jack's life—and O'Brian's—become inextricably linked to this gradual movement into the "dark" areas. The effect is not felt immediately, though the plot of *Far Side* does meander in the Pacific Ocean around essentially a singular conflict between Jack's ship and an American ship during the War of 1812. The ship has import here

2. Scars, History and Historical Fiction

as well, for in this novel we learn that the H.M.S. *Surprise* has been deemed no longer worthy of battle; it has outlived its practical usage, and Jack "knew that this was almost certainly the last leg of her last voyage, but he had known that she was mortal for a great while now and the knowledge had become a kind of quiet heartbreak, always in the background, so that at present he took very particular notice of her excellence and of each day he passed on her" (79). The paying off of the crew would make "all her people, paid off at last, changed from members of a tight-knit community to solitary individuals" (80). The sadness, presented with no irony, becomes quite evident, and we can also notice that the significance of the loss extends beyond the ship itself to its figurative aspects: the ship has become a metonym for Jack—it was the ship of his youth, and its mortality mirrors Jack's (I will take up this relationship between ship and Jack more fully in Chapter 5). The loss of the ship means the end of a way of life, the loss of community. In the novel that follows, *Reverse of the Medal*, Stephen buys the *Surprise* in order to let Jack use it as a "letter of marque," essentially a privateer, once Jack loses his place in the navy. That novel, which ends with the dramatic punishment of Jack, provides a key to a kind of wish fulfillment in Stephen's gesture. In the appropriately named *Letter of Marque*, the subsequent novel, Jack grows to enjoy a certain degree of independence. When Stephen reflects on Jack's possible return to the navy, "He would most probably be given a command after the South American voyage: and perhaps it would be another independent commission—his genius lay that way" (239).

Jack enjoys "independence" for many of the novels that follow. In *Thirteen Gun Salute*, though Jack must take an envoy—Fox—on a diplomatic mission, that mission takes Jack and Stephen to Pulo Prabang, which, while clearly located in the vicinity of Malaysia, was invented by O'Brian. Yet, here they confront one of the central villains of the series, Andrew Wray, and a single French ship. Thus, the series finds itself in a historical world we recognize, but I cannot quite call it an actual historical world. In this space, though, the kinds of restrictions normally faced by the historical novelist begin to drop away. Perhaps not by coincidence, this novel contains one of the most simultaneously absurd and yet strangely beautiful moments in the entire series when Stephen meets orangutans in Kumai. In fact, King notes that O'Brian's editor had asked him to remove Stephen's experience in a "prenaturally peaceful valley" because O'Brian had "sprung off into the realm of fantasy" (291). O'Brian declined (292). The novels do not remain exclusively in this semi-imaginary historical space, but they certainly stay at remove from the main action of the war. In the novel that follows, *Nutmeg of Consolation*, Jack, Stephen, and the crew must overcome a shipwreck and eventually make their way to Australia. Essentially, O'Brian keeps Jack and Stephen in the margins of the war until the eighteenth novel in the series, *The Yellow Admiral*, in which history returns with a threat to the livelihood of Jack and O'Brian—in the form, namely, of the war's end: "Unless Napoleon wins yet another of those shattering unexpected victories by land all over again, it looks like this war was pretty nearly over, with the French cleared right out of Spain and Wellington already well into France" (18). In fact, the last three completed novels of the series take place clearly in the confines of historical space, and they bring both the series and the war to a conclusion.

Or so it would seem. In a certain kind of way, it appears that the pressure of historical time and mortality—first raised in the Author's Note for *Far Side of the World* and thematized in that very novel—has exuded its ultimate influence. Thus, the last novels of the series, with their return to history, suggest that O'Brian feared that perhaps he might die before giving the series a sense of an ending (if I may borrow a phrase from Frank Kermode). However, the key to understanding some of the tensions of the late novels may lie in the fact that we only ever get "a sense"—such as Jack learning he has been made an admiral in the twentieth novel of the series, *Blue at the Mizzen*. Perhaps, then, we can see one more postmodern complication in O'Brian's seeming resistance to closure. On the one hand, we might consider the degree to which the path into the "dark areas" of history the novels take have something to do with a compound wish fulfillment—both O'Brian's and the reader's. The novels on some level are bound by history, as is the author. O'Brian began these novels late in life and clearly never expected to spend the remainder of his life writing them (the first three novels really feel like something of a trilogy—though the gap in writing between the third and fourth novel may account for this feeling), and placing Jack and Stephen in this in-between state allows them to stay alive and thrive even as the books trace the way in which they age. (And, of course, something like that same thing is happening in the very mortal body of the author himself.) Hayden White argues that "the demand for closure

2. Scars, History and Historical Fiction

is a demand ... for moral meaning, a demand that sequences of real events be assessed as to their significance as elements of moral drama" (21). Although O'Brian's series stopped—because of O'Brian's death— they never did fully end (he was writing another book when he died), and so in that way he refused to ever offer the kinds of moral judgments White implies more classic historical stories have tended to provide. A very telling passage from *Nutmeg of Consolation* speaks to the problems of endings, which come in the form of Stephen's ruminations on them: "The conventional ending, with virtue rewarded and loose ends tied up is often sadly chilling; and its platitude and falsity tend to infect what has gone before, however excellent" (256). If we look at both the way the novels end and the way the series resists a true resolution of the action, we can see that these remarks from Stephen must align closely with the thoughts of the author. King introduces the question of how O'Brian might wish to end the series, as he discusses *Nutmeg of Consolation,* the fourteenth novel in the series, written while O'Brian was in his seventies. King sees the passage I cite from the novel as a direct discussion of this problem of finding an end, and proclaims, "Those who knew O'Brian well did not expect him to tie up the series in a neat bundle" (311). Perhaps more importantly to the questions I have been raising between morality, history, and the resistance to closure, King adds, "So inextricably interwoven was his life with his fictional characters and their world that for him this would be tantamount to saying: 'Right, I've had a long wonderful life. It's time to end'" (311). Even in a *Times* article King cites, O'Brian talked, as *Blue at the Mizzen* appeared, of his desire to keep writing (312). Most significantly, though, is O'Brian's desire to follow the advice Stephen offers to resist "the conventional ending," one that prescribes and closes off possibilities. Therefore, though in the bodies of the characters we have the signs of history, we have not been told how to interpret those signs. Of course, there is also the strange, Beckett-like gesture in this fact of "I can't go on, I'll go on."

3

"The Virtuous Shrub"
The Drug Problem

Let's Start with Coffee

It's hard to think of coffee as invisible in our culture. Not with a Starbucks squatting on every corner. Not with Starbucks spreading like a green-tinged plague throughout even England. Anyone who has stood on a corner in Manhattan and simultaneously seen two Starbucks within strolling distance would not call it invisible. Instead, if anything, coffee is everywhere. We have made it into a fetish, a joke (usually featuring some combination of the words low-fat and latte), an accessory (we sport cups of coffee like a walking stick, a cane, a decorative or ceremonial sword), and sometimes, simply, as a beverage (often with so many sweeteners and flavorings that the coffee serves mostly as a kind of filler, a conveyance). We do not, however, think of it as a source of addiction—at least not at the forefront of our thinking.

Yet anyone who drinks coffee on a regular basis comes to recognize its role in one's life. Like most coffee drinkers, I need my coffee. And I mean *need*. If I do not get my coffee at its regular morning hour, I begin to show symptoms of withdrawal. I am sluggish, more so than normal, and eventually a headache comes to fully bloom, a stinging headache akin to a mini-migraine. Like many a writer, I am writing this essay under the influence of caffeine. There it sits, quietly, to my right. Perhaps Marcus Boon has a more apt way of considering coffee's—and, more specifically, caffeine's—presence in our culture. In his extended study on the relationship between drugs and writers, *The Road of Excess*, Boon suggests that caffeine has a kind of "transparency," and "this transparency is characteristic of our attitude to stimulants, the most ubiquitous, yet least understood, of the psychoactive drugs used in modern life" (170).

3. "The Virtuous Shrub"

In this chapter I will focus on the body in its more material and less figurative sense (putting aside the fact that the bodies in the novels always remain on some level figurative), and, in particular, I will examine the ways in which the novels describe and reflect upon the relationship between the body and four addictive substances—namely, coffee, alcohol, opium, and cocaine. Due to its prominent role in the series, and in particular the life of Stephen Maturin, opium will be the subject of our most extended discussion. As we consider the depictions of these addictions, I will consider the extent to which O'Brian has drawn upon historical precedent in presenting these substances, and the degree to which attitudes toward addiction might seem to be more twentieth century than eighteenth. It will be my contention that these addictive substances become a part of the long meditation in the series about the relationship between the human mind, to which we tend to ascribe a great deal of agency, and the often quite animal body in which that mind is housed. Drugs help raise these issues through the way their presence invites discussions of the very nature of addiction, and questions of whether the mind or the body is the source of addiction. Coffee will be our starting point—our gateway drug.

To a coffee drinker, one of the comforts of the Aubrey-Maturin's novels is the joy and pleasure that the main characters take in their coffee. Tea, that oh-so-British drink—never mind its origins for a moment—gets dismissed again and again as that "vile wash." Avoiding anachronism, there is no talk of caffeine (what both tea and coffee impart to their drinkers). They may drink tea, but certainly tea provides no joy, and sometimes it makes for quite the opposite situation. Early in the series (in the second book, in fact), Jack and Stephen find themselves suddenly on a crack ship, *The Lively*, on which the crew drinks hot chocolate. They send Killick, the captain's steward, scurrying through the ship looking for coffee, only to come up empty. This failure is met with horror on both Jack and Stephen's part. Late in the series, a similar sequence is repeated when, after a long, tiring and trying voyage, Jack and Stephen are somewhat put out and ordered to dine aboard an admiral's ship for breakfast. The ship, however, does not possess coffee. Stephen, nearly inconsolable, asks if he can have a beer instead.

We might see coffee as another of the many examples of ritual and routine aboard ship, thought it remains largely confined to Jack and Stephen. Inevitably, in almost every one of the O'Brian novels the narrative arrives at a moment we might call "clear sailing," in which the ship cracks on at a rigorous pace, no enemy or land appears in sight, and readers find themselves greeted by the narrator's rhapsodies of the pleasure of such open seas and the reliability of routine. Coffee, at the beginning and end of the day, fits clearly into both Stephen's and Jack's sense of routine and the everyday. After all, my own description of coffee's role and its effect upon me if it is absent could be said to fall somewhat into the same pattern. It is something we have everyday and often at the same time of day. If we eat at the same time or shower or shave, we can certainly put that activity off if something comes to prevent us from doing it on any given day. For Jack and Stephen, coffee is no different. They frequently share breakfast (or at least Jack's second breakfast, as Stephen routinely fails to arise before Jack has been up on deck, observed his current situation, ordered the necessary adjustments, and then returned for his morning meal—often with an officer or a midshipman in tow). When they drink their coffee with breakfast, O'Brian frequently has them indulge in "pot after pot."

Of course, part of the comfort of these scenes is the routine and repetition—both for the reader and the characters—as well as the typically luxurious nature of the breakfasts (a man of Jack's size and appetite seems to require—should stores allow—many eggs, much toast, and some selection of meat: a chop, fresh fish, or perhaps a steak). Consider this aside from *Treason's Harbor*: "As he turned to go below for his breakfast, the first wonderfully reviving cup of coffee—the genuine Mocha, straight from the interesting port—that he had already smelt, he caught the eyes of his four young gentlemen fixed thoughtfully upon him" (176). Yet coffee also appears throughout any given day. In the midst of rough conditions, or an exhausting chase, or difficult maneuvers, Killick will appear, unbidden, with the balm of coffee, a fresh hot pot, ready to restore, revive, or simply sustain the body of the captain, which craves this succor even beyond the level of his conscious mind. In the evenings, too, coffee makes its appearance and has its own place in the rituals of the two men. Typically, in the best of situations, they also end the day together. Perhaps they play some music, and Killick—whose skills extend essentially to two culinary procedures, the making of coffee and the making of toasted cheese—delivers a fresh hot pot, after the cheese has been consumed, perhaps with the last of some port.

Coffee, then, is clearly part of a ritual, but it is also needed both to

3. "The Virtuous Shrub"

complete the ritual and because the body needs it (perhaps as the mind needs the ritual). Does this make Stephen and Jack somehow lesser figures or problematic figures? No more so than any other coffee drinker. But it is a drug—or at least it transports a significant one, caffeine, to our system—and we need it, to some extent, like any body that needs a drug. Stephen, of course, needs or comes to need several other drugs throughout the series, and these addictions are treated with a great deal more seriousness by both Stephen—at least when he recognizes their effects or cannot help but recognize them—and likely the reader. Yet coffee is the one addiction both Jack and Stephen share.

What, then, do we make of all this coffee drinking? If the narrator does not treat it as a drug—in, say, the way he treats laudanum or coca leaves—does that mean that we as readers should not treat this consumption as one of the many forms of addiction we witness over the course of twenty volumes? If O'Brian wishes us to see it as addiction—whether he highlights it as such or not—what is he after? Is he asking us to turn away from our own consumption? Like yours, no doubt, my cup has already been drained as I've been typing away. We do not see any ill effects of coffee consumption in the novel except for tiredness and irritability when it is not consumed. This may upset the human community, but certainly the effects do not lead to much beyond occasional discomfort.

Perhaps we might say that the repetitions of coffee drinking fill several roles in the novels. First of all, as I have noted, they are a ritual, and the novels again and again suggest a basic human truth: humans enjoy routine, find comfort in it, and can become anxious, irritable and perhaps many things worse when they are denied this comfort or are thrust out of a routine. To those who have chosen a life at sea, routine might be one of the many things that distinguishes time aboard from time on shore (often seen as a place of chaos, a place where the unexpected comes to intrude upon the individual, usually for the worse). When we begin to think of coffee as a part of this repeated cycle that provides comfort, we are certainly not surprised to read that among coffee's original uses was "as an aid to prayer," another routine often associated with (among other things) a desire for comfort and safety (Boon 172). Coffee in the novels can also be seen in light of two other associations or effects it has. First, as Boon points out, coffee has long been seen as part of community building in its central place in the coffee house (172). While

Aubrey and Maturin form nothing like a European intellectual circle of writers, coffee is a frequent witness if not a cause to their small community. If coffee also, as Boon says, "promoted clarity of thought and sobriety," we can understand why both the ship's captain and the ship's surgeon have frequent recourse to its assistance (172).

However, while I have conceded that coffee is not cocaine, and we would be ill advised to treat it as such, we also cannot deny that it contains a drug, one that possesses the power to affect the human beings who take it. Throughout the long history of coffee consumption, its use has not always been "transparent" or innocuous. It is perhaps also important to note that, according to Rudi Matthee in the essay "Exotic Substances," caffeine, like tobacco, tea, and alcohol, first found its way in the West as a "medical agent rather than as ingredients of tasty beverages" (30). Boon informs us that in Constantinople, coffee houses and coffee drinking inspired a great deal of debate, and coffee houses "were shut down for promoting intoxication and for being a social institution that rivaled the mosque" (173). However, in Europe it was seen as a counterpoise to "opium and wine," and instead was regarded for "promoting health, moderation, clarity of thought, and energy" (Boon 173). Boon goes on to cite figures like Michelet who praised coffee as a kind of spark for the Enlightenment, which Stephen in many ways comes to represent throughout O'Brian's series. Again and again we might cite writers who praised coffee for its ability to enhance our ability to think, as reflected in a phrase from Stephen in *Far Side of the World*: "I have felt my mind glow, my mental and no doubt physical powers increase" (160). However, this comment from Stephen does not apply to coffee; it describes the effects of Stephen's beloved coca leaves.

Thus, I would say that one of the other effects achieved by O'Brian, whether intended or not, by the repeated documentation of coffee consumption is to connect it to other drugs and drug consumption. In addition, coffee's very "transparency" and relatively benign reputation may allow O'Brian to persuade the reader to feel some sympathy for other drug use in the novels, particularly Stephen's indulgence and reliance on other, more powerful stimulants, as well as opiates. In fact, as we shall see, O'Brian on multiple occasions has Stephen make direct links between these multiple drugs.

3. "The Virtuous Shrub"

The Bottle Stands by You, Sir!

As a society, we have long since moved beyond a time where alcohol had the kind of "transparency" that caffeine and coffee can be thought to have. In fact, it might be more accurate to say that, despites its ubiquity, it never has had anything like such a status, even if our awareness of the dangers of abusing alcohol have increased a great deal in recent decades. This is also the case with drinking onboard a King's ship, at least in the portrait of such a life that O'Brian provides us. To some extent, everyone on board ship drinks, and it forms as much a ritual to all as, say, the coffee drinking does to Jack and Stephen.

Let's consider for a moment the role of alcohol in the lives of the majority of the crew—and we may call them the crew because this condition essentially applies to each and every one of the crews we meet through the twenty novels. At various points throughout the series, Jack makes it clear that one can run short of various supplies aboard ship. While it is unfortunate to drink rain water that has mixed with tar—and it may in fact taste quite vile—Jack can live with such a situation; however, he cannot flirt with running shy of either rum for the crew's grog or their ration of tobacco. Every day the crew must have their grog, which, of course, includes their tot of rum. Many of the crew members will cut various deals, with other crewmembers usually, in order to get more of a ration on any given day, and occasionally the crew will receive more as a reward, as ordered by the captain. Now, we can see this again as part of the routine of the ship. The crew—at least in O'Brian's vision—wants everything regular, regimented and repeated, and will grow disconsolate with any break (salt pork is to be served on a particular day, seemingly, in a phrase of O'Brian's narrator, since time immemorial). Are the men really getting drunk on their one glass of grog a day (at least that's their ration anyway)? Of course, it is hard to say—and, of course, these are imagined versions of historical figures. Yet, I think we can dismiss the need to choose whether they are being offered this regular draught because of routine or because of a need, a need derived from the chemical responses of the body, of the mind, or some combination. In essence, the grog serves the same end. It pacifies, it satisfies, it comforts. And, as Dr. Maturin complains again and again, it also injures; it also kills.

Throughout the series, and particularly early in the series, Stephen complains about this practice of the Navy (among others), and his main complaints arise from his having seen the results of the grog upon these men. After all, they drink during mid-day, in the fine European tradition, and then they return to work. This work, of course, requires these men to climb to great heights, to stand on narrow beams, and all in a moving vehicle swaying, often in a kind corkscrew pattern, and often in violent winds and storms. During a particularly ugly rash of injuries during bad weather as the *Surprise* goes round the Cape in *Far Side of the World*, Stephen laments that, after he tells the crew that "you must throw your nasty grog into the scuppers, if you are to go aloft within two hours," they, unfortunately, "do not attend" (196). We see this cycle of drinking and work documented many times in the series. At least in this instance, then, we have a pattern, a routine that is seemingly inevitable. The implication is that without grog you are certain to have a mutiny or, at the least, a great deal of insubordination; but you are also going to have men putting their lives at even greater risk as a consequence.

While it does not seem necessary to go into a great amount of detail regarding the crew and its use and abuse of alcohol, we should perhaps also take a brief note of the regular behavior of the crew when given shore leave, particularly shore leave after a successful cruise in which a prize was taken. Like in Freud's hydraulic model of the mind, with its sense of pressure that builds up requiring release and a return to stasis, discipline is maintained not simply by threat of violence, patriotism, respect for authority, or any of the other popularized notions of military service. Instead, O'Brian clearly suggests that discipline is maintained by allowing the men a release from the repression of the iron hierarchy aboard ship; they must be freed to go ashore so that they can spend their money indiscriminately (despite Jack often pleading that they send their money home), fornicate, and, inevitably, drink and drink.

Since my primary focus throughout this study has been to consider in particular the ways in which O'Brian makes use of the bodies and the behaviors of the bodies of Stephen and Jack in the construction of his extended narrative, I would like to consider alcohol consumption from the perspective of our main characters for a few moments. Unlike coca leaves and laudanum, to which I will turn shortly, alcohol is not regularly abused by either character—and by abuse I mean consuming drink to the point of incapacity. In the case of Stephen, we can say just about never. While Stephen's eyes grow paler and paler—except when masked

3. "The Virtuous Shrub"

by blue-tinted glasses—he is, in a strange way, known for his sobriety aboard ship, known for never drinking too much, for never making a show of himself in that regard (as opposed to his pratfalls and astonishing ignorance of the workings of the ship). In contrast, Jack certainly has his moments, but not very many. Early in the series he makes a bit of an ass of himself at a formal function after drinking quite a lot, and he is seen to grow in enthusiasm over the course of a formal meal (turning redder and redder); but, for the most part, Jack's great size helps him negotiate the worst effects alcohol can have in store for the human body.

When we speak of alcohol consumption, and particularly the manner by which it is most often consumed by Stephen and Jack, we enter territory that can resemble the ingestion of coffee. As I have suggested, certainly coffee and caffeine have little of the stigma that alcohol has—we have yet to witness the first person who has had to check themselves in for rehabilitation for having made coffee too much of a part of her life—but we can see them connected in their pervasiveness in our culture, as well as that of Jack's and Stephen's world (and, one assumes, of O'Brian's as well). Stephen and Jack more often than not drink wine with their dinner, and they are both connoisseurs. This fascination with wine likely derives from O'Brian's own (he owned vineyards in the south of France), but their fondness for wine, their treasuring of it, suggests a few elements of their characters and their relationship. As demonstrated in this somewhat playful passage from *Thirteen Gun Salute*, Stephen sees wine in terms of culture and what humanity can achieve: "'When they are making good port wine, and the better kinds of claret and burgundy,' said Stephen, looking at the candle through his glass, 'men act like rational creatures. In almost all their other activities we see little but foolishness and chaos'" (22). Throughout the series the narrator and the characters take note of what they drink, and offer praise or criticize the wine where it is necessary (to them at least). A wine connoisseur can take pleasure in Jack and Stephen imbibing Chateau Haut Brion from the eighteenth century, and consider the implications of their choice to treasure Hermitage and Chambertin (certainly two of the heroic wines of France, no matter what the era).

Those who drink wine as Jack and Stephen do seek pleasure from the wine—as, arguably, on some level the pot smoker and the heroin addict do—however, they are not responding to wine primarily in terms of its possessing alcohol, and that consumption is not primarily being driven by the body's need for more (a desire for the physical effects alcohol has on the system). Instead, we can say that it is driven by many esoteric qualities, and we can say it is driven by the sensations it creates in the body. Perhaps on some level it produces a kind of need to repeat that experience—though again this is not the need of the alcoholic. No one experiences the shakes because they have been denied the bouquet of a fine Gevry-Chambertin for too long. Instead, this is more of a psychological need, a treasuring of experience, of sensation, of the rich variety produced by the earth. In fact, Stephen, in a moment that can only be labeled hypocritical from *Letter of Marque*, while denying the addictive qualities of laudanum (we'll return to this passage and Stephen's obtuseness on this matter later on in this chapter), compares those who would fall victim to laudanum to those who would "become the victims of intoxicating liquors" and labels them all "moral imbeciles" (55–56).

Despite Stephen's disregard for those who would fall victim to alcoholism—and we should admit that Stephen here is speaking from a clearly rationalizing and self-deceiving position at this point—and despite the fact that he largely treasures wine for its smell, taste, and finer points, he himself can be seen to respond to the undeniable effects that alcohol carried along in that very fine wine, be it Boone's Strawberry Farm or Domanee Romani-Conti. In other words, no matter how much of a wine connoisseur any human may be, they cannot drink wine without its having physical effects on the body that have little to do with the sensations and pleasure of a long finish. This becomes clear, for example, during an episode relatively early in *Far Side of the World* in which Stephen "felt the effect of the wine well before his glass was emptied—a very slight swimming in his head, the faint birth of a certain benignity, a willingness to be pleased with company" (52). In this same novel, Stephen, in a peevish mood, finds his mind is not strong enough to counter the effects of food and wine: "And Stephen noticed, not without irritation, that as he ate and drank his civility was growing less artificial, his deliberately urbane expression more nearly a spontaneous smile, and that he was in danger of enjoying himself" (251). Such moments speak not so much to what the body needs—though one can see how this infusion of joy could be something a body might desire again and again—as to the ways in which alcohol and other powerful drugs undermine or work against the individual's desire to shape his or her own mood and behaviors. While Stephen does often desire such control, he also

3. "The Virtuous Shrub"

sympathizes with a need to change one's mood, sometimes as a matter of health, and he also takes too much human enjoyment in wine to become a figure like Jack's literary predecessor, Horatio Hornblower, who we are told in *Beat to Quarters* was a "naturally abstemious man" because "he hated the feeling of not quite being the master of himself" (112).

Whereas the desire for control dominates Hornblower's behavior and attends him at all times—he again and again seeks to appear the master of himself to the point of revealing a true insecurity in the matter—Jack and Stephen typically only seek such control in moments of public or professional performance. As we have discussed, Stephen seems to become something other than himself, something almost reptilian, when he must use force as a part of his intelligence work, and Jack too realizes the need to be a figure of authority—if not outright invulnerability—as he controls his ship. As the passage from *Letter of Marque* I have cited above attests, Stephen sees a giving in to liquors as something of a moral failing, and it is clear throughout the series that being able to handle one's wine or liquor is a significant sign in one's favor. Inevitably, the expansive dinners aboard ship put many a man to the test. As we are told frequently, in a well-stocked ship, with a fairly well-off Captain and officers of like status, there can be much entertaining aboard ship: the Captain inviting his officers to dine with him; the gun-room, the dining quarters of the officers, returning the compliment to their Captain. Such affairs—especially those involving Jack—tend towards the extravagant whenever supplies afford. At such dinners, wine, port, Madeira, and brandy are often consumed in great quantities and often help fill the gaps or awkward pauses common to such events, for "Small things [Jack] had to find, since by convention all the sailors sat like so many ghosts, never speaking until they were spoken to, this being a formal occasion, with a comparative stranger present: fortunately, if he ran out of topics he could always fall back on drinking to them" with the declaration, "A glass of wine with you sir," or the friendly reminder, "the bottle stands by you, Sir" (*Far Side of the World* 83). Thus, we see alcohol filling its time-honored role in social gatherings, as it works to ease the inhibitions of its consumers. This can have some rather clear consequences aboard ship, especially if a midshipman whose voice has not yet broken (or, of course, has only recently done so) is in attendance. Yet, anyone can fall victim to such affairs. Consider the fate of a young

Marine officer during a meal in *The Letter of Marque,* who, while others were conversing, "[had] chosen the same moment for gliding under the table, a smooth plunge into smiling, speechless coma" (65). Succumbing in this way is, of course, not a way to distinguish oneself, but there are certainly worse ways to be overcome. It is also clear that Jack and his fellow sea officers respect those who can withstand the effects of alcohol, as Jack makes clear to Stephen after a dinner with Envoy Fox in *Thirteen Gun Salute:* "'The club's port was the best I have drunk for years,' said Jack. 'Fox stood it remarkably well: never a tremor as he went downstairs, which is more than could be said for Worsley and Hammond and some other members'" (108).

It is fair to say that alcohol in its many forms has a more complicated role in the series than coffee does, and that its role touches upon several recurring interests of the texts. It plays a role in routine, in maintaining control and the hierarchy aboard ship; it affects the body in ways pleasurable and damaging. Its over-indulsence on occasion is seen as more or less the run of life, but its chronic over-dependence is seen as a weakness, a sign of the frailty of the person—at least to the majority of the novels' characters. However, in the wider lens and sympathy of O'Brian's narrator—and let's go ahead and call the narrator in light of Wayne Booth's seminal text, *The Rhetoric of Fiction,* the implied author—we cannot help but feel sympathy for the body's weakness, weaknesses that can take the great joy of wine and make it a demon haunting the individual to the point of death (if not creating a life of misery). There are few sadder moments than when we see Jack gaze upon a crewmember or officer and realize that he has—either under the pressure or stress of the moment, or even from simple ill-judgment or weakness—managed to get himself drunk at a crucial moment. Inevitably, Jack looks upon these figures as pathetic and rarely, if ever, does more than push them aside in that particular moment (of course, their long-term fate can be much more severe).

Just My Usual Dose

Of all the addictive substances of the novels, the one that receives by far the most extended contemplation and description throughout the series is opium, most often in its preferred form—preferred by Stephen

3. "The Virtuous Shrub"

Maturin, in any case—of the alcoholic tincture of laudanum. Although we do not find out about Stephen's use of laudanum at the inception of the series, we hear of it in *Post Captain,* and it is a fully established fact by the time we reach the fourth novel in the series, *The Mauritius Command.* Throughout the series we see Stephen taking laudanum, trying to quit it, doing so for a time, and consistently finding excuses again and again to return to it. Before going into depth about how O'Brian depicts Stephen's opium addiction, its effects on Stephen, and the implications of that addiction, it seems appropriate to make a few remarks about O'Brian's choice in this matter.

So much of the novel is told through the perspective of either Jack or Stephen, despite being usually in the third person. These inside views, as Wayne Booth would call them, tend to have a remarkable effect on how we as readers respond to Stephen's addiction. We should note that Jack seems entirely oblivious to Stephen's habits. He makes many a comment about Stephen's behavior in the mornings—loathe to awaken, short, crabby, taciturn, even hostile before coffee has had its full effect (a classic passage from downer to upper)—and he will occasionally remark on the effect of trying to read the face of a man sporting colored glasses, but other than that Jack never utters a comment about Stephen's use of laudanum, either in his first-person narration—his serial letters home to his wife—or in the many, many passages narrated from his perspective. It is possible Jack knows—there are multiple ways he could have learned of it (the depth of its use, that is); however, if he does so, this is never made explicit in the series, and he certainly never intervenes with his friend on this matter. Because the taking of laudanum would have been seen as a medical matter, and because Jack ascribes a kind of omniscience to Stephen when it comes to such matters, he might also simply defer to Stephen in regard to this as with all medical procedures (except those having to do with Jack's own alimentary canal).

However, this lack of knowledge about Stephen's addiction may not be exceptional. In her exploration of the history of its use, *Opium and the People,* Virginia Berridge points out that Samuel Taylor Coleridge's consumption of the drug—and he was a habitual user for years—"was not well-known even to his close friends" (54). These issues aside, we can also say that the fact that O'Brian has chosen to depict Stephen's drug use from almost an exclusively inside view has two important effects. First, we are often somewhat uncertain whether to label Stephen's use an addiction or some other label implying regular use, perhaps even some dependence. Second, we are led to have a great deal of sympathy with this drug user—perhaps not sympathy for his use or addiction, if we wish to call it that, but general sympathy for his character and for his weaknesses, and generally for the reasons that drive him back to laudanum with such frequency.

In choosing to depict Stephen as a chronic user of opium, O'Brian draws Maturin in terms consistent with physicians of his era. When looking at Maturin's drug use, it is necessary to shrug off or divest ourselves of the steady stream of anti-drug propaganda that has dominated the past century and will likely continue into this one (unless the recent campaigns to legalize marijuana reflect a noticeable shift). As an opium user, then, Stephen was simply one of many. Writing of Dr. Samuel Johnson, for example, Marcus Boon informs us that though he was "better known as a tea drinker," he "was, like many doctors throughout history, a habitual opium user" (20). And this was not an entirely new phenomenon in the eighteenth century either. Boon reminds us that "references to opium in belle lettres after the Renaissance reflect the ubiquity of opium use in Europe at that time" (19). In addition, Matthee charts the remarkably commonplace use of the drug throughout his chapter "Literary and Middle-Class Society." While, as Boon suggests, opium might have frequently been seen as connected to the East—as both a dark menace and an exotic path to transcendence—it made its way through society in large part because physicians frequently prescribed it. In fact, Boon argues that two physicians of the eighteenth-century, Erasmus Darwin (Charles' grandfather) and John Brown, were largely responsible for popularizing opium (23). Considering Stephen's own interest in theories of evolution and "natural philosophy" more generally, the connections between Darwin and Stephen seem particularly noteworthy (though Stephen loves Dryden, he is no poet—however, some, like the Romantics or really anyone who has spent much time with his work, might say the very thing about Erasmus Darwin). While some of the beliefs regarding opium (and drugs in general) may look naïve to us now, we should also note that its negative effects were not entirely ignored. Consider this evaluation of opium's effects from Darwin: "In small quantities it exhilarates the mind, raises the passions, and invigorates the body: in large ones it is succeeded by intoxication, languor, stupor and death" (qtd. in Boon 24). On the one hand, we have the mistaken belief that opium

3. "The Virtuous Shrub"

acted as something of a stimulant (like caffeine, for example); on the other, we have some sense that real dangers lie in its use (though here there is no mention of addiction; more on that later). Throughout his discussion of opium and narcotics in general, Boon suggests that there is a great deal of inconsistency in how writers have discussed opium. And though writers may be a particular group in some ways, we can extrapolate that most users of opium had recurring doubts about it (he cites Coleridge as providing a fine example of this—with especially early praise of its effects and a gradual view of it as a burden overwhelming him).

The problem is that even if opium was a problematic medicine—and opium certainly did not act as some of its proponents, like the Scottish physician Brown (who also thought it was a stimulant), thought it did—its use for the population did not stop at the medical. "Many Romantics," Boon writes, "took opium—but as I have already noted, so did many people in England in the late eighteenth century and early nineteenth—as a 'medicine,' but one whose nonmedical effects might also be enjoyed" (31). As Mike Jay describes it in *Emperor of Dreams: Drugs in the Nineteenth Century*, a somewhat flawed distinction was made "between those who used it to treat pain and those who used it to pursue pleasure" (54). It also undoubtedly does work as a medical aid, as the continued use of opiates and narcotics for pain relief demonstrates. However, as Matthee points out, during the time that O'Brian sets his novels, we find "the widespread use of the drug for every variety of complaint." In fact, Matthee concedes that "it would be almost easier to list those areas where it was never employed than to attempt to deal with every therapeutic possibility" (66).

Of course, even if many people, and particularly physicians, living during the time in which O'Brian set his novels took opium, O'Brian need not have felt any compulsion to make Maturin a drug user. In other words, O'Brian certainly seems to have been interested in depicting drug use; and by giving drug use to a character we inevitably sympathize with (we see so much of the events of the novel through his eyes, how can we not?), he invites us to examine his drug use from a position that goes beyond simply condemnation (or commendation, for that matter). As I have suggested, O'Brian then invites his readers to consider what drives Maturin to opium use and what effects it has upon him. Throughout the series there appears to be nearly countless passages in which Maturin rationalizes his drug use and finds yet one more excuse for using it. The most common is simply that he cannot sleep. However, inevitably, we realize that it is not the absence of sleep that drives him to laudanum, but the thoughts that invade Stephen's mind while he lays sleepless, swaying in his hammock.

What then is Stephen looking for when he turns to the tincture of laudanum? Ultimately, if we were to generalize, we might say that he looks for comfort, for escape—however temporary—and a calming of his spirit. The traditional uses of opium as a medicine—that is, as pain relief—fall then into a more figurative type for Stephen. It is clear throughout the series that Stephen sees the mind and the body as inevitably interconnected. As a physician, one simply cannot treat one aspect of the person. His propensity to dispense sugar pills is just one small bit of evidence to support this claim. If he takes opium as a kind of spiritual pain relief, then we can see the ways in which this interconnection becomes complicated in the series, especially if Boon is correct in claiming that "pain relief is a kind of transcendence of the body" (34).

Although we cannot identify it as the sole cause of Stephen's pain, one recurring source is Diana, the woman who eventually becomes Stephen's wife (though she continues to cause him a great deal of pain and heartache afterwards). In choosing heartache as a primary source of pain that can only be quelled by opium, O'Brian may be drawing directly upon the work of Thomas De Quincey, since, as Martin Booth points out in *Opium: A History*, De Quincey may have sought out opium in part to deal with his "misery over the loss of his companion, a prostitute with whom he lived in penury" (36). When I examined O'Brian's collected notes at the Lilly Library (housed at Indiana University), I found that they included a sheet recording laudanum doses transcribed from De Quincey's *Confessions of an Opium Eater*, indicating that De Quincy's text was clearly something of a source for the writer.

Let's consider how O'Brian develops Diana as a source of recurring pain for Stephen. Stephen first meets Diana in the second novel of the series, *Post-Captain*, where she quickly becomes a point of contention and strife between Stephen and Jack (to the point that the two nearly have a duel, which would have ended the series quite prematurely). As we are told throughout the series, Stephen and Diana are an ill-matched couple; however, one of the clear impediments to Stephen in trying to woo Diana is his own body—namely, his ugliness. Throughout the series,

3. "The Virtuous Shrub"

O'Brian's narrator goes to great lengths to establish how physically unattractive Stephen is. In our first meeting with Stephen, he is seen from Jack's point of view, who conceives of him as "the ill looking son of a bitch" in *Master and Commander* (8). Consider also this introduction to Stephen in the fourth book of the series, *The Mauritius Command*:

> Sitting sideways upon his horse with his feet so withdrawn from the mud that he appeared to be crouching on his back, like an ape, rode Dr. Maturin, Captain Aubrey's closest friend, the surgeon in many of the ships he had commanded, a small, indefinably odd and even ill-looking man with pale eyes and a paler face, topped by a full bottomed wig that marked him as a physician, if a somewhat old-fashioned one [16].

Later in the series, in *Treason's Harbor*, the spy Lesueur will refer to Stephen as "a nasty looking crocodile" (19). I could go on. Stephen comes to internalize this judgment as the series progresses. For example, when evaluating the causes and responses to the flirtation he is engaged in with Mrs. Fielding on Malta in *Treason's Harbor*, he declares to himself that she cannot possibly find that she is "enamoured of my person" (89).

Although Stephen could do something about how he presents himself—and he does upon occasion, or at least Killick tries to—he can do very little about his own comeliness. Fairly early in *Post Captain*, however, Diana—a very attractive woman herself—makes it quite clear that, for her, looks do matter. In comparing Jack and Stephen, she says to Stephen, "You are very good company: I like being with you. But he is a handsome fellow" (54). She stops short of uttering "and you are not," but the point becomes quite clear. On the very next page we find Stephen's retort and perhaps muted cry of despair: "But I am averse to giving pain, Villiers, which you are not" (55). By the end of this novel, Diana's ability to impose a kind of chronic pain upon Stephen becomes clear in his despairing philosophies: "Life is a long disease with only one termination and its last years are appalling" (449). Thus, unable to transcend his body in the everyday world, he seeks such transcendence at night, trying to self-medicate and manage the disease of living his life outlined here.

His marriage to Diana does little to stifle the flood of insecurity and pain she evokes in him. This passage from *The Letter of Marque* outlining his views of the relationship make the problems plain: "Stephen knew very well that in their relations the very strong feeling was all on his side: she had a certain liking, friendship and affection for him, but certainly no passion of any kind. Passionate resentment of his supposed infidelity, perhaps, but no other" (241). He will spend much of the series pursuing Diana, and though he will appear to get her to accept him despite his looks—character will out—their marriage and relationship remains tumultuous, and we find him twice having to find her and return her to England. Once she ran away to Norway in response to her mistaken belief that he has had an affair, and once she fled England to Ireland in desperation at her inability to cope with their apparently mentally disabled daughter, which, like Stephen's adultery, proves to be a misapprehension. With each moment of despair involving Diana—his inability to woo her, his need to rescue her in some way, his need to convince her that he has been faithful, his need to convince her that their daughter is healthy, and finally his difficulty in dealing with her death—he will return to laudanum and its ability to, however temporarily, quell the pain and impotence he feels. Although the pain is seemingly of the mind and not the body, Stephen comes to see the two as essentially interconnected, as he pronounces in *The Ionian Mission:* "'Indeed, the effect of the mind on the body is extraordinarily great,' observed Stephen. 'I have noticed it again and again; and we have innumerable authorities, from Hippocrates to Dr. Cheyne. I wish we could prescribe happiness'" (107). Seemingly, then, for himself in any case, the closest he can come to such a prescription is his beloved laudanum.

Laudanum, Medicinal or Recreational

As Boon and Jay suggest, the problem with the use of laudanum was, in part, that people enjoyed it. To this point, Martin Booth directs us to Dr. John Jones' *Mysteries of Opium Reveal'd*, which he calls "probably the earliest book specifically dealing with opium." It came out in 1700, and in that text we already see the author describing both what would be, to a modern reader, signs of its addictive qualities as well as its pleasures, opium "being a vehicle of pleasant fantasies, the dulling of pain and release from anxiety" (31). In other words, the problem from the start was that people might enjoy taking laudanum or other opiates not simply as a medicine but as something beyond that, and hence it has the ability to become something much more recreational—something to do, something for its own sake. As Alethea Hayter notes in

3. "The Virtuous Shrub"

Opium and the Romantic Imagination, "Eighteenth-century doctors hearing such tales [of regular opium eaters] as these and knowing how essential opium was as an occasional analgesic in their ordinary medical practice, were puzzled whether it could be safely confided to the general public" (28). Hayter, nevertheless, also cites "celebrated physicians" like John Brown, who were wholeheartedly enthusiastic about opium as a "wholly beneficent drug" (29).

Often, at least in terms of his medical practice, Stephen would seem to line up with folks like Brown. However, as for its use as a recreational drug, for the most part (with one exception that I will get to shortly) Stephen thinks of his laudanum use in terms of the medicinal, as something his body—even if driven by his mind—needs for healing. Throughout the series we witness Stephen's attempts to leave his use of laudanum behind—clearly a sign that he is aware that it can have negative consequences for him—and we inevitably find, subsequent to such moments, others in which Stephen performs great mental acrobatics in order to rationalize its use. Consider for a moment these passages from *Far Side of the World.* At one point the narrator informs us that Stephen's laudanum "had consoled him in anxiety, happiness, privation, pain and insomnia for many a year but which he had given up (except medicinally) on his marriage to Diana" (129). In this description we have one of the moments in which the narrator seems both inside Stephen's thoughts, while also playfully or ironically teasing him, as the narrator highlights how laudanum "consoled" Stephen not just in negative moments but also in "happiness." When he says that Stephen only used it now medicinally as opposed to in these other moments, we suspect the narrator is just simply poking fun at his character and perhaps more broadly at all of us, as humans are prone to such play.

This kind of satire continues as Stephen struggles to deal with his suspicions that Diana has left him because she believes he has had a public affair with Mrs. Fielding on Malta. After attempts to fight his desire to return to the laudanum, Stephen rationalizes his return to its use:

> The laudanum he had returned to at last because after mature and wholly objective consideration he had been brought to see that as a physician he was required to sleep well enough to perform his duty the next day; furthermore the poppy had not been created idly, and a rejection of the natural balms provided was contumelious pride, as heretical as the notion that because a thing was pleasant it was also sinful [154].

97

Here we have two distinctive but clear self-deceptions. The first, of course, is that by not taking the laudanum and being without sleep, he would be derelict in his duty (the obvious hole in this claim is the fact that when he does take laudanum, he sleeps late and is not only loathe to wake up, but he is nearly comatose with sleep). The second, however, corresponds to his more broad philosophical positions of the world, those clearly inspired by the views of Gottfried Leibniz and popularized by Alexander Pope, among others, in his "Essay on Man." Although neither writer is cited or invoked directly in these texts, Stephen's thinking seems in line with their worldview. Following these beliefs, then, to Stephen, God's creations are good, and this corresponds with his many nonjudgmental positions on all of humanity, though his appeal to this position obviously makes little sense in the particular (even if the philosophical position in favor of the pleasures of the world more broadly can stand up to inspection).

In order to contextualize the long narrative path—one that crosses several novels—of Stephen's escalating opium use, please bear with me while I flesh out some of the competing and complimentary narrative strands. The moment in the series that comes closest to something other than the medicinal arrives only as part of the denouement to a long narrative arc—one that spans several novels—involving the seeming loss of Diana to a Scandinavian army officer named Jagiello, who is described, unsurprisingly, in terms of his beauty when we first encounter him in *The Surgeon's Mate*: "the sweet young gentleman, a slim officer in a mauve coat with silver lace; he had surprisingly golden hair, bright blue eyes, large and set wide-apart, and a complexion any girl might have envied" (182). The significance of his appearance, for this discussion, resides in his contrast to Stephen. As I have alluded to before, this long narrative thread begins in *Treason's Harbor* where Stephen pretends to carry on an affair with the wife of a British naval officer. Some clarifying of this arc will be necessary in tracing out its relation to Stephen's drug use, as the two arcs—his eventual overdose and his near loss of Diana—mirror one another: Stephen entrusts a letter to Diana explaining the situation to Wray, seemingly a British intelligence officer but in reality a spy for the French (a plot point not revealed to Stephen for several novels and one that O'Brian utilizes to point towards the limits of Stephen's ability and insights). Thus, Wray fails to deliver the letter, and Stephen grows more and more depressed—about the loss of Diana, his

3. "The Virtuous Shrub"

views of marriage in general, his inability to deduce the traitor in the "house" of British Naval Intelligence, and, perhaps more figuratively, the way his own "house," his private state of affairs, has exceeded his control. Until he returns to Britain towards the beginning of *The Reverse of the Medal*, Stephen only suspects Diana has not received his message (he has received one from her voicing her displeasure at his conduct); however, once ashore, he learns that she has left and receives a letter essentially signaling the end of their marriage.

I have recounted these plot points so that we can be sure of the context into which O'Brian places the corresponding extensive narrative arc involving Stephen's use of laudanum. O'Brian uses this arc to trace Stephen's reliance upon laudanum, the nature of addiction, and, to some extent, the enchantments and transcendence possible as a result of its use. The third thread in this complex weave of themes involves marriage, adultery, and sex, and I will largely relegate those discussions to the fourth chapter, which focuses upon that subject. Ironically, as the first novel in this section of the series, *Treason's Harbor*, commences, Stephen is in a foul mood—not related to any of these things—but from his attempts to give up tobacco. In such a mood and in retort to the scholar Graham trying to convince him to take up smoking again—as an assertion of free will and individual choice—Stephen declares, "How I hate enthusiasm and romantic vistas" (11). If this first novel sets the stage, introducing these various themes, the second in this sequence, *Far Side of the World*, is perhaps the masterpiece, particularly in its treatment of sex, marriage, and adultery. However, in terms of this chapter, this novel is notable for Stephen's rising depression, his discovery of coca leaves (which I will return to later in this chapter), and his return to laudanum, which I have outlined above.

As is often the case in the series, but perhaps a bit more unusual in general, O'Brian builds at least three narrative streams in this novel in tracing issues of adultery, marriage and sexuality. Only Maturin's narrative involves seeking solace in drugs, and only one is truly tragic; however, the unusual part of this construction is that in terms of the novel, Stephen's story is a subplot. Much more of the novel focuses on the events involving Horner. However, in the series itself, Martin's story and Horner's story are subplots to Stephen's. As *Far Side of the World* progresses and Stephen has given himself over once more to the charms of the poppy, he discovers coca leaves. In evaluating their worth, Stephen concedes that it might be best to shed his use of laudanum. The coca leaves, he thinks, can help him kick the laudanum, "a somewhat troublesome habit": "I do not think there is any question of abuse, still less addiction, yet it creates a certain need not unlike that for tobacco; I should be glad to be set free of it, and I am confident that these valuable leaves will prove efficacious" (172). We need to go back a full novel and a half, to the beginning of *Treason's Harbor*, to recall the effects of attempting to give up tobacco had on Stephen, but we can see O'Brian's ability to layer these various needs and cravings.

We can also see the kind of mental agility available to the addict. Note that he has already left behind the Leibniz rationale for using the laudanum he had evoked a mere dozen or so pages earlier. Here, as elsewhere, though, Stephen will insist that he not be considered an addict. As the novel progresses, however, Stephen does not trade one drug for another, but, almost by instinct, finds how the stimulant and the tranquilizer compliment one another in his attempts to deal with the psychological pain of his apparent break with Diana: "Most fortunately he had his leaves of coca, that virtuous shrub, which kept him going by day and abolishing his hunger, and his laudanum by night, which made the darkness a refuge at least" (204). Again, we see Stephen's ability to manipulate himself, and by O'Brian going inside Stephen's mind here as he does, he exposes us to both Stephen's case and Stephen's own attempts to manipulate us (as we become a reflection of the more scientific and logical part of Stephen's mind). We have by this time—and if we have been reading through the series, it truly has been a long time—come to respect Stephen's knowledge and judgment. Yet the over-praise here, the shrub becoming "virtuous," seems a clear sign that we need to hesitate, to raise questions about what it is Stephen is doing to himself. It is noteworthy that earlier in the novel, perhaps as a kind of corroboration, we witness Jack turning down Stephen's offer of some leaves. Later, even our sense that we should excuse this return to the laudanum as the result of truly severe mental anguish is called into question when we see Stephen finding refuge in his opium as a means of dealing with the disappointment of not being able to visit the Galapagos (249).

This examination continues to build through the next novel, *Reverse of the Medal*. Here again, Stephen's story is really a backdrop. Instead, after the first hundred pages or so, O'Brian seems largely preoccupied in retelling the events that involved the trial of Lord Cochrane,

3. "The Virtuous Shrub"

except with Jack largely standing in for Lord Cochrane (one of the central sources for Jack's character throughout the series). Nevertheless, we get to see Stephen's heartbreak at having his worst fears regarding Diana realized. Early in the novel, though, when the *Surprise* is at a station in the Caribbean anticipating its return voyage, we find Stephen administering laudanum to a sick physician, and it fails to meet his intent. In one of the more extended descriptions of his drug use in this text, we see that its consumption is clearly tied up in habit, in the rituals of activity, and that it appears to be escalating in use. Stephen tries to put off taking the opium,

> but the association of diary-writing (an evening occupation in general) and opium-taking was so strong that he turned back at the door, walked swiftly to his bedside table, took a wine-glass and filled it to the half-way mark from the square bottle. He drank the pleasant-smelling amber liquid in three voluptuous gusts and walked downstairs as Sir Joseph came into the hall [230].

This passage is telling for a number of reasons. First, its link with the diary recounts the fact that Stephen has used his diary too as a means of coping with his private pain, as a kind of self-therapy. We also know, though, that because he is an intelligence officer, he believes that he should not be keeping a diary and thus its use here—like the use of the laudanum—is a potentially dangerous self-indulgence, but also a kind of despairing means of trying to cope with and control that upon which he cannot otherwise exert an influence. Furthermore, as we have seen previously, he has not typically indulged in laudanum before he has headed to bed. Here we find that the drugs have come to play a role in his everyday life much more than they had previously. Lastly, the adjective "voluptuous" to describe his draughts of the liquid speak to the sensual pleasure he is taking from the laudanum; such an adjective seems to suggest that the drug is moving beyond the simply medicinal.

Laudanum and Addiction

This brings us to the climax of this extended narrative thread centered on (at least in part) Stephen's use of laudanum and the nature of addiction more generally—namely, *The Letter of Marque*. While this novel is neither the beginning nor the end of Stephen's laudanum imbibing, it investigates and dramatizes the use and effects of laudanum more than any single novel in the series. The main plot of this novel ostensibly involves Jack (as it is almost always Jack whose career and life propel the main narrative thrust of the series), his attempts to gain reinstatement into the Navy, his taking over the *Surprise* once more (but this time as a Letter of Marque, a hired vessel of the government, not unlike a privateer), and his somewhat secret mission to cut out a French ship, the *Diana* (yes, the naming of ships in the series sometimes lacks subtlety). Eventually, the novel will be taken over by the plot involving Stephen's attempts to cut out a Diana (namely, his wife, who has left England for Norway, apparently in the company of Jagiello). Relatively early in the novel, O'Brian introduces a third plot; though this one is clearly a subplot, it allows for some very clear commentary on Stephen's own plot, particularly as it relates to his opium use, and eventually these two narrative strands intersect in somewhat spectacular fashion. This subplot involves Stephen's loblolly boy, Padeen, who, after he is severely burned, is treated with laudanum by Stephen. Eventually, Padeen becomes addicted to the point that he steals it repeatedly—replacing it with plain alcohol—from the ship's stores.

The introduction of this incident leads to multiple extended contemplations of laudanum, particularly as Stephen discusses it with Martin, his surgical assistant. Here Stephen goes to treat Padeen after the injury and discusses the benefits of laudanum. First the narrator informs us, with Stephen's sensibility clearly leaking through, that "the doctor dealt with pain, the very severe pain, by an heroic dose of laudanum, the alcoholic tincture of opium, one of his most valued medicines." From there, though, Stephen begins to extol its virtues in Latin to Martin, raising up the "amber liquid" and declaring it

> "the nearest approach to a panacea that has ever been found out. I occasionally use it myself, and find it answers admirably in cases of insomnia, morbid anxiety, the pain of wounds, tooth-ache, and head-ache, even hemicrania." He might well have added heart-ache too, but he went on, "I have as you perceive, matched the dose to the weight of the sufferer and the intensity of the sufferer. Presently, with the blessing, you will see Padeen's face return to its usual benevolent mansuetude; and few minutes later you will see him glide insensibly to the verge of an opiate coma. It is the most valuable member of the whole pharmacopoeia" [55].

Now, as we have established, there is not too much unusual in this particular discussion. Stephen, like many of the physicians of his era, looked

3. "The Virtuous Shrub"

upon opium as producing remarkable medicinal benefits. In the particular case of pain relief, they were certainly right—or at least we continue to believe them to be so, as opiates continue to be a "most valuable member of the whole pharmacopoeia," at least as far as dealing with severe or chronic pain is concerned. However, perhaps the most telling moment of this passage itself is the brief interjection of narrative commentary here. Now, this brief aside—"He might well have added heart-ache"— does not necessarily translate into some kind of admonishment of Stephen on the narrator's part; however, the narrator is clearly reminding the reader that, when it comes to the praising of laudanum, Stephen is certainly no unbiased judge, and he is one who has attempted to heal himself, and in terms of injuries that go beyond the simply physical.

Martin, who has no personal allegiance to laudanum—it has never helped him deal with heartache—raises the question of addiction, of opium-eaters, only to meet with a strong rebuke from Stephen in a passage we have referred to earlier in its grouping together of alcohol, coffee, and sex with opium:

> The objections come only from a few unhappy beings, Jansenists for the most part, who also condemn wine, agreeable food, music, and the company of women: they even call out against coffee, for all love! These objections are valid solely in the case of a few souls with feeble will-power, who could just as easily become the victims of intoxicating liquors, and who are practically moral imbeciles, often addicted to other forms of depravity; otherwise it is no more injurious than smoking tobacco [55-56].

Reading this, we can see Stephen's brief allusions back to his Leibniz-influenced position, but we are forced to shudder a bit at Stephen's hypocrisy. While leaving aside for a moment the question of whether Stephen is an addict, he is, at least, a fairly habitual user. The Irishman, Padeen, while in many ways illiterate, is repeatedly depicted as an astonishingly compassionate soul, one who cries in sympathy with the pain of others and who generally avoids the many forms of "depravity" to which other members of the crew succumb. Thus, in this subplot, O'Brian positions an individual whose character contradicts that identified with addiction by Stephen and gradually depicts his life becoming destroyed by the substance. By the end of the novel, driven mad by his need for opium, Padeen attacks a pharmacist and is eventually sent as a prisoner to Australia—only Jack's influence prevents him from being executed for his crime.

This storyline thus allows for an introduction of addiction as a topic in the novel, and eventually to a questioning of how we should classify Stephen and his use of laudanum. The novels are set at the very time in which addiction, as we now know it, was being introduced into the larger vocabulary (though notions of body and mind in relation to addiction will be again reassessed in the twentieth century). Marcus Boon quotes Coleridge in 1814 when he identifies opium as a "free-agency-annihilating Poison" (36). Boon claims that Coleridge "was discovering, through the struggle in and with his own body, the phenomenon we now familiarly term 'addiction,'" and thus Coleridge, in asking questions like "Is not the Habit the Desire of a Desire?" is beginning to lay hold of a concept that we may consider relatively modern (36). As Berridge notes, Coleridge made several "attempts to reduce or break off his habit," indicating his growing awareness of his unhealthy reliance on the drug (54). So, while it may be a bit unusual for O'Brian to begin similar investigations in his own novel, such thoughts do historically correspond; this is not an outright anachronism. De Quincey's famous book on the taking of opium, among other things, does not appear until 1821 and, according to Boon, does not show a grasp of addiction in the terms hinted at by Coleridge some time earlier. However, Berridge argues convincingly that both De Quincey and Coleridge reveal the intertwining of medical use, and the indulgence and reliance more commonly associated with addiction (52).

In the course of this novel, however, Stephen does not make links between Padeen and himself, but the narrative invites the reader to make such connections. For example, on the same page we see that Stephen has grown distressed because "his laudanum was having less and less effect and since he did not want to increase his usual dose he spent much of the night in musing, not often happily." And though Stephen, having seen Padeen with a brandy bottle and "sometimes a strange dreamy exhilaration," thinks Padeen has taken to drink, we are told by the narrator that "in fact Padeen was now a confirmed opium-eater or rather a drinker, a sixty-drops a day man" (159). Of course, Stephen is unaware that, since Padeen keeps stealing his laudanum, Stephen is growing increasingly sober in inverse proportion to Padeen's intoxication. Thus, the following morning after these musings, Stephen "was up very early and clear-headed, a rare thing for him, though somewhat less unusual now that his effectual night-draught was so diminished" (160). This

3. "The Virtuous Shrub"

might seem almost comical except for the devastating results this exchange has upon Padeen.

In essence, in terms of Padeen, we see the altering role of laudanum, as it moves from medicinal—a cure to the pain of his burned hands—to recreational and addictive, as he cannot control his desire for laudanum and, presumably, its effects upon him. We do not, however, get inside Padeen's thoughts, so, outside of his actions, we cannot know his experience with the drug. Stephen, in his privileged position as a physician, and as a member of the educated and—despite his many democratic principles—ruling class, can traffic in laudanum without any public stigma. After all, no one questions a physician, certainly not a physician of Stephen's standing and reputation, who desires to acquire the tincture of laudanum. Although Padeen tries to essentially follow in Stephen's footsteps (and as his longtime assistant, he quite knows of Stephen's need for his "night draught"), "since he could neither read nor write he had no success" in acquiring the laudanum at a chemists. Thus, Padeen, relatively unfamiliar with its dangers and forced to acquire it through essentially covert means, finds an end much more dire than that of Stephen.

We are also invited in this novel to repeatedly question Stephen's rationales for taking opium. Later in the novel, as the *Surprise* is about to launch its attack on the *Diana* and during which Stephen is to participate for intelligence reasons, we find Stephen once more wrestling with a desire to take laudanum and finding reasons to justify it. Stephen "turned over the question of whether the present conjuncture allowed him to depart from his rule and take an extra dose, not as a soporific—very far from it—but as a means of doing away with the illogical purely instinctive uneasiness and thus enabling his mind to deal more freely with any contingencies that might arise in the new situation" (187). Yes, Stephen proceeds to regret that he lacks his recently discovered coca leaves; yes, laudanum might calm his nerves; yes, Stephen may feel the need for laudanum because Padeen is largely denying him its use in the main part. While we may grant him all of those points, we cannot dismiss how absurd Stephen's logic is here—that laudanum is likely to allow him to act more precisely and unemotionally in the battle to come. Having won the battle with himself nonetheless—desire will out—"he finished his glass of laudanum with pleasure though without the fullest satisfaction," no doubt due to it being largely alcohol (187).

This particular narrative thread concludes with Stephen's approach to Diana. After his bottle is surreptitiously dropped and broken in a nervous grab for it to calm him before he shaved and met Diana, he seeks out more in the local port. Of course, since he has not been actually consuming his regular dose for some time, and since he feels he needs more than usual to calm himself, he takes too much. Thus, following his initial rapprochement with Diana, still aflame with anxiety, he takes a second draught and "was astonished at the strength of his draught" (270). The initial dose made him blame the apothecary and his apparent use of "aquavit" for its powerful effect on Stephen; the second makes him wonder if the opium is somehow stronger, different than what he is used to (270). With much more opium in his system than he had been used to in recent times, Stephen falls down a stairwell to a tower, "pitched headlong into the void" (271). I will return to Stephen's experiences during this period of what we might call overdose in the next section. However, I want to take note of two elements of this episode first. When Stephen falls, we are told that the bottle "broke" and that "It nearly killed you—a most frightful gash in your side" (276). Rarely can we criticize O'Brian for his lack of subtlety; however, the symbolism here is, shall we say, at the very least pointed.

The implied meditation on whether Stephen's use has ventured into addiction climaxes in what we might otherwise consider the denouement of the novel. Stephen, now confined to bed, is visited by the physician who has been called in to treat him. The physician, a Dr. Mersennius, begins by saying, "I trust you will not ask me to prescribe laudanum, colleague," and he goes on to mention instances that he has known of where laudanum had caused "extreme and lasting mental distress," which has produced on occasion "lunacy and death" (276). Stephen's response—"Have you any reason to suppose that I had taken laudanum?"—reveals Stephen's defensiveness. He acts as if he were hiding something, as he normally does with tinted glasses, glasses that would have prevented Dr. Mersennius from recognizing Stephen's drug use made evident from his "pupils" (276). As the physician goes on to assert that he will not further the problem by prescribing more laudanum, it is clear that Stephen senses the implied accusation of the physician—that Stephen is an opium addict. Aloud, Stephen attempts to defend himself by asserting that "many medical men use the tincture against pain and emotional disturbance" (276). Internally, the narrator goes on to reveal Stephen's thoughts on the matter:

3. "The Virtuous Shrub"

> Within the limits of his information, Mersennius was right; he obviously thought that his patient was addicted to laudanum, and he had no means of knowing, as Stephen knew, that this frequent and indeed habitual use was not true addiction, but just the right side of it. The boundary was difficult to define and he did not blame Mersinnius for his mistake, the less so as his body was at this moment feeling more than a hint of that craving which was the mark of a man who had gone too far [277].

The "Stephen knew" here seems to be our narrative clue that this judgment is Stephen's and not O'Brian's, and thus the entire passage becomes somewhat suspect. As we have established, Stephen's abilities of self-analysis cannot be entirely trusted when it comes to his opium use. As the end of this passage suggests, even his body seems to be contradicting his mind. What are we to make of this ambiguous line and Stephen's place on "just the right side of it?"

If Stephen's body can be said to speak here—in contradiction to what his mind has to say—then perhaps O'Brian is introducing very modern, arguably anachronistic notions of addiction into the novel. The body speaking its addiction resembles something more akin to the positions attributed to someone like William Burroughs in the 1950s, for whom, according to Boon, "addiction was physiological, a cellular craving" (75). Whether O'Brian has slightly shown his hand here, the response of Stephen's body, its clear desire for the laudanum, coupled with Stephen's rather coy defensiveness suggests the undermining of Stephen's claims regarding addiction. Of course, this episode stems ironically as much from how much he took at this time—two strong doses, more than is certainly typical for him—as from the fact that he had not been taking his full dose for some time prior to this overdose. In this passage, O'Brian seems to desire to leave some doubt. He offers us Stephen's claim that he is not an addict, and some clear evidence that undermines this claim or at the very least complicates our ability to make clear judgments upon it.

Only later in the series, such as in *Nutmeg of Consolation*, some two novels further along, does the narrator offer firmer judgments. After Stephen refuses to take opium when he is ill, the narrator says, "He had been very deeply addicted to the drug for years and years, reaching such monstrous doses that they hardly bear repetition, and suffering in due proportion when he gave it up" (22). By taking us inside Stephen's reasoning and his responses, and withholding clear judgment until later in the series, O'Brian encourages us to sympathize with Stephen's trauma. And, of course, since we know that it is in part spurred by the apparent loss of Diana and Stephen's heartbreak, we are generally willing to offer our sympathy. However, we are also led to examine the very nature of addiction. By giving this condition to Stephen, O'Brian invites us to remove the kind of character stigmas about those who become addicts that Stephen espouses. He also leads us to consider the very range of addiction and ways of coping with it. In Stephen, we never have a figure who gives himself so totally over to his addiction that he cannot function. In fact, with some very rare exceptions, which I have noted, Stephen's work and daily life are largely unaffected by his use of opium (since we rarely have a glimpse of his work from someone with his training, our information is admittedly limited, but from what we do have, he continues to work at a high aptitude within the limits of what a physician at that time could do). Although Stephen turns to opium as a means of attempting to control the pain and personal anguish that seems to overwhelm him when alone and not working, he also manages to, more or less, control and monitor his addiction in a way, say, that Padeen obviously cannot. He knows what he takes and when he takes it, and perhaps on some level why he takes it, with something of a scientific preciseness. Yet all of that is about his mind, and the telling passage from the close of *The Letter of Marque* suggests that since the desire for the laudanum is lodged within the body itself, his sense of control in its use is ultimately an illusion.

A Visionary Moment

This overdose marks the end of Stephen's fairly profligate use of laudanum. He returns to it, again and again, for various reasons, but largely resists allowing its usage to become regular again (the same cannot exactly be said of his beloved coca leaves). It seems odd, then, that such a moment would be the time O'Brian would also give to the only drug-influenced passage in perhaps the entire series. 18th and 19th-century authors who wrote of the effects of opium dwelled largely on these kinds of visionary moments, where, according to Boon, folks like De Quincey "offered dreams that money can buy, a fabled, mythical substance from the East [which] would allow transport to the realms of the

3. "The Virtuous Shrub"

imagination" (37). Throughout the series we see Stephen dispense laudanum, consider taking it himself, groggy the next day from it, imbibing it; but, generally speaking, the narrative breaks off before we go inside the perspective of someone on it. However, after Stephen falls down the stairwells, we join him in his disjointed vision that features sailing with Diana in a hot-air balloon, a scenario based in both his desire to have such a flight and his worries that she is recklessly flying herself. The descriptions of this vision recall wondrous visions akin to moments in "Kubla Kahn" in that Stephen sees "heightened colour" to a "miraculous degree," and "It was though he had never seen rope before, or as though he had recovered his sight after many years of blindness, and when he looked across at Diana, the perfection of her cheek fairly caught his breath" (271-272). Boon talks about the relationship between opium use and the kind of gnosticism promoted by Novalis where "opium may come from nature but its essence belongs to the transcendental night, and by taking the drug, the user is able to negate his or her own body and environment temporarily" (30-31). In constructing this vision for Stephen, it also seems that O'Brian follows the arguments about the effects of drugs mapped out by De Quincey. Jay sees De Quincey's central claim to be that "the drug does indeed have an innate spectrum of effects, but these interact with the personality of the user and are always to some degree subject to the user's control" (61). Thus, this vision both resembles those of others, but also fits well with the concerns and personality of Stephen.

While I am uncertain about whether O'Brian wished to see this vision in terms of a kind of gnostic fantasy outlined by Boon, it is clear that there is a kind of transcendence of the body at work in the passage. The narrator notes, "This was a world of silence," and that Stephen and Diana "were perfectly in tune" (272). Here, "there was no time," and "there was no sense of duration" (272). Of course, this vision cannot last. Stephen senses "some disagreement and although at one time a rocky landscape had been seen below they had not made any attempt to descend and now there was nothing in sight but grey ocean stretching from sky to sky" (273). Thus, just before the vision fades—"this dissolved to an unknown room"—it turns to something of the sublime, which Boon rightly identifies as Burke's conception of "a kind of pleasure taken in painful, overwhelming, or intense situations experienced at a distance" (38). Stephen, while somewhat revolutionary in his youth, is not much of a Romantic, so it is unlikely that he would be attracted to what opium could bring in the way of such visions. Perhaps that is why O'Brian reserves such a moment for the close of this chapter in Stephen's life. It does tie up with various kinds of opium-related language and images. Stephen does have a kind of transportation that takes him seemingly outside himself, but the balloon itself suggests the kinds of limits of such transcendence and such feelings of unity—with the body, with others, with the larger, vaster world. What goes up must come down.

"That Virtuous Shrub"

It is not until *The Far Side of the World*—nearly mid-way through the series—that Stephen discovers the wonders of the coca leaves. As we have seen, by this time he has been consuming opium in the form of laudanum for ages—to the point of habitual, addictive use begun and maintained by various forms of self-medicating. If—relative to laudanum—Stephen comes to the coca leaves late, he is not alone. Although, according to Jay, coca leaves were described in an account by Nicholas Monardes in 1569 as part of the "first wave" of substances discovered in the New World, Jay notes that they "remained an ethnographic curiosity" for some time (147–148). Its eventual popularity comes well after Maturin's use of it. In the seventeenth century, another physician, Abraham Cowley, spoke its praises in verse: "Our Varichocha first this Coca sent,/ Endow'd with leaves of wond'rous Nourishment,/ Whose Juice succ'd in, and to the Stomach tak'n/ Long Hunger and long Labor can sustain" (qtd. in Boon 177). This early characterization of the drug, as we shall see, does not deviate tremendously from Maturin's later one. As Boon outlines, the major interest in the coca leaves among Europeans who discovered it and its use in South America was as a means of energizing slaves and fighters (a seemingly cost-efficient method, as the leaves also alleviated hunger, as Cowley noted). Although this usage is not the main focus of O'Brian's interest in the leaves, we do witness such a situation in the last novel of the series, *Blue at the Mizzen*, when Stephen administers the leaves to soldiers in the midst of trying to promote Chilean independence (225). European and thus Western interest in coca came primarily in the form of cocaine, which was not discovered

3. "The Virtuous Shrub"

until the 1880s (Jay 154). Its use and history—in both forms—however, according to Boon, had been studied and recorded earlier, and more often than just about any other comparable substance (176).

Why? Boon speculates that cocaine "is a social drug, and wherever people gather together to take a substance, they like to talk about its qualities" (177). We never learn about when Stephen first tried laudanum, and we do not see him take it in anyone's presence. Except as a part of his pharmacy and medical practice, laudanum is a part of Stephen's private world. Coca leaves do not function simply as an opposite. There are no coca leaf parties anywhere in the series. As Jay describes, chewing a coca leaf is comparable to coffee, "a mild stimulant," and suggests that it is "almost impossible to abuse" because of the way it is typically consumed (148). Since its effects are far less drastic than laudanum, it makes sense that one would not hide consuming it (no more so than any of us hide our coffee intake). Thus, Stephen is far more likely to sing its praises in public, and certainly there is no European-based stigma about its use like laudanum at around the time the O'Brian novels take place. In Peru particularly, there is no stigma at all, as the eating of coca leaves is a part of the culture (and, to some extent, continues to be). As Stephen says in *The Letter of Marque,* by way of defending his eating of the leaves, "it is as usual as tobacco" among the Peruvians (277). When Stephen first tries the coca leaves, it is indeed a social situation, and he takes the time to discuss and praise the leaves to the man who offered them to him: "Ever since the first acullico that you were so good as to give me I have felt my mind glow, my mental and no doubt physical powers increase. I have no doubt that I could swim the river that lies before us.... I prefer to enjoy your conversation and my present state of remarkable well-being—no fatigue, no hunger, no perplexity of mind, but a power of apprehension and synthesis that I have rarely known" (160). Shortly after, however, and as a matter of course, Stephen confesses that now "my sense of taste is entirely gone" (161).

For the most part, descriptions of the powers of the leaves in the series remain static. Later in this same novel, when Stephen has split his drug use by time of day—leaves during the day, opium at night—the narrator, capturing Maturin's perspective, notes that "most fortunately he had his leaves of coca, that virtuous shrub, which kept him going by day and abolishing his hunger" (209). Again and again we are told throughout the series about how the leaves sharpen the mind, give "clarity," forestall hunger and help one overcome tiredness. Many books later, in *The Commodore*, Stephen outlines the psychological effects a bit more broadly, delineating how those physical effects regarding hunger are "followed by an increasingly remarkable and evident *clarity* of mind, a serenity, and a perception that almost all worries are of little real consequence, most of them being the result of confused, anxious and generally fallacious notions that crowd and increase in direct proportion to the decline of pure single-minded reason" (41, emphasis mine).

These descriptions are not unusual in the history of coca/cocaine literature, particularly in the literature of stimulants. Recall how these descriptions—involving clarity, the ability to bring together thoughts, and to strengthen—resemble discussions of that other, much more culturally pervasive stimulant, caffeine. Then recall the intertwined histories of coca and caffeine. Boon describes the creation of Vin Mariani, the "athlete's wine," a "wine" developed by Angelo Mariani that had "a cocaine base" (179). Eventually this "wine" from the mid-nineteenth century had immense popularity and the endorsement of what we might call celebrities of the day.[1] Consider, then, the pattern traced by Boon: "the matrix of stimulant, exoticism, advertising, and worldwide distribution invented by Mariani was carried forward into the twentieth century by Coca-Cola—but coca itself was replaced by the everyday stimulant par excellence of the West: caffeine" (179).

A Virtue Even Rats Can Love

Although effects of the coca leaves are much closer to those of its fellow stimulant caffeine, in terms of their role in the series (and in particular Stephen's interaction with them), we need to think of them more in relation to laudanum. After all, they make their first appearance in the middle of the extended narrative arc involving laudanum that I have sketched out earlier in the chapter. Stephen does not seek out the coca leaves because he is addicted to laudanum (as I have mentioned, he does not necessarily seek them out at all); however, he is receptive to them in part because of his problems with laudanum. In a passage I mentioned earlier as evidence of Stephen's own wrestling with the possibility of being an opium addict, he sees the leaves as a means of escape, for he concedes that the laudanum "creates a certain need not unlike that for

3. "The Virtuous Shrub"

tobacco; I should be glad to be set free of it, and I am confident that these valuable leaves will prove efficacious" (172). Therefore, though Stephen does not fully acknowledge his opium addiction—in fact, he denies it—he sees the coca leaves as a path away from it. Of course, he is looking simply to exchange one drug for another. That most famous of cocaine users and enthusiasts, Sigmund Freud, "suggested that cocaine was an antidote to morphine addiction" (qtd. in Boon 182). Thus, O'Brian keeps Stephen's responses to opium within the same realm of the attitudes of those who have enjoyed coca in one of its forms (although, as Boon notes, the medical craze for cocaine—rather than coca leaves—takes place much later in the nineteenth century than Stephen's time, and its claim to being a "panacea" lasted far shorter than that of opium [182]).

As readers, we can certainly understand why Stephen feels that the coca leaves may be a "healthy" alternative to opium. While opium deadens, helps with sleep, makes one subject to visions, and tends to be associated with isolation, the coca leaves appear to help Stephen participate in the world more—he feels good about himself, he converses more, he believes he is thinking more clearly, and he shrugs off lethargy and the demands of hunger. However, as the series progresses and Stephen begins to shift his primary drug use from opium—following *The Letter of Marque*—to coca leaves, we become aware that Stephen has once again begun to tread a dangerous road.

The marked turn from opium to coca appears fairly soon after the culmination of the opium plot—namely, two novels later, in *The Nutmeg of Consolation*. Here we find Stephen falling ill and refusing to be treated with his former panacea because "he had been very deeply addicted to the drug for years and years, reaching such monstrous doses that they hardly bear repetition, and suffering in due proportion when he gave it up" (22). Later we are told that "he had abandoned it on his reconciliation with Diana, doing so for many reasons, one of them being his belief that a man ought to manage without bottled fortitude. Plain fortitude from within, that was the cry." But even here he feels the temptation (77). The language here resembles some of Stephen's earlier critiques of those who are susceptible to addiction: they are subject to it because of moral, constitutional failings, and he wishes not to be grouped in with them. Yet the coca leaves begin to fill the void—not coincidently, along with coffee:

"Strong black coffee," said Stephen some minutes later. "How well it goes down: and how glad I am that I did not indulge myself in my coca-leaves on finishing with the sick-birth as I had intended. They calm the mind, sure, but they do away with one's sense of taste. I shall chew three when the pot is out, however." These leaves, which he had first encountered in South America, were his present, purely personal, catholicon and although he traveled with enough, packed in soft leather bags, to last him twice around the world, he was remarkably abstemious: these three leaves, now to be chewed so late in the afternoon, were an unusual treat [117].

Here we see a familiar pattern begin to emerge. At the very least, Stephen has some sense that the leaves alter his body in not entirely positive ways—the loss of taste—but he quickly provides a space for them. We also see the narrator return with his somewhat ironic, mocking tone in discussing the kinds of logical contortions that tend to accompany Stephen's thoughts or voiced opinions on his current panacea. Stephen comes across as equal parts addictive personality and overall enthusiast.

However, there are some significant differences in how O'Brian maps out Stephen's interaction with coca leaves. We might say that he simply seems less patient with Stephen, as if he is a friend one has suffered with, helped through a major problem, only to find him returning to his old ways. As the friend, our patience becomes exhausted, as we seemingly ask, "Hasn't he learned his lesson by now?" This impatience and frustration shows up in a number of ways—plot, narrative commentary, and conflicting commentary from two of Stephen's friends, both his surgical assistants. While Stephen's problems with opium linger for many novels before O'Brian brings the problem to a head and reveals its troubling effects (perhaps most significantly through Padeen), he begins to assert the problems with the leaves much sooner—in *Nutmeg of Consolation*, in fact.

This process begins when Stephen discovers that rats have eaten his store of coca leaves (223). He denies, however, that they could be addicted: "Oh no: it does not cause a vehement addiction, as tobacco does; though curiously enough some of its effects are not unlike; and it quite does away with the need to smoke. I still enjoy my occasional cigar after a good dinner; but if I have my little ball of lime-sprinkled leaves in the morning I am perfectly content" (225). Again we find the naïve denials and the claims of the coca as something that frees one from addiction rather than imprisoning one in it. Later, though, Stephen

3. "The Virtuous Shrub"

records the following in his diary: "It is now clear that they [the rats] had become slaves to the coca. Now that they have eaten it all, now that they are deprived of it, all their mildness, lack of fear and what might even be called their complaisance is gone. They are rats and worse than rats: they fight, they kill one another, and were I to unblock my ears I should hear their strident screams." Thus, Stephen the scientist, the observer of natural phenomena, must begin to concede his position to observable evidence, and he goes on to compare his own behavior to that of the rats: "So far I have killed no one, nor have I desired to do so; but in other ways I too feel my lack: I eat exorbitantly, my eyes starting from my head (whereas coca imposes moderation); I smoke and relish it extremely (whereas coca does away with tobacco); sleep is near to closing my stupid eyes (whereas the coca keeps one contentedly awake until the middle watch)" (226). It becomes clear to others as well that the lack of coca leaves is altering Stephen's personality—as his previous attempts to leave behind addictive substances (tobacco and opium, for example) had. Thus, Killick later reports Stephen's "crabbedness," and Bonden notes Stephen's cruelty to Stephen's adopted daughters Sarah and Emily, as well as a long-time shipmate, Plaice (229).

Later in the series we witness the chiding or correctives about the nature of the coca leaves, provided by two of Stephen's friends and surgical assistances, Martin and Jacob. In *The Wine-Dark Sea*, the *Surprise* is heading once more for South America and facing some of the usual deprivations associated with the long and dangerous journey. Stephen consoles himself with the thoughts of attaining his beloved leaves: "Yet providing we do not die of thirst, I comfort myself with the thought that even this languid pace brings us nearly a hundred miles closer to my coca-leaves—a hundred miles closer to wallowing in some clear tepid stream, washing the ingrained salt from my person and chewing coca-leaves as I do so, joy" (68–69). However, Martin, in a somewhat contrary mood for various reasons, fails to tolerate Stephen's habit: "I have no notion of these palliatives, which so soon become habitual. Look what happened to poor Padeen, and the way we are obliged to keep laudanum under lock and key" (69). Martin goes on to decry drinking too, the "curse of the nation." "What I deprecate is the persistence of indulgence," he confides (69).

Nevertheless, Stephen continues to resist the evidence and opinions placed in front of him. In *The Wine-Dark Sea*, when he is trapped in a snow storm while trying to pass through the Andes, he turns to the leaves for illness and fortitude. In *The Commodore,* we find him once more praising them in much the manner he had once praised laudanum:

> I do not present them as a panacea, but I do assert that they possess very great virtues in the cases of melancholia, morbid depression of spirits whether rational or irrational, and the restless uneasiness of mind that so very often accompanies fever: it brings about an euphory, a sense of well-being far more lucid, far superior in every way to that produced by opium; and it does so without causing that unhappy addiction we are all so well acquainted with. Admittedly, it does not procure sleep as opium does—a most unhealthy sleep, I may add—but on the other hand, the patient does not *require* sleep: his mind rests of itself in a remarkable calm clarity [98–99].

Here he seems to have completely repressed the prior incidents. In *Blue at the Mizzen,* he will ask Jacob if he knows about whether coca leaves cause hallucinations or knows of effects of taking the coca leaves, and receive this response: "No—apart from habituation, of course" (208). From Jacob, then, we get the implication that it is fairly common knowledge that coca leaves are habit forming; someone of Maturin's experience and worldliness would thus have to fairly actively seek to repress or misunderstand this property of the substance.

Losing Control

Throughout the series, then, we see many of the principle characters ingest various substances that alter the behaviors of the human body—whether they principally affect the mind or the body or both. The most powerful of these substances—namely, opium and coca leaves—affect Stephen Maturin principally. For a time there is something of an open question of how we should read or perceive Stephen's use of these substances, and the use of coffee, alcohol, and, to a lesser degree, tobacco all come to reflect upon one another: they demonstrate the limits of control any individual has over his or her own body, the degree to which we are all subject to desires driven by the body, and the degree to which we wish to escape from the limits of the body itself. As I have argued, we get to see Stephen's issues with these substances largely through his own eyes, and the usually sympathetic but increasingly ironic voice of the narrator—who can report inside Stephen's perspective and step out-

3. "The Virtuous Shrub"

side it. After the close of the primary laudanum arc—which ends with the overdose and vision in Norway—the narrator settles the question, unhesitatingly calling Stephen's use of laudanum an addiction. However, though Stephen shows clear signs that he knows he has overstepped the line of casual or simply medicinal use, the word "addiction" does not pass his own lips (except in that brief interior monologue of denial after the close of his vision). The modern sense of addiction was, of course, slowly coming into being at the time during which the novels are set, and this may play some small part in O'Brian's shaping of Maturin's attitudes. However, they seem to largely stem from a sketching out of the kind of mindset of the addict—a mindset we are told Stephen is aware of: "Like most medical men Stephen Maturin had seen the effects of addiction, full-blown serious addiction, to alcohol and opium; and like many medical men he knew from inner experience just how immensely powerful that craving was, and how supernaturally cunning and casuistical the deprived victim might become" (*The Truelove* 35). Stephen can read the signs in others, but the ability to fully read them in oneself is, of course, exceedingly difficult; and for O'Brian to give Stephen that kind of unmitigated self-knowledge would be, on some level, to elevate him to an extraordinary degree.

Instead, Stephen's behavior seems eminently frustrating—to him, to O'Brian, to us as readers—but also extremely human in its fallibility. Yet, as the novels progress and as Stephen continues to indulge, and as the figures around him who understand his use of these substances become less indulgent (at least those around him with some medical knowledge), the narrator too seems to hide his feelings and opinions far less. Thus, in one of the final novels in the series, *The Commodore*, the narrator describes the extent of Stephen's drug use:

> Yet he had some faults, and one was a habit of dosing himself, generally from a spirit of inquiry, as in his period of inhaling large quantities of the nitrous oxide and of the vapour of hemp, to say nothing of tobacco, bhang in all its charming varieties in India, betel in Java and the neighboring islands, qat in the Red Sea, and hallucinating cacti in South America, but sometimes for relief from distress, as when he became addicted to opium in one form or another; and now he was busily poisoning himself with coca-leaves, whose virtue he had learnt in Peru [188].

Here we have several significant elements. On the one hand, Stephen's use comes from his intellectual and scientific curiosity: he explores the physical world and its drugs. We also see, though, that inevitably this experimentation—perhaps for its own sake, "the spirit of inquiry"—shifts to "relief from stress," from desires to affect and escape the body that inevitably lead one into the cycle of becoming entrapped by the desires of the body. Perhaps most telling, however, is the narrator's phrase "busily poisoning himself," which marks the most overt and stern judgment against Stephen in the entire series. This moves beyond mocking irony, a playfulness at the foibles of a beloved character or friend: this is distress and exasperation with a friend who continues to harm himself despite his better judgment and immense capacity for judging behavior and character (often his own).

In the last completed novel of the series, *Blue at the Mizzen*, we find a return of the more ironic tone in a passage quite similar to the one I have quoted above:

> Dr. Maturin had certain practices that he would have condemned in others as unhealthy, self-indulgent and even immoral, such as the smoking of tobacco and Indian hemp (or bhang), the drinking of alcohol in all its forms from mild ale to brandy, the taking of opium and coca, and the frequent inhalation of nitrous oxide; but in his own case he had nothing to say against any of them. Indeed he judged their effects wholly beneficial: and this was because he never (or very rarely) countenanced the least excess [73].

We again see the distress, though perhaps subtle or more mild, in the sense that Stephen is a hypocrite in these matters; we again witness this nearly epic catalogue of his drug experimentation that spans the globe; and we again see the mild prodding of the narrator, showing the kind of "conniving" mind of the addict in the phrasing "he never (or very rarely) countenanced the least excess." Perhaps so very late in the series there is a return to acceptance, however begrudging, that Stephen cannot change, signaled by this return to the narrator's choice to mildly prod rather than more broadly scold ("poisoning"). Ultimately, the novels seem to suggest that we, like Stephen, are subject to the frailties and desires of the body, and the mind becomes inevitably complicit in the end-goal of satisfying that body.

4

Sex at Sea, at Sea with Sex

Situating Sex

After the height of the action in C. S. Forester's first Horatio Hornblower novel, *Beat to Quarters*, the eponymous hero and his crew of the *Lydia* enjoy a relatively peaceful and routine trip back around the Horn. During this period, the slow fizzle of the falling action, Forester provides ample time for much interplay between Hornblower and the Lady Barbara, a well-connected aristocrat who has more or less demanded passage on Hornblower's ship, and who proved her *sang froid* and mettle by acting as a nurse following a particularly violent single-ship action. Thus, the romantic pattern of this novel resembles that of Forester's *African Queen,* in which a more middle-class but strong-willed man develops a relationship with an upper-class, apparently spoiled woman. In this novel these frequent rendezvous lead to a great deal of purple prose and lots of kissing; but in Hornblower's only notable moment of cowardice—the author's prejudice in this regard is underscored subtly by calling the chapter "Cowardice"—he pulls back from anything further, and thus Hornblower remains, at least in this novel, chaste and loyal to his wife. In the two hundred and seventy or so pages of this novel, that is about as close to sex and sexuality as one is likely to get—unless one counts Hornblower's speculation, before he gets to know Lady Barbara, that she is possibly "unsexed" or "masculine" because she has traveled to Panama without a proper escort (why she is there in the first place is never really explained).

I think no one is likely to come to the Patrick O'Brian novels looking for sex. These tales are not *The Story of O* or *Lady Chatterly's Lover,* nor would I even say they are bawdy in the manner of some swashbucklers or Fraser's satirical Flashman series. In fact, it is fair to note that at no time in the twenty-volume series does the narrator directly depict a sexual act. However, even in the first volume of the series, matters of sex appear nearly everywhere (well, not in the extended discussion of sails and cordage, but with greater frequency than one might expect). Unlike Forester's hero, Jack Aubrey not only follows through with his romantic aspirations in the first novel of the series, he does so with Lady Harte, the wife of his admiral. This will not be the last of his participations in adultery, and they will often have some kind of consequence (though usually only temporarily). Later, after his encounter with Lady Harte, for example, we find out that she "has been too liberal with her favours, too universally kind," for she has passed on a venereal disease to Jack (349). Early in the series at least, sex and class are also intermingled in O'Brian's narrative. Aubrey, though an aristocrat and an officer, found himself, we are told, turned before the mast—made to serve as a regular member of the crew—for apparently keeping "a likely black girl called Sally" on the ship when he was but a midshipman (*Master and Commander* 145). In fact, this is a story that O'Brian returns to again and again, though we hear later that Aubrey may have been punished for stealing the captain's tripe rather than fornicating. It is as if the novels say to us, be it sex or food, the body will betray us, or at the least overwhelm our good sense.

The novels do have a repeated and recurring interest in Jack's sexuality, and it seems to be both part of his legend and a kind of hallmark of his character. I will return to Jack's sexuality, and the depiction of male, heterosexual sexuality overall, more extensively later in this chapter. However, before we turn to that and other matters of sexuality in the series, I want to offer a few thoughts on point of view. Much of the discussion of sexuality, and much of the perspective on it shared with the reader, comes from Stephen. As a medical man and a naval surgeon, he can hardly ignore sexuality. At various points he even tries to describe himself as relatively immune to the charms of the opposite sex because of his ability to see women's bodies as objects of scientific inquiry (as with Jack's, we'll return more fully to the question of Stephen's own sexuality later in the chapter). This attitude towards examining women can be seen as part of Stephen's larger views toward sexuality. To a modern reader, Stephen's views might appear to be remarkably liberal or open-minded. When it comes to sexual practices—with rare exceptions of

4. Sex at Sea, at Sea with Sex

temper shown at the profligate indulgences that lead to venereal disease—Stephen seems to largely withhold moral judgments. For the most part, his views align with materialist philosophers of the eighteenth century like Denis Diderot and the physician Julien Offray de la Mettrie, author of such tracts as "Machine Man" and "Man as Plant."

In the previous chapter I noted that O'Brian's choice of having a physician as a proponent and consumer of drugs was entirely in line with the historical circumstances in which the novels are set. In terms of Stephen's view of sex and sexuality, we can again see that there is historical precedence. La Mettrie, who saw humans as essentially made up of material, creatures to be studied like any other animal, was a physician. Scholars of the period see Enlightenment views on sexuality as mirroring those I have identified with drugs. In *The Facts of Life: The Creation of Sexual Knowledge in Britain, 1650–1950*, Roy Porter paraphrases the view as "If Nature was good, then erotic desire, far from being sinful, itself became desirable" (19). Porter, in another text, *Bodies Politic*, cites famed physician—and prolific father—Erasmus Darwin's view on sex being "the purest source of human felicity, the cordial drop in the otherwise vapid cup of life" (77). In Diderot's somewhat infamous philosophical dialogue, *D'Alembert's Dream*, he puts the most explicit and accepting views of sex into the voice of the eighteenth-century physician Bordeu. Let's consider the core of his views for a moment. Bordeu argues that the differences between the sexes are minimal; he credits and acknowledges female sexual pleasure—referring to the "internal pouch" as the "seat of pleasurable sensations" (192); he condones—well, practically prescribes—masturbation, dismisses "chastity and absolute continence" (227), and finds that logic leads him to conclude that little differentiates sexual congress between members of the same sex and members of the opposite. Thus, Bordeu concludes, in words echoing those of Porter,

> Nothing that exists can be against nature, and I don't even exclude chastity and voluntary continence which, if it were possible to sin against nature, would be the greatest of crimes against her as well as being the most serious offences against the social laws of any country in which acts were weighed in scales other than those of fanaticism and prejudice [230–231].

Thus, Diderot's incarnation of Bordeu offers a vision of sexual practice that aligns with the philosophy we have seen Stephen take in discussing the benefits of opium—namely, the views expressed by Gottfried Leibniz and popularized by Alexander Pope, among others, in his "Essay on Man" concerning the positive light in which all aspects possible in nature are to be treated. In addition, Bordeu sees the failures to engage in sex as a kind of sin against the social contract. Diderot and la Mettrie—despite their oppositions to one another at various times—both largely endorse a vision of the world that is strictly materialist.

Stephen's philosophies are not so easily pegged down. For one thing, throughout the series he remains, more or less, a practicing Catholic—something neither Diderot nor la Mettrie would accept (in fact, their materialism is often used primarily in the service of critiquing the foundations of religion). However, despite Stephen's faith, his everyday practice of living seems to match up more with that of his fellow eighteenth-century materialists than with his fellow believers. Thus, as we will see, there is a definite resemblance between Stephen's take on sexuality and sexual practices and those of Diderot's Bordeu. Considering the fact that Diderot's physician even speculates on the possible offspring produced by humans and goats, and the fact that early in the first novel of the series Stephen demonstrates his own tolerance for an individual who has taken up relations with a goat aboard ship, it seems not much of a stretch for the reader to draw a clear line between Bordeu and Dr. Maturin.

As we then think through O'Brian's choices here, we see how his presentation of sexual attitudes and behaviors resembles his choices about depicting drug use—though the problems with drugs can be both more various and lethal. If there were people in this society who were more likely to see the ways in which individuals respond to the needs and desires of the body, it would certainly be physicians. We can extend this even a step further. If there were people who, through observation of and interactions with a variety of people, bore witness to the astonishing breadth of sexual practices to which humanity has proven capable, and who came to be tolerant of those practices and see them as normal in the run of existence, it would certainly be physicians. Since, as I have just elaborated, there is also historical precedence for physicians holding such opinions about human sexual practices, O'Brian is certainly not violating any aspect of historical realism in giving these broad-minded views to his naval surgeon.

However, just as he need not have made his doctor experiment with drugs, he need not have made Stephen look at the world in the way in which he does. There was certainly no uniformity of opinions on sex—not all physicians could be said to line up with the most liberal views of the Enlightenment thinkers—to which O'Brian needed to conform in creating those of Stephen. We should also bear in mind, as we established in the previous chapter, that because so much of these views and opinions come from a figure whose authority on the body is so strong and who—for the most part—the reader trusts so fully, we come to find these views often endorsed in the novel, and not, as with the use of drugs, satirically called into question by the doctor's own practices. There is little of the sly gestures, or even outright ironic moralizing comments from the narrator, that mark his treatment of Stephen's drug use in the later stages of the novels (of course, Stephen is practically chaste sexually in comparison to his drug use). Having established that both Bordeu and Stephen share remarkably similar opinions on sexual relations between members of the same sex, let us begin our discussions there.

Homosexuality

As the film *Master and Commander: Far Side of the World* opens, the camera, tracking forward, takes us through the decks where the enlisted men and boys sleep, side by side, swinging near each other in hammocks. Later in the same film we are taken again via the camera—in a kind of sympathy with the perspective of Hollom, who will soon kill himself—through the crowds of men, mostly shirtless, squeezed near to each other in extreme quarters. I invoke these scenes because they speak to the extreme, forced intimacy among and between men who sailed on a warship in the Royal Navy—or any other navy, for that matter—at the time in which these novels are set. I suppose that, to some extent, this has not changed tremendously in modern times, though it has seen the introduction of women into these worlds. In these historical circumstances, however, for the most part, the world of the ship is the space of men. The novels only mention the practice of shipping some very few women aboard a ship, and, with very few exceptions, Jack always rails against this practice (as he does other similar practices like allowing prostitutes aboard a docked ship). I will discuss what we might call the threat of women's sexuality later in this chapter, but for now let's consider some of the consequences of this isolation.

We might consider that any situation—be it sports teams or the armed forces—in which men are either forced or volunteer for a kind of intimacy among only men has bred a kind of fear of homosexuality, perhaps a fear that springs from (considering a relatively naïve view of sexuality) its apparent opportunities and the limitations placed upon other outlets for sexual gratification. Now, aboard ship, this situation is of course amplified because the isolation is so much greater and the sense of the fragility of the community (both literally and figuratively) becomes fairly pervasive. The narrator repeatedly tells us throughout the series of the captain's weekly reading of the *Articles of War;* these explicitly ban sodomy, a crime, which, like most crimes enumerated in the *Articles,* can be punished by death. In fact, the article, "Buggery and the British Navy," by one of the foremost authorities on this subject, Arthur Gilbert, highlights how little mercy was typically shown to those convicted of this crime (81).

Of course the U.S. military's own infamous "don't ask don't tell" policy can be thought of as what we might expect to find in what can most superficially be labeled adventure novels of the sea, and, if Gilbert is right, this silence largely pervades the historical record, since, due to the dire consequences of conviction, most likely many officers "never reported known cases" (72). In *Beat to Quarters* we find that one of Hornblower's officers has a rather obvious crush on him, but the novel never acknowledges it beyond characterizing it as admiration for Hornblower's abilities as a captain. Perhaps. O'Brian, though, draws our attention to the possibilities behind such admiration in the very first novel of the series, through the depiction of the ship's master, Marshall. A reader coming from the Hornblower series, though, could be somewhat taken aback to encounter the depiction of Marshall in *Master and Commander.* Rumors of Marshall's sexuality had reached Aubrey. However, because Marshall is "a big, good-looking, capable middle aged man," Jack suspects that his informant "had probably gotten the whole thing wrong" (30) and that Marshall is not a pederast or homosexual.[1] However, it is not long before the entire crew is aware of Marshall's "crush" (200). In a comical scene in which Stephen calls Jack "portly" (which I cited in the first chapter of this book), Marshall openly rebuts this characterization, suggesting that "the captain has an uncommon genteel figgar" (219). Marshall does not remain a significant character in the series, but he is but the first of many suspected homosexual characters in the

4. Sex at Sea, at Sea with Sex

novels. In Jack's response to him, we see the novel's acknowledging the pattern of making judgments based upon the body, its appearance, its carriage, as well as the pattern of raising questions about such sense-making. For Jack, if Marshall appears masculine, then he should not be considered homosexual.

Much later in the series, in one of the novels that most extensively deals with homosexuality, we see a similar pattern, but through the eyes of Stephen. Reflecting upon Captain Duff, a suspected "sodomite," Stephen, through the mediation of the narrator's voice, observes that

> Duff was an unusually good-looking, manly fellow of about thirty-five, rather larger than most, with no hint of those traits usually associated with unorthodox affections; he seemed to have been totally unmoved by the Commodore's ribaldry and at times Stephen wondered whether the *Stately*'s officers were not mistaken [in thinking that he had sexual relations with his younger officers] [181].

Since the novel seems to go on suggesting rather broadly—sometimes comically—that Jack has been wrong in his judgments, then we are led to uncouple stereotyped but seemingly positive characteristics of masculinity from sexual preference or practice. However, in this second passage we can also see how O'Brian highlights how difficult this process is, for while Jack might have a great deal of the naval officer's inherent prejudices derived from bodies, Stephen's own tend to be much more measured. Stephen must rely on the symptoms shown by the body—hence his willingness to raise questions about these rumors—but he also has been trained to observe the complexities involved in diagnosing the body, whose signs can send a multiplicity of messages, some disguising others.[2]

In addition to this problem of reading an individual by his or her body, of seeing it as a sign that indicates character, sexuality, and other more vague meanings, we also see in the depictions of Marshall something of the reverse problem—of applying labels. O'Brian, as I have mentioned, trying to be historically accurate, never uses the term homosexual anywhere in the series. We have instead the more historically accurate terms of sodomy, sodomites, and pederasts. Of course, this choice of wording is not the same as looking back at Shakespeare and considering his depictions of particular behavior in light of his society and his society alone. O'Brian clearly has something of a contemporary sensibility about homosexuality and perhaps sexuality in general, but we have some challenges in negotiating his perspective because of that difference—a staple problem one supposes with any text that takes its use of historical materials seriously. Likewise, as readers, we have similar problems. The line, for example, between pederasts—those individuals sexually attracted to young boys or girls (and in this context, almost always boys)—and homosexuals (men sexually attracted to grown men) becomes somewhat confused and blurred.

This blurring of pederasty and homosexuality becomes more confused by the presence of midshipmen aboard all of the Royal Navy vessels. The midshipmen are often referred to as squeakers, in part because their voices give every indication of the onset of puberty. They hold a strange place in the ship—they are neither regarded as outright boys nor as grown men; they are at the bottom rung of authority in some ways (in that they are often made to essentially go to school aboard ship), but they are also officers, and as such often find themselves giving orders to men old enough to be their grandfathers. Along with the ship's boys, they are also clearly the most vulnerable to sexual advances, unwanted or otherwise. In depicting the midshipmen in this light, O'Brian appears to be aligning himself with the historical facts. Matt Cook's *A Gay History of Britain* notes that "in fourteen of the seventeen cases [of reported sodomy aboard Royal Navy ships] an adult man had sex with a boy sixteen or younger" (98). O'Brian, thus, acknowledges this pattern.

Throughout the series, then, we find ourselves being introduced to boys of particular beauty (often marked in contrast to boys pocked with acne or possessed of a singular awkwardness). Here, for example, is a representative description taken from *H.M.S. Surprise* at a time when Jack rounds the ship during an inspection: "Young Conroy was the last in the division: a blue-eyed youth as tall as Jack but much slimmer, with an absurdly beautiful mild smooth girl's face; his beauty left Jack totally unmoved (this could not be said for all his shipmates)" (111). We see similar remarks elsewhere in the series, such as when Jack thinks of another midshipman, Reade, in *The Truelove,* as "a pretty boy" who is indulged by the crew (13). These attractive midshipmen seem to hold a mixed place aboard ship. In some cases they play a role similar to that of an attractive woman who comes aboard ship, though in a more muted form, whose infrequent presence tends to compel an over-reaction in the crew.

4. Sex at Sea, at Sea with Sex

These attractive midshipmen, then, have the men giving in to them due to their physical beauty and thus can be seen as manipulative flirts or coquettes, but they also may be the victim of unwanted advances—from those with some power over them, like officers such as Marshall or Duff. Jack's view here seems to be fairly casual. In his many years in the navy he has seen more than his fair share of Conroys and Reades. The homosexuality involved in their positions—as objects of attention, as manipulators of others—often gets somewhat repressed or is left unsaid (in its full implications). It is as if there remains a kind of shared understanding—yes, men aboard ship will find themselves attracted to young men, not fully past puberty, whose beauty is akin to that of women; it cannot be helped. A captain like Jack should only interfere in such matters if they get out of hand—if the boy is in jeopardy of abuse at the hands of an older superior, or if the boy is playing the coquette or flirt to such an extent that he is undermining the discipline of the ship. No one, however, identifies this behavior in terms of its possible implications regarding human sexuality. Yet we may wonder at the implications of such recurring—nay, seemingly perpetual—moments. Do they suggest that the need for sex is so strong that one's sexuality always needs an outlet? Do they suggest that, at best, most human sexuality can be considered in terms of a dominant? In other words, that most men might be considered at most largely heterosexual, but, given the right circumstances, capable of much broader sexual interests? Does it simply muddle our attempts to see people as falling more or less into definable and distinguishable categories of sexual behavior?

These discussions, though, center largely on young boys, figures who arguably are in the process of discovering their sexuality, who are largely feminized, and whose agency is more limited than the adults of the novels. Therefore, I would like to take a bit more time now to discuss the representation of the adults in the series whose behaviors we would today associate with homosexuality. We might say that these figures tend to fall into two main categories in the series: minor figures, treated in the text by more sweeping generalizations, and major figures whose behaviors, attitudes, and character find themselves the subjects of the extended musings of the main characters of the series. With the grouping of the minor figures, we tend to get a great deal of broad gestures, off-hand remarks and casual references. However, especially when seen by Stephen, these figures are objects of sympathy. Hence, we get moments like this offhand descriptor of Pratt the loblolly-boy in *Far Side of the World:* "a gentle, unpracticising paederast" (203). While this is a very minor allusion, and Pratt is a character of little consequence in the novel, we can see that, from Stephen's point of view, one's sexuality does figure in to how one conceives of another individual's identity. Thus, Pratt is an assistant in the surgeon's orlop, but he is also someone who desires to have sexual relations with men or boys—it is not made entirely clear who he desires (but, apparently, he is one who resists such desires aboard ship). Or we might consider this quick reference from *Treason's Harbor:* "Most were condemned to glum celibacy or to what local solace they could find" (8). Such a musing—taken from Stephen's perceptions once more—helps set the tone for the novel's treatments of these figures. We can gather a lot from this quick phrase. Their "celibacy" is "glum" perhaps because Stephen, like his fictional counterpart Bordeu, sees celibacy as glum (though Stephen, depending on his mood, is capable of arguing the exact opposite position). To phrase it slightly differently, the implications are that these men, like all men (and I think Stephen would be likely to include women in this mix as well), need sexual gratification, that the mind becomes affected by the body's needs, its lacks, and thus the absence of bodily fulfillment breeds a depression, one that seeks what "solace" it can find. In this dilemma, Stephen would see no difference in the type of sexuality: whatever one's preferences, we are all susceptible to the same needs, the same effects from those needs, and the same imposition to satisfy those needs. That, the novels seem to suggest, is the human condition.

Later in that same novel we see that O'Brian has set forth his theme. *Treason's Harbor* will be a novel featuring a great deal of discussion of sexuality, as it will feature both Stephen and Jack flirting with adultery, only to see Jack's failure to achieve it and Stephen thinking the better of it (though Stephen nonetheless finds himself believed to be guilty of the acts he had not committed; such is life). This novel begins a long sequence—one of the extended narrative arcs of the series—in which Jack (and, to a lesser extent, Stephen) will find themselves caught up in intrigues set in motion by French intelligence agents. The central figure in this plot is Wray, who even earlier in the series became an adversary of Jack's after he cheated Jack out of money and then refused to accept, well, publicly acknowledge, the implied challenge Jack had made. Thus, when Wray makes his appearance in this novel, now as one of Stephen's

4. Sex at Sea, at Sea with Sex

superiors in Naval Intelligence, we, as readers, are suspicious of him. Relatively early in the novel, the two men meet up on the island of Malta. As they have a meal together, Stephen detects Wray's sexuality:

> From behind his green spectacles Stephen watched Wray when the young man of the house, a beautiful youth with caressing ways, brought them their drinks, their cigars, their lights, and then unnecessary lights again, and it occurred to him that the Second Secretary was probably a paederast [sic], or at least one who, like Horace, might burn for either sex [245].

However, as we have come to anticipate, "This [fact regarding Wray's sexuality] aroused no virtuous indignation in Stephen; no indignation of any kind," for Stephen possesses "the usual tolerant Mediterranean attitude" (245).

This introduction to Wray can take us down several paths, and I would like to pursue two more extensively. As I have noted, Wray's importance to the series really begins in this novel, the ninth—despite his earlier appearance—but this arc will not run its course until at least the fifteenth novel in the series (and this despite Wray's death in the thirteenth novel, *The Thirteen-Gun Salute*). In all of these machinations and plots, Wray remains primarily a villain. Thus, clearly, one central question we must pose is whether there is a relationship between Wray's sexuality—however Stephen might feel about it—and his villainy. I will return to this question shortly.

The other main path set before us by this passage evolves from the narrative judgment upon Stephen's views—namely, his holding of "the usual tolerant Mediterranean attitude" (245). Let's consider this statement in a bit more detail. While our larger discussion needs highlight the phrase "tolerant" most, I want to discuss two other descriptors in this passage: "the usual" and "Mediterranean." Whose judgments are these? Clearly, here we have a moment when the narrator steps outside of the frame of Stephen's perceptions so that his attitudes are labeled as common, but common to a particular region; in fact, we get a broad generalization. Such language leads to other questions more difficult to answer. In labeling Stephen's views in this way, is he praising the more tolerant-minded regions of Southern Europe (however unreliable such blatantly broad claims might be), or is he critiquing them but labeling them as a viewpoint shared by groups outside of the dominant major group of the novel—namely, the Northern European British (and, to a lesser extent, Irish)? As I have suggested, I am not certain we can firmly answer any of these questions. The novel tends to sympathize with Stephen's positions. He's extremely intelligent and perceptive; however, he is also very, very human, and he makes mistakes. In particular, he misjudges Wray, as the narrator rather pointedly informs us at the opening of *The Reverse of the Medal*: "Simplicity was not perhaps one of Stephen's outstanding characteristics; yet his mind was not wholly free of it and he had never even suspected the possibility of Wray being a French agent," and Stephen "had not perceived that Wray did in fact possess a malignant, revengeful mind" (55). The narrator, though, does not extend this critique, does not question (any more than he has already) Stephen's tolerance of Wray's sexuality. Nevertheless, that passage introducing the matter from *Treason's Harbor* does at the least raise some questions of where the novel stands on the matter.

The evidence of Stephen's tolerance, though, goes far beyond this passage. We see many examples throughout the series. At the end of *Reverse of the Medal,* Pullings, one of Jack's officers, recalls Stephen's defense of "sodomites," for "you told him [Jack] that there were many good, brave and gifted men among them" (240). Such a scene puts Stephen in a familiar setting throughout the novels, as he frequently becomes a voice of tolerance, compassion, and enlightened views towards those different to himself. These moments stand side by side with other comparable moments, such as his many pleas against corporal punishment. They also generally follow the pattern I have outlined above of Stephen's willingness to accept that which occurs in nature as a good, especially if it imposes no limits on others.

The measure of Stephen's influence, I suppose, would be his ability to convert Jack to his way of thinking. Of course, Jack is not exactly predisposed to hate others; however, he certainly comes from a more conservative background than Stephen and has an extraordinary capacity to defend tradition (simple gestures, like how Jack wears his hats, speak to his desire to uphold certain ways of doing things). And, of course, Jack's very position as a captain in the Royal Navy means that he is supposed to root out and punish anyone who practices sodomy aboard ship. Throughout the series, Jack vacillates about whether he will have religious services formally conducted aboard ship on Sunday mornings—he sees a hypocrisy involved in conducting such ceremonies aboard a ship during war and abides by the naval suspicion that religious reads on board ship are bad luck—but only battle or bad weather would pre-

4. Sex at Sea, at Sea with Sex

vent Jack from making sure that the *Articles of War* are read each week. Nevertheless, Stephen does have an impact on Jack, as we see when he returns from serving as a judge at a court martial dealing with charges of sodomy. Jack proudly reports, in *The Hundred Days,* on how he altered the verdict: "I repeated your 'No penetration, no sodomy,' which floored one and all; though I must say that most of them were glad to be floored. I persuaded the others to find no more than gross indecency" (35).

Perhaps the most expanded discussions regarding Jack and Stephen's views towards what we would call homosexual practices—and particularly those practices aboard naval vessels—takes place in *The Commodore* in regards to the aforementioned Captain Duff. In many ways this novel, the seventeenth in the series, is a return to some of the main issues of the fourth book, *The Mauritius Command.* In each novel, Jack receives a commission in which he serves as a commodore, a kind of stand-in or temporary admiral who thus commands his own ship but also a few others (forming a squadron). Thus, in each text much of the conflict revolves around Jack's interactions with these other captains—unfailingly drawn to be quite dissimilar to Jack and usually assigned to him despite his objections. In each novel one captain is a tyrant who whips and abuses his crew while simultaneously revealing his incompetence. We see this type of captain many times in the series: they are sadists and bitter men who are despised by their crews and by Jack. Also, each novel features a feminized captain who has some difficulties maintaining order aboard his ship. In the case of the earlier novel, this particular captain, Clonfort, is treated much more circumspectly by the novel; however, the implications are that he is homosexual, and that he somewhat narcissistically admires his own beauty, dressing himself as a dandy and practically costuming his midshipman. We learn that Clonfort had sailed with Jack when they were both younger, had betrayed Jack in an act of cowardice, and has never owned up to it. In this early novel he seemingly overcompensates for this cowardice and ends up leading his ship into a massacre, one that also results in his own disfigurement and subsequent suicide. Although not made explicit by the novel, we are left to wonder about the relationship between his possible sexual preferences, his feelings of inadequacy, his possible cowardice, and his inability to act rationally in a need to compensate for his apparent weaknesses.

In the later novel, published approximately seventeen years after the earlier one, the issues are made much more explicit. The nature of the mission forces interactions among the various ships, particularly their officers, who must frequently gather aboard Jack's ship to discuss strategy and logistics, as well as disseminate orders and information. Quickly the rumors regarding Duff and the favors disposed upon the officers who sleep with him spread throughout the squadron. Thus "sodomy" becomes a relevant—if rather loaded—topic of discussion. O'Brian's narrator records for us one such moment at a dinner in Aubrey's gunroom—the dining hall for officers—led by one of the visiting officers:

> "You may say what you like," said the tall, thin lieutenant, second of the *Thames*, "but they are never really *men*. They may have pretty ways and read books and so on, but they will not toe the scratch in a fight. I had two in a gun-crew when I was in the *Britannia*, and when things grew rather hot they hid between the scuttle-butt and the capstan." Other views were heard, other convictions and experiences, some tolerant, even benign, but most more or less violently opposed to sodomites [220].

There is perhaps nothing surprising in this conversation. It brings forth the obvious stereotypes we might presume to hear, and if there is anything that might catch us off-guard, it is the few voices of acceptance (whose actual words go unreported). However, perhaps most noteworthy here is that these stereotypes align with the motivations that forced Clonfort to such extremities of behavior in the earlier novel—extremities that led to widespread death, including his own.

Although Jack normally maintains clear boundaries regarding what he consults with Stephen about (because Stephen is both his best friend and an officer serving under Jack's command), he decides that he can consult with Stephen regarding Duff and sodomy because Stephen is a "medico": "As you know, I hate the way sodomites are hanged or flogged around the fleet, and I like Duff: but you must not do it with the young foremast jacks, or discipline goes by the board" (76–77).[3] Later in the novel Jack once again speaks frankly about the practice aboard ship: "But when you consider what the lower deck is like—three or four hundred men packed tight—the cloud of witnesses when hammocks are piped down—and the very public nature of the heads—it is difficult to imagine a more unsuitable place for such capers. Yet it does occasionally happen in what few holes and corners a man-of-war possesses, and in cabins" (248). Thus, Jack's position on "sodomy" stands in marked con-

4. Sex at Sea, at Sea with Sex

trast to the stereotypical positions offered by the visiting officer. He does not question Duff's masculinity, and while he wonders how it is at all possible aboard a crowded ship, he eventually confesses that it does indeed happen. I will return to this question of discipline in a moment.

Stephen, like Jack, has heard the rumors, but when he meets Duff he begins to have some doubts about their validity. He approaches the situation like a detective or forensic investigator: "Stephen could detect no sign of the tastes attributed to him. Indeed he would have sworn that Duff would have been most attractive to women." In this initial passage, Stephen seems to view homosexuality as purely a choice, and a choice made out of desperation—as if to say a man would only become attracted to men if he could find no woman who would have him. He also seems to fall into the trap we have seen many times before of looking to the body for clearly readable signs. Stephen, however, as usual, continues to push past his first, superficial impressions: "Yet the same, he reflected, might have been said of Achilles." From here, then, Stephen does a kind of scientific cataloguing in his head: "His mind wandered over the varieties of this aspect of sexuality—the comparatively straightforward Mediterranean approach; the very curious molly-shops around the Inns of Court; the sense of furtive guilt and obsession that seemed to increase with every five or ten degrees of latitude" (92). Thus, Stephen reworks his initial considerations based upon stereotypes and tries to fit this encounter with Duff into a larger context of understanding this behavior. We may say that there are lines to be drawn between tolerance, sympathy, and understanding, and to the objection that we cannot expect Stephen to understand human sexuality in the same way that we do in the twenty-first century I bow.

Now let us return to the question of discipline and villainy. As I have outlined above, Jack's frequent objection regarding sodomy in the Royal Navy is that it has a negative effect upon discipline. Above nearly all else, Jack believes discipline to be key to the efficient running of a ship, and—putting aside all other moral and ethical considerations—we would be hard-pressed to seriously question a captain's worries about the need for discipline aboard a ship-of-war. We can even extend our defense of Jack's viewpoint in this matter in two ways—his frequent attempts to lighten punishments derived from charges of this practice, and, perhaps more importantly, his even more fervent beliefs regarding heterosexual behavior on board ship. In other words, Jack sees sexual activity—whoever is involved—as creating breaches in discipline (if you'll pardon the pun); he certainly does not single out sodomy in particular. We even have a contrasting example from the opening of *The Reverse of the Medal*, when the narrator informs us, "It was also known that the Admiral was fond of beautiful young men; but as this fondness was reasonably discreet, never leading to any disorder or open scandal, the service regarded it with tolerant amusement, much as it regarded his more openly-avowed but equally incongruous passion for Handel" (10). So, then, Jack's reactions to and beliefs about how Duff's behavior might affect his ability to run and sail his ship properly and effectively do not necessarily imply a critique of homosexuality or a specific sexual practice.[4]

However, I think we cannot also deny that there is a pattern that begins to emerge over the course of the novels. As I have noted, we have at least two clear examples of problems raised by the presence of a captain suspected of being a "sodomite," and we also have the example of Wray. Wray emerges as one of the primary villains of the novels. Yet he is no monster. We see his many weaknesses, some of his strengths, and we certainly can concede he is a fairly well-drawn figure to whom O'Brian lends the kind of humanity he grants all his well-developed characters. However, the long, over-arching plot that features Wray involves at least four characters who would be identified as "sodomites." There is Wray, his French co-conspirator Ledyard, the highly placed English Lord, and the Sultan featured in *The Thirteen-Gun Salute*, the novel that sees a direct confrontation between Stephen and Ledyard and Wray, as the French and English compete to gain influence with the Sultan of Pulo Probang. After observing the Sultan's interactions with one of his serving boys, Stephen realizes that the Sultan of Pulo Probang is "a paederast," for, as Stephen's contact, Van Buren, informs Stephen, "such things are as usual here as they were in Athens" (203). Eventually, in the plot of this novel, their affairs prove to be their undoing, as jealousies surface, and the Sultan and the French spies are found out. Stephen and Van Buren, a fellow naturalist, end up rather ignominiously dissecting Ledyard and Wray after they have been assassinated. Likewise, the high-placed English Lord becomes identified because his sexual practices and interactions with Wray lead him to a whorehouse in which Clarissa Oakes worked, and she passes on this information to Stephen. Let me reiterate: none of these characters is directly implicated in their villainy by way of their sexuality. However, what do we do with the fact that they are all "sodomites?"

Thus, as attentive readers of these novels, we are left with some difficult questions. I will put aside for now the general ones regarding sexuality in all its many guises. Undoubtedly, O'Brian's consistent attention to these issues speaks to their larger importance to the series. However, in the matter of the novels' depiction and treatment of homosexuality, we are left to consider how two clearly opposing elements mesh. On the one hand, we have the views of "sodomy" and "paederasty" espoused by the two main characters of the novel, Jack and Stephen. As I have tried to argue, their views are typically tolerant and sympathetic. They are not threatened by these practices as such, and they do not judge individuals on the basis of their sexual orientation or predilections (unless that orientation or behavior carries over into areas they believe they should not). While, as I have pointed out, the narrator sometimes— and rather ambiguously—separates himself from the point of view of his characters on this issue, we can certainly find no evidence of independent critiques or indictments of homosexuality coming from the narrator (as we do, for example, come to see such moments in regards to Stephen's drug use). Nevertheless, the novels do have a definite pattern of antagonists, weak characters, or sometimes outright villains being "sodomites." Clearly, not all such characters are, but enough are to make us wonder if there remains in these novels an ongoing suspicion of homosexuality, despite an overt desire to simultaneously preach tolerance through the novels' primary characters. We might also wonder if this suspicion is tied to a larger doubt about the ability to control the body, and that it is not coincidental that these negative homosexual characters are repeatedly undermined by way of giving themselves over to their sexual desires.

"Poor Soul": Women and Sexuality

Rum, Sodomy, and the Lash. Besides being the title of the finest collection the Pogues ever produced, these are things a reader coming to a series of novels about the Royal Navy during the Napoleonic Wars might reasonably expect to encounter. In other words, the Aubrey-Maturin novels may investigate these matters with a depth and broadmindedness that challenges our preconceptions and expectations; however, we feel no shock at reading of them. In contrast, we probably would not expect to read as much about women and sexuality as we do. Evidence for O'Brian's interest in the subject can be found among his archived notes where he has included an unlabeled photocopy of two "lectures" on the nature of women's sexuality. Those photocopies, it turns out, come from *Tableau de l'amour conjugal* (*Conjugal love; or The Pleasures of the Marriage Bed*), written by a French physician, Nicolas Vennette, in 1686, but not translated into English until 1750, after which it remained popular until the end of the Eighteenth century.[5]

Therefore, with some reconsideration, we can see that such discussions of women's sexuality do fit within the larger framework of the novels. I have discussed elsewhere how Stephen's focus shifts over the course of the novels from a primary concern with flora and fauna, with animal life more than human life (besides his professional obligations), towards the study of humanity, much as Doctor MacAdam, the proto-psychoanalyst, suggests he do in the fourth book of the series, *Mauritius Command*. As Stephen's ruminations turn toward what shapes human behavior, and as the novels give greater room for Stephen's perspective, the novels would then seem to inevitably need to turn towards the workings of women as well as men. It should also be no surprise that the novels, especially in these reflections from Stephen, avoid clichéd notions of the essential unfathomable nature of women. Instead, here too we find a general broadmindedness, a willingness to reject or challenge received wisdom, and a wide-ranging sympathy.

The difference in this subject more than others lies in Stephen's lack of comfort with it, at least early in the series, such as in this concession in *Mauritius Command* where Stephen first considers whether he should have something to say on marriage: "'Since it has physical effects, the sorrow and woe that is in marriage no doubt belongs to the province of the physician,' said Stephen. 'But I am as little acquainted with it as I am with gardening, or domestic economy'" (35). However, as Stephen observes Jack's marriage and eventually marries Diana himself, his speculations on marriage, women, and sexuality grow more expansive. After brief asides, such as Stephen contemplating "upon the sexual nature in elegant females" (*Treason's Harbor* 120), we get a lengthy consideration on marriage, "that difficult state," as part of his discourse with his friend, the Reverend Martin, in *Far Side of the World*: "He had

4. Sex at Sea, at Sea with Sex

heard of a race of lizards in the Caucasus that reproduced parthenogentically, with no sexual congress of any kind, no sexual complications" (144). Later in the same novel, Stephen again admits that his mind has return to the complications of marriage, particularly courting rituals:

> I have been contemplating on the mating ceremonies of our own kind. Sometimes they are almost as brief as the boobies,' as when two of a like inclination exchange kind looks and after a short parley retire from view.... At other times however the evolutions of the ceremonial dance, with its feigned advance and feigned withdrawals, its ritual offerings and symbolic motions, are protracted beyond measure, lasting perhaps for years before the right true end is reached; if indeed it is reached at all and not spoilt entirely by the long delay. There are endless variations according to time and country and class, and the finding out of common factors running through them is a fascinating pursuit [242].

Whereas these kinds of passages are often undercut by Stephen himself, in this particular passage Martin offers the puncturing comment: "the act itself, which is nasty, brutish, and short" (242). Nevertheless, the passage is telling. We see Stephen in essence making the transition in his own larger philosophical attentions. He takes what he knows—the mating habits of birds, his beloved "boobies"—and uses that as a lens to consider the endless variation of humanity's practices. He also observes with the practiced eye of the naturalist. Here, at least, we also find Stephen approaching his subject with wonder and not judgment, certainly not moral judgment. Thus, as the novels continue—and perhaps this is also tracing a kind of underlying shift in O'Brian's own attentions—Stephen comes to provide a greater and more specific lens for examining human sexuality and, through his attentions to marriage, the sexuality of women.

The discussions of Sophie and Diana, however, begin fairly early in the series, really in the second novel, *Post Captain*, in the introduction of the two most prominent women of the series, Jack's future wife Sophie, and Stephen's future wife Diana. In that first novel, Stephen and Jack nearly fight a duel in their passion for Diana, while Jack also courts— in a far more conventional way—the seemingly more innocent cousin, Sophie. Diana's first appearance has her riding in on a horse, and the men notice—"for she was the prettiest thing"—that she also stands out because of her seemingly male behavior. She utters things that "Jack had never heard a girl say—before," and the narrator, through Jack's perspective, remarks that she sat upon "her horse with the unconscious grace of a midshipman at the tiller in a lively sea" (19). Although Diana is regularly idealized for her grace of movement, it is not, however, a "studied," self-conscious and conventional way of moving, as this passage from *H.M.S. Surprise*, in which Stephen sees Diana for the first time in Bombay, highlights: "At all events that remembered perfection of movement was there: nothing studied about that sinuous turn, nothing that loosened all his judgment so" (212). In contrast, Sophie "was a reserved creature" with a "wonderful sweetness of expression" (*Post Captain* 22).

Thus a pattern starts that continues throughout the series. Diana appears to be a kind of Hemingway ideal of womanhood—she is masculine in her attitudes, behaviors, and sexuality, but is unmistakably a woman, beautiful and heterosexual—the Brett Ashley type; whereas Sophie is a fairly conventional figure of the period in which the novels are set, shy and lacking Diana's knowledge of the world and her own body. With regularity, then, throughout the series we see a comparison of opposites within marriage (or relationships), with the experienced and seemingly sexually avaricious Diana paired with the seemingly passive and unmotivated Stephen; and the innocent, reluctant sexual partner Sophie in a marriage with Jack and his powerful "animal spirits."

I will discuss Jack and Stephen at greater length shortly, but we might here consider some typical passages on this matter from *The Commodore*. The narrator lets the newcomer to the series know that Stephen "was not at all agreeable to look at and from the physical point of view he had never been much of a lover—a state of affairs much influenced by years of addiction to opium, which he neither smoked nor ate but drank in the form of the alcoholic tincture of laudanum, sometimes, in his despair over Diana, reaching heroic doses." Still, he has been married to Diana and her "naturally ardent temperament" (11). Of Sophie, we are told she "had been brought up so straight-laced that she possessed no very exact notion of how babies were made in the first place or born in the second until she learned from personal and startling experience" (60). Earlier in the series, in *The Mauritius Command*, Stephen contemplates that "Jack must be strangely put about," as he decides that Sophie is frigid and, like other Englishwomen, has "an ignorance of the warming, ripening delights of physical love" (29). Jack even seems despondent at the thought of having another child (31).[6]

4. Sex at Sea, at Sea with Sex

I do not want to give the impression, however, that the novels rely on this static consideration of the two women and construct a stereotypical division among them. If anything, as the novels proceed, these investigations grow deeper, the portrayals more rounded, and the issues more complicated. By the fifth novel of the series, in which the spy and acquaintance of Diana, Louisa Wogan, finds herself being transported to Australia for her prison sentence aboard Jack's ship, the novels begin to incorporate the presence of women on the ships in order to examine the relations between the sexes and to point a lens towards women as well as men. One of the central threads of the middle work, *Far Side of the World*, considers a love triangle involving the gunner's wife; and in *The Truelove*, the fifteenth novel in the series, we again have a plot that revolves around the fractious presence of a woman on the ship—this time the stowaway and fiancée of an officer, Clarissa Oakes. She becomes Stephen's patient and confides her past to him. While she resembles Wogan in many ways—including how she disrupts life aboard ship—Oakes differs greatly from Wogan in terms of her sexuality. If anything, Wogan is a more typical *femme fatale*, willing to use her sexuality as part of her power grab, dangerous to both herself and others; Oakes, however, had suffered sexual abuse early in her life and had grown up in a brothel. Thus, she "could not associate [sexual intercourse] with the least degree of pleasure, however short: and so a great deal that I read and heard—romantic attachments, swimming the Hellespont and so on—remained incomprehensible, in so far as they were for that end, the right true end" (165). Living in a brothel, she tries to get a sense of the world from literature, but she cannot comprehend the literary descriptions of "physical love" because she found "chastity or unchastity neither here nor there—absurd to make fidelity a matter of private parts: grotesque" (167). Through Stephen's ruminations, then, the novel takes up questions regarding human sexuality, and particularly the consequence of abuse, as, for instance, when Stephen writes to Diana that "I do not think I could ever make him [Jack] understand that for her the sexual act is trivial, of no consequence" (208).

Thus, it is not surprising to find that such a focus has shifted from a minor character—albeit one central to that particular novel—to a greater and more complicated discussion of sexuality and women, in particular Sophie a few novels later, in *The Yellow Admiral*. In fact, the novel features a lengthy discussion between Diana and Stephen on the matter, instigated by the troubles Jack and Sophie experience when evidence of his infidelities surface. Stephen offers a somewhat typical take: "Poor soul, poor soul. But it was an ill-fated marriage. She has never taken pleasure in the act itself: she has always dreaded pregnancies: and her deliveries have been extremely painful. It has long seemed to me that jealousy and frigidity or at least tepidness are in direct proportion to one another. And Jack is what is ordinarily called a very full-blooded man." However, O'Brian challenges the conventional wisdom established in the novel by giving Diana a full voice in the conversation:

> I dare say you are right about frigidity and jealousy. But I believe you are wrong in calling Sophie frigid. Certainly, when her mother is by, I think she would be a poor companion for a lively, eager man—indeed, Jack would never have got her into his bed at all if she had not run away in a ship far from her mother's eye. And then again I have it on the best authority that Jack is no artist in these matters. He can board and carry an enemy frigate with guns roaring and drums beating in a couple of minutes; but that is no way to give a girl much pleasure. In better hands she would, I am sure, have been a very likely young woman; and oh so much happier [185-186].

The passage continues with the Diana discussing sexual pleasure and her conversations with other women about the matter. Diana's commentary, however, puts a lie to the assumption that the problems in the sexual life of Sophie and Jack lie with Sophie and her discomfort, her "frigidity," when it comes to sex. Instead, the novels further undermine Jack's conventionally heroic status, and suggest his own attitudes and sexual behaviors have been instrumental in the failure of this aspect of his marriage.

While this passage is rather unusual, it is not, however, an anomaly. The novels, although male-biased in perspective and largely in sympathy, do offer a complex and often sympathetic portrait of the position and lives of women—often directly tied to their sexual lives. A passage from *Far Side of the World* can stand as an appropriate representative. In it, we find Stephen and Martin discussing the practice of "emasculation"— the near castration of Jack, in particular—carried out by "Amazonian" women Jack and Stephen encounter. After Martin expresses some horror at the extremity of action undertaken by the "Amazonians," Stephen retorts:

> Oh, as far as unsexing is concerned, who are we to throw stones? With us any girl cannot find a husband is unsexed. If she is very high or very low

> she may go her own way, with the risks entailed therein, but otherwise she must be either have no sex or be disgraced. She burns, and she is ridiculed for burning. To say nothing of male tyranny—a wife or daughter being mere chattel in most codes of law or custom—and brute force—to say nothing of that, hundreds or thousands of girls are in effect unsexed every generation: and barren women are as much despised as eunuchs. I do assure you, Martin, that if I were a woman I should march out with a flaming torch and a sword; I should emasculate right and left [301].

I do not want to make too much of Stephen's proto-feminism here. After all, there are plenty of Jack's biases towards women afloat in the texts—though often challenged by Stephen—and I do not want to judge whether we should offer some kind of golden palm to the novels for their broad-mindedness. However, such passages speak to O'Brian's recurring interest in both human sexuality and in exposing the hypocrisies implicit in the typical moralizing judgments and categorizations that accompany the labeling and assessment of human sexual practice. Perhaps even more central to our larger discussions here, we see that women are seen as much subject to human desire and the conflicting needs of mind and body as men, and thus these depictions fit within this larger framework of understanding human sexuality and humanity more broadly in the series.[7]

The Sexuality of Jack and Stephen

Perhaps the most obvious question that I have side-stepped in the previous section is what of the relationship between Jack and Stephen. It is not mere whimsy that leads Diana to say to Stephen, "Anyone would think you were married to that man" (*Post Captain* 77). Quite clearly they love one another, and in their relationship we can see many of the kinds of traditional tropes of masculinity and homosocial bonding common to male-oriented genre fiction like *noir* and the Western. No doubt they prefer each other's company to all else; no doubt women serve to complicate their lives; no doubt they understand each other as no one else does. Again, I have no doubts that they love one another, that the novels celebrate a kind of bond among men, but we simply cannot make any arguments regarding the relationship being sexual, based on the evidence of the texts. Thus, for the sake of the conversation of this chapter, I will leave off some of these questions for now.

As he does in many aspects of their characters, O'Brian draws Jack's and Stephen's sexual make-up as somewhat diametrically opposed, although they are both heterosexual. From the outset of the series, Jack's sexuality gets a great deal of attention from the narrator and, to some extent, Stephen (always one of our likely vantage points into Jack's character). The earliest descriptions of Jack's nature in this regard from *Master and Commander* are almost cartoonish in how stereotypical they are. This behavior is also part of his stereotyped masculinity: "In times of stress, Jack Aubrey had two main reactions: he either became aggressive or he became amorous; he longed for either the violent catharsis of action or for that of making love. He loved a battle; he loved a wench" (245). At such moments we may be tempted to groan at the seeming "man's man" construction of Jack. However, we must also recall that any such moments become complicated by various factors: the constant presence of Stephen and his deflating wit, and the strange mix of beauty and obesity that comprise Jack's physical nature. In this same novel we have lush descriptions of Jack's flowing blonde hair in the breeze (69), a physical attribute that leads the men to call him Goldilocks (248). Thus, he's beautiful almost to the point of feminine beauty, yet we have the description I invoked in the first chapter of Jack's size—"like so many sailors he was rather fat, and he sweated easily on shore" (80)—and the later details of Jack, after some successes and acquiring a French cook, "putting on weight like a prize ox" (229).

As the series progresses, we find that Jack develops a reputation. At the opening of *Reverse of the Medal,* O'Brian alters the perspective so that we watch the *Surprise,* with Jack and Stephen aboard, come into port, but from the perspective of those on shore, particularly Captain Goole and his wife. Goole, clearly somewhat jealous of Jack, tells his wife, "You would never think so to look at him now, but Aubrey was once considered handsome." However, Mrs. Goole's perspective seems to lend credence to Jack's continued attractiveness:

> She did not at all find it surprising that he was considered handsome; even now, although his scarred, weather-beaten countenance had nothing, but nothing of the bloom of youth and although he weighed too much, he was not ill-looking; he had a certain massive, leonine style, and he fairly towered over Goole, who had no style of any kind; and his blue eyes, all the bluer in his mahogany face, had the good-natured expression of one who is willing to be pleased with his company [30].

4. Sex at Sea, at Sea with Sex

Most telling though is Goole's lament about Jack: "'But the real trouble with Aubrey,' said the captain after a long pause during which he watched the distant frigate go about on to the larboard tack and head for Needham's Point, 'is he cannot keep his breeches on'" (13). The novels only dispute this account to a moderate degree.

A brief survey of some descriptions of Jack's responses to women make the point. From early in *The Letter of Marque* we find: "Although Jack Aubrey could never fairly be described as much of a whoremonger, he was no celibate and from his earliest youth until the present he had taken the liveliest pleasure in beauty, and this spirited girl, half standing and all alive with excitement, was absurdly beautiful" (8). In the *Wine-Dark Sea*, after traveling with Clarissa Oakes, the eventual wife of one of his officers, Jack confesses to Stephen: "Lord, Stephen, that was a fine young woman. How shamefully I lusted after her: but it would not do, of course, not in my own ship" (62). Lastly, and as late as the eighteenth novel of the series, *Yellow Admiral*, the narrator informs us that Jack "was not a man to whom chastity came easy—had to impose a most rigorous self-command" in order to not go after Clarissa Oakes (76).

In terms of the novels' treatment of Jack's sexuality, it is hard to differentiate matters of sex from matters of marriage. While the series begins with Jack single and his reputation already in place (thanks to his affair with his Admiral's wife and his notorious smuggling of a woman onboard when he was a midshipman), he rather quickly becomes a figure out of a Jane Austen novel, a man who needs a wife, a place of his own, a settling down. In the second novel of the series, as I have described, Jack and Stephen both compete for the affections of Diana, while Jack also pursues Diana's less adventurous cousin, Sophie. By the end of the third novel Jack has married Sophie, Stephen and Jack have just barely escaped fighting a duel but have repaired their friendship, and Stephen has failed in his attempts to wed Diana. However, as the passages from throughout the series regarding Jack's sexual desires show, his appetites are in no way curbed or sated by marriage. In part, this derives from the situation of his life—inordinate amount of time spent at sea and away from his family—and from Sophie's supposedly limited interest in sex.

I will come back to these matters in a few moments, but here I would like to explore how Jack's sex drive is then depicted in the novels. To be specific, Jack's "animal spirits" are treated like a medical condition and thus examined by Stephen. These circumstances are played out in the novel *The Surgeon's Mate*. The novel finds Jack and Stephen in Nova Scotia following their escape from an American prison in Boston during the War of 1812. Jack had reached a real, depressive low during his imprisonment. Early in this novel the narrator describes Jack's marriage: "Their marriage, firmly rooted in very deep affection and mutual respect, was far better than most; and although one of its aspects was not altogether satisfactory for a man of Jack's strong animal spirits, and although it might be said that Sophie was somewhat possessive, somewhat given to jealousy, she was nevertheless an integral part of his being" (18). Stephen fears that Jack needs to "renew your animal spirits" (41) to lift him out of his depression, and when Stephen's prescribed walks fail to help him, Jack's subsequent affair does.

By the time of the fourth novel of the series, *The Mauritius Command*, this pattern has already been established. After Jack expresses his disappointment about the lack of openness involved in marriage (32), Stephen feels at a loss to help him. It seems worth looking once more at his response, which I cited earlier in a different context: "Since it [marriage] has physical effects, the sorrow and woe that is in marriage no doubt belongs to the province of the physician,' said Stephen. 'But I am as little acquainted with it as I am with gardening, or domestic economy'" (35). Stephen's conclusion about how to answer his concerns about Jack's well being seem to be pretty simple: he needs to act upon or live within his typical sexually active mode. Thus, Stephen expresses his concerns: "Then again there is the diminution not only of his animal spirits but also his appetites: I am no friend of adultery, which surely promises more than it can perform except in the article of destruction; but I could wish that Jack had at least some temptation to withstand" (171). Throughout the series Jack does commit adultery a seemingly countless number of times, and, besides the hurt it causes Sophie when she becomes aware of such an incident, he feels little guilt for the act itself. For example, after Sophie discovers letters resulting from one of Jack's liaisons, "He felt no particular guilt except for this foolishness [of not having gotten rid of them]" (149). Similarly, at various points in the series, as in *The Truelove*, when Jack goes through a period of sexual frustration he becomes depressed and physically ill. After we are told, "Throughout the voyage from Batavia to Sydney Jack Aubrey has been chaste: necessarily so, given the absence of anyone to be unchaste with" (12), he com-

4. Sex at Sea, at Sea with Sex

plains to Stephen: "I am most damnably hipped" and wonders, "Is there a medicine for good temper and general benevolence?" (15). Eventually, Stephen prescribes an enema for Jack.

As this discussion suggests, then, the novels' treatment of Jack's sexuality—at least as we encounter it through the eyes of Stephen—is seen as part and parcel of the life of the body. Like the needs for food and drugs, we are inevitably at the mercy of the body, although the mind may seek to rationalize the behavior and may be affected by the body's needs. There is not, however, much moralizing on the subject. It is as if to say, well, Jack has a lot of testosterone (a more modern word for "animal spirits"), and that is common enough. We expect largely heroic figures like Aubrey to be of this ilk, but perhaps we have never quite gotten as close a sense of the inner workings of such a being, seen not just as a throwaway characteristic but a physical phenomenon, one that can help the hero thrive but can also send him into—to borrow his phrasing—a blue funk.

While Jack's sexuality is tied very obviously to his body, to his active, heroic, soldierly demeanor, Stephen, as a rather physically unattractive man (one who squeaks when he laughs, wears dirty clothing and a rather disastrous old-fashioned wig), comes across quite differently. To be blunt, the novels focus far less on Stephen's sexuality in part because Jack far less frequently turns his attention to Stephen's sex life than Stephen—in his medical capacity—does Jack's. In addition, Stephen's sex life can hardly be distinguished from his drug use. Although the novels do take some pains to make it obvious that Stephen is heterosexual, that he quite clearly desires Diana, we also get a definite sense that he does not convey his sexuality with anything like the robustness of Jack. As you may recall, in *The Surgeon's Mate* a French spy says of Stephen, "Madame Dangeau is sure he is a paederast, and I think she is right. He is a friend of La Mothe's" (157). This accusation may result from his acquaintance with the known "paederast" La Mothe, but it nevertheless speaks to the kind of public figure Stephen presents.

In the matter of drugs and sexuality there appears to be some question of cause and effect. In other words, does Stephen have less interest in sex because he has become addicted to laudanum, or has he taken to laudanum as a means of coping with his sexual frustrations? This question emerges fairly early in the series in *The Mauritius Command*, the novel that follows upon Stephen's heartbreak with Diana, as Stephen encounters another physician, Dr. McAdam, who comes across as something of a proto-Freudian. While Stephen takes to consulting him regarding the case of Captain Clonfort (outlined in a previous section of this chapter), the discussion inevitably finds its way back to Stephen. During their initial consultation, McAdam offers a pointed and loaded critique of Stephen's primary interest of study: "The proper study of mankind is man. And I may observe, Dr. Maturin, that this eager prying into the sexual organs of vegetables on your part seems to me ..." (92).[8] Towards the end of the novel the implications of this exchange become more explicit. From McAdam's perspective, Stephen's drug use is clearly a coping device. At one point he declares, "It is the pity of the world, Dr. Maturin, to see a man of your parts obnubilate his mind with the juice of the poppy" (243). Then, at the end of the novel, when Stephen directly asks his advice, wondering if McAdam is familiar with a man "Who takes a disgust to the world?.... He sees his own animal functions will not interest him either. Do you understand me?" McAdam responds, "Sometimes his perception of the void is intermittent; but where it is not, then in my experience spiritual death ensues, preceding physical death sometimes by ten years or more. Occasionally he may be pulled out by his prick." After Stephen inquires further, "You mean he may remain capable of love?" McAdam has had enough of the game: "'As between men and women I use the term lust: but call it what you like: desire, a burning desire for some slut may answer, if he only burns hard enough. In the early stages, however,' said McAdam, leering at the geckoes, 'he may tide himself over with opium, for a while'" (342). While I would not wish to suggest that such a scene or an exchange as this is as common as those involving Jack, I do wish to consider just how obviously similar these discussions are. Clearly the implication of Jack's case is that if he does not find sexual satisfaction or some kind of sexual outlet, then this leads to other physical and mental problems, frustrations, and a depression of sorts. Perhaps the case for Stephen is a bit more clouded, but the relationship between sex—from McAdam's point of view—and Stephen's overall well-being seems clear. Stephen can see this readily enough in Jack's case, and Jack can also recognize what he wants and needs; McAdam suggests that Stephen, however, seeks to repress those needs or the pain felt from the inability to satisfy those needs, and thus deceives, even poisons, himself.

Like the long arch of drug addiction I charted in the previous chapter, Stephen's sexual frustrations, drug use, and general physical lethargy takes a long time to work its way out. In the subsequent novel, *Desolation Island,* Stephen finds himself in daily contact with a convicted spy named Louisa Wogan. On the surface, he claims to have no confusion about having a woman as a patient, declaring, "When I am called in to a lady, I see a female body, more or less deranged in its functions. You will say that it is inhabited by a mind that may partake of its distress, and I grant your position entirely. Yet for me the patient is not a woman, in the common sense. Gallantry would be out of place, and what is worse, unscientific" (243). However, during the course of the novel the former companion of Wogan is discovered aboard ship, and, like Stephen, he has been a former opium addict (Stephen is in one of his brief periods of quitting). After Herapath discusses how opium diminishes the sex drive, Stephen rationalizes that it is his obligation to go back on drugs so that he will not compromise his intelligence work with Wogan (to whom he has become attracted, despite his earlier protestations). Although here Stephen refers to an outbreak of scurvy, we cannot help but notice the larger implications of this statement: "'I must confess, Mr. Herapath,' he said, 'that nothing grieves me more than the dependence of the mind upon the body's nutriment. It points to a base necessitarianism that I rebel against with all the vehemence my spirit can engender" (271). So this despair about the inability of the mind to transcend the body echoes throughout the novels, and clearly the relationship between sexual health and mental and physical health becomes an ongoing theme.

Stephen finds himself repeatedly in a pattern akin to this one with Louisa Wogan. In *Treason's Harbor* he flirts with Mrs. Fielding for similar, intelligence-based ends. As that novel begins, Stephen is in a foul mood, perhaps because he is "sexually starved and that recently his amorous propensities had been stirred" (15). With women, Stephen "was convinced he could govern any untimely emotion that rise in his heart" (26). He acts this out later by fending off Mrs. Fielding by declaring that she cannot possibly find that she is "enamoured of my person" (89). Nevertheless, Stephen is upset when Jack wakes him from an amorous dream involving Mrs. Fielding (94). Later, Stephen calls his decision to remain chaste, to not act on the apparent flirtations of Mrs. Fielding, perhaps "untimely, unnecessary, foolish, unprofitable, sanctimonious" (132). Stephen—as we saw particularly in his somewhat contradictory views about drug use—can clearly see that human beings must give in to the needs of the body, but he can also be capable of criticizing those who too easily give themselves over to said body. So he can claim that he has no weaknesses to women, but then he must face the fact that he has needs, his body practically demands that he respond to them (or drug it so it need not respond). And he can also see through his own moral hypocrisy.

Later in the series, after he has worked his way out of the nadir of his laudanum use, Stephen suddenly finds his sexuality rekindled. As *The Thirteen-Gun Salute* opens, he now realizes the effect his opium use had upon him and "what a shamefully inadequate husband it had made him, particularly for a woman like Diana." Again and again in the series we are told how mismatched Stephen and Diana are, and one of the clear divisions between them is sexual appetite. However,

> The change in his behavior, the very decided change (for when undulled by laudanum he was of an ardent temperament) had added an almost entirely new and almost entirely beneficent depth to their connection; and although it was in all likelihood the cause of the heat with which they argued, each preserving an imperiled independence, it was quite certainly the cause of this baby [18].

However, whereas we might expect Stephen to embrace this new fire in his sex life, he seems to practically despair at it. Later we learn of Stephen: "He had awoken not long since from the most unusually explicit and vivid erotic dream; they had become increasingly frequent of late, with the laudanum dying even in its remotest lingering effects, and the vehemence of his desire quite distressed him. 'I am becoming a mere satyr,' he said. 'Where should I be without my coca-leaves? Where indeed?'" (38). For Stephen, then, the problem seems to lie in the matter of controlling the body. To feel passion too strongly, to feel his body respond with sexual desire, is to feel his ability to control his body slipping away. This tension between respecting the body's needs and trying to repress those very same needs seems to be at the heart of the matter—a pattern akin perhaps to Freud's take on the means by which civilization deals with its "discontents."

Conclusion

I began this chapter by suggesting that it is hard to imagine a reader who picked up his first O'Brian novel in hopes to find extensive discus-

4. Sex at Sea, at Sea with Sex

sions of sex and sexuality. Nevertheless, as I hope this chapter has made clear, if that reader sticks around for very long, she will come to expect frank discussions and long reflections on human sexuality, despite the absence of similarly frank depictions of actual sexual behavior. In terms of action adventure, I am more likely to view the depiction of sex acts as more likely than the reflections on human sexuality. Yet we might see such reflections as a staple of a novel of ideas or more philosophical fiction writing, in which a character spends much of his or her time in repose and pondering. Therefore, in one sense, the novels' interest in sexuality provides yet more proof of the complications of trying to affix an easy label to what O'Brian has written; however, as I hope the larger claims of this chapter have suggested, these discussions of sexuality are in many ways of a piece with the novels' attention to what it means to be human and to inhabit a body. We see in these discussions attempts to understand the needs of the human body as they relate to sexuality, and the complications of human sexuality in that humans do not see sexuality as exclusively a bodily need, but still must negotiate with the fact that—from the perspective of these novels—sexuality is tied directly to bodily needs and wants. Although, as I have done here, readers can certainly raise questions about whether the novels do direct suspicion at some forms of human sexuality, I would still contend that the overall tenor of the texts does align with tolerance and empathy—empathy for figures in the midst of trying to navigate the complexities of human consciousness and animal desires and needs. In fact, we might conclude that the novels suggest that the attempts at creating a dichotomy simply deceive us about who and what we are.

5

The Captain's Bodies
Desolation Island, *a Case Study*

Introduction

"I like being at sea." In a crucial scene in Hal Ashby's 1973 film *The Last Detail*, Billy Buddasky mutters this comment to his fellow Navy man, Mule Mulhall. Buddasky, played by Jack Nicholson, sits on a picnic table facing the camera at a remove from Seaman Larry Meadows, whom Buddasky and Mulhall are escorting to naval prison. Snow covers everything, and the sight of the men's breath indicates how cold it is. Not exactly picnic weather. "Bad Ass" Buddasky, in a seemingly philosophical bent of mind, continues: "I was in a weather ship once, off the coast of Greenland. Right in the middle of winter." To the question from Mulhall, "How was it?" Buddasky only replies once more: "I like being at sea."

The Last Detail can be viewed in much the manner of the many anti-establishment, often anti-war or anti-military, films coming out of Hollywood at this time. Thus, it has clear connections to films like *Easy Rider*—also starring Nicholson—and *M*A*S*H*. The film reveals the mindset of these two military lifers, as they revel in an apparent freedom of action and power granted them by their status in the U.S. Navy, only to find themselves compelled to follow orders and bring Meadows to prison. After the build up of their relationship with Meadows—a man being sent to prison for 8 years for having attempted to steal 40 dollars—the audience cannot help but be deflated by the sudden arrival at the Portsmouth prison. The scene I have described above concludes with Meadows, after hearing Buddasky's comments about the abuse he is likely to receive in prison, attempting to run away, only to be caught and beaten by the two men who have become his friends. Their frus-

5. The Captain's Bodies

tration and violence seemingly must have an outlet, and as part of the critique of the way such systems work, Ashby makes sure that we see that those frustrations find an outlet in those at the lowest end of the hierarchy. My own personal desire for a different outcome manifested itself in a peculiar way. Having recently re-watched this film, I realized that I had relieved my own dissatisfaction and frustration with the film by repressing and reconstructing the ending. I had gotten it into my mind and memory that they had let Meadows go in a brave act of defying the establishment. If only it had been so.

Patrick O'Brian's fifth Aubrey and Maturin novel, *Desolation Island* (1978), published but a few years after Ashby's film debuted, produces similar frustrations in the reader. In it we also find a Jack in the position of escorting prisoners, a commission he did not want (what Buddasky and Mulhall would call a "shit detail"). But like Buddasky, Jack Aubrey, too, likes being at sea, and thus accepts this duty out of obligation, to both the Royal Navy and to his friend, and a chance to once more sail independently (Jack even seems on the verge of saying no, but his wife convinces him that he needs to take the commission for Stephen's sake; both Stephen and Sophie, though, feel that Jack *needs* to be off at sea once more). Our frustrations as readers, however, emerge from the frustrations Jack experiences in the novel. He tries again and again to exert his will and maintain control, but this novel, in various ways, depicts the limits of that power. He can say "Make it so" with all sincerity, but he is ultimately no God.

Especially over the first half of O'Brian's twenty-volume Aubrey-Maturin series, there is usually a scene in which the captain of the Royal Navy, Aubrey, receives a new commission. As readers—especially if we have become accustomed to the series—we anxiously await this moment, first because our protagonist is so awkward and fallible on land that we cannot wait to get him back out to sea, and second because we know that Jack's relation to this boat and its crew will set the tone for the rest of that particular narrative. We might see this as almost a kind of courting ritual in which Aubrey has various degrees of say in his ability to choose—both with the ship and with his crew. I do not use this metaphor here simply to be glib; as the novels progress, clearly we see that Jack has two lives—one at home and on land with his wife, and the other at sea, and he often has an arguably even more intimate relationship with his ship than he does with his wife. As I've noted, the books often follow a process in which he must forsake—though this may be more his wife's word choice than Jack's—his wife for the sea.

Once Aubrey has received his commission and his orders, O'Brian usually establishes his relationship with that ship quite early. He either falls in love with it, or he must maintain a troubled relationship with it. Part of this relationship seems to come from Aubrey's ability to make over the ship in his own image: to make it conform to his ideas of sailing, to his ability to maximize its sailing and gunnery potential. The H.M.S. *Sophie*, as his first command, is his first love (and, not coincidentally it seems, Sophie is also the name of his wife), and he is blind to her faults and treasures her small gifts—such as having something like a partial quarter deck. The *Surprise* is his most beloved—in part because he sailed upon her as a midshipman (literally leaving his mark in the form of his initials at the top of one of its masts), and it most fully responds to him and his desires (expressed in many rhapsodic passages about its sailing abilities). In *Treason's Harbor*, for instance, Jack thinks that "[the *Surprise* was] a difficult and temperamental frigate, but wonderfully responsive, fast and mettlesome for those who knew her ways; she never failed in an emergency, and he would never know a more sea-kindly ship, by or larger, in light airs or strong gale" (230). In contrast to a ship like the *Surprise*, we find a ship like the *Polychrest*, Jack's commission in *Post-Captain*. Of the *Polychrest* we learn, "She had the strangest motion, a kind of nervous lift and shudder like a horse about to shy, as she rose to the swell, a kind of twist in her roll that he had never known before" (216). Jack "could not love her" (231–232). Through the first half of the series, Jack seems to swing between these kinds of commissions—the ships he cannot "love" and those for which he feels passion. The ships that he feels a certain distance to tend to feature in novels that contain a great deal of strife (*Post-Captain*, for instance, sees Jack's and Stephen's relationship near collapse over their competition for Diana's affections). As the series expands and O'Brian comes to place more and more of his narratives in obscure locales and within obscure historical incidents (as I discussed in Chapter 2), Jack also spends more time with his beloved *Surprise*, and that ship's aging comes to mirror Jack's.

A similar process to Jack's courtship with his ships takes place as Jack fills out his crew for any particular voyage. In some scenarios he finds himself named the captain of a ship with an already preexisting crew. In more favorable situations, he is allowed to select some of the

5. The Captain's Bodies

officers; but even in these situations he finds himself often taking on officers or midshipmen on the orders of superiors or as favors. As Aubrey gains in reputation, his ability to attract a strong, experienced crew also increases; however, often the Admiralty interferes in this process, taking away experienced sailors to give to other ships or forcing him to take on impressed men or landsmen as part of his crew. In the best of circumstances, Jack's crew consists largely of individuals—both in terms of the officers and the regular sailors—who have sailed with him before. These "followers," as they are known, clearly allow Jack a great deal more comfort. In any case, just as Jack typically must test, master, and attempt to make over the ship in his own idealized conception of it, he must also make the crew a reflection of his desires so that they might become an extension of his will. Essentially, this process resembles what Michel Foucault refers to in *Discipline and Punish* as disciplining the body—and not by coincidence does he use the figure of the soldier as a primary example. Foucault locates the transformation of how bodies were treated in a time very close to when O'Brian's novels are set, proclaiming, "The human body was entering a machinery of power that explores it, breaks it down, and rearranges it" (138). As Jack seeks to make his various ragged crews over into something that will work as a unit, he must "discipline" these men, and, in Foucault's words, "Thus discipline produced subjected and practiced bodies, 'docile' bodies. Discipline increases the forces of the body (in economic terms of utility) and diminishes the same forces (in political terms of obedience)" (138). Essentially, the consequence of this process as Foucault describes it clearly corresponds to the outcome that Jack too seeks: this process "dissociates power from the body; on the one hand, it turns it into an 'aptitude,' a 'capacity,' which it seeks to increase; on the other hand, it reverses the course of the energy, the power that might result from it, and turns it into the relation of strict subjection" (138). To put it plainly, Jack's goal is to both increase the power inherent in this group of men by reshaping their behaviors via military discipline, and to make those bodies "docile" by "subjecting" them to his authority.

In each of these recurring scenarios we see that there comes to be a metaphoric relationship between Jack Aubrey and both the ship and the people he commands. I have been contending that throughout this series O'Brian shows a preoccupation with bodies. We have the great attention paid to Jack's own expansive and expanding body, as well as the body of his close friend and ship's surgeon, Stephen Maturin, whose body, in contrast, is slight, small, and tends toward shrinking. Stephen, as a surgeon, is famed for his ability to take bodies apart, severing limbs, opening brain pans, for the purposes of saving those bodies; Jack, conversely, uses his great, if over-sized, frame to deal damage to the bodies of England's enemies. They are also susceptible to the needs and weaknesses of the body, as Jack exemplifies in his carnal appetites and Stephen displays in his addiction to opium. In particular, Jack's body becomes both literally and figuratively tied up in the welfare of his ship and his crew, recalling the medieval conceit of the King's two bodies.

In thinking through these issues of the body in O'Brian's novel, it is useful to place this discussion in light of Michel Foucault's analysis of Kantorowitz's conception of the "King's Body" as Foucault discusses it in the section of *Discipline and Punish* entitled "The Body of the Condemned." Foucault reminds us that Kantorowitz's analysis sees the King's body as "a double body according to the juridical theology of the Middle Ages, since it involves not only the transitory element that is born and dies, but another remains unchanged by time and is maintained as the physical yet intangible support of the Kingdom" (28). In other words, there is the literal body of the king—which is subject to mortality—and the more figurative body, a sort of mystical conception of a transcendent notion of the king. The phrase "The King is dead; long live the king!" captures Kantorowitz's notion. Thus, it takes little imagination to realize that, at sea, the captain of the ship comes to resemble something of the role of the King in this conception; he is a mortal, literal body, but he is also something more, and if the "imagined community" that forms the nation can be read metaphorically across this imagined body, so can the bodies of the captain's ship and crew.

While we might locate the patterns I have described above throughout much of the series (and I will try to draw in some of the echoes of these patterns found elsewhere), I will focus primarily in this chapter on the fifth novel of the series, *Desolation Island* (1978), which proves to be something of a spectacular example of the complicated levels of relationship O'Brian uses to organize his narrative and to unpack the relationships among his principal characters. In the context of this novel, O'Brian uses this complex trope to examine gender constructions and the disruption of the typically male universe aboard ship, political conceptions—through the references to the King's two bodies, but also

5. The Captain's Bodies

through competing theories as played out in the leadership crises aboard the ship—as well as the complicated psychological desires for controlling what is perhaps uncontrollable, one's unconscious and one's physical self.

At Sea on Land

As with many of the novels in this series, *Desolation Island* begins on shore. In doing so, O'Brian helps reiterate several recurring themes, but perhaps most importantly it helps establish the distinctness of the two worlds in which Jack Aubrey lives. Each new novel and each new visit to shore helps the reader chart Aubrey's progress in the world. When this novel begins, he has been on shore following his highly profitable—in terms of money and prestige—command in and around Mauritius and has been given a relatively comfortable position with the Fencibles, a group that essentially impresses men into the Navy. Although O'Brian is quick to chart the continued renovations to Aubrey's home—Ashgrove Cottage—he also wishes us to see how unstable and problematic life on land can be for Jack. At the start of *Desolation Island*, in his time on shore, Jack has begun contractual negotiations with a charlatan involving lead mines, a situation that will financially and legally haunt him for some time; he has begun regular card games in which he loses a great deal of money and creates an enemy in Andrew Wray after calling out this intelligence official who has been cheating him in these games; he has also continued to throw money on schemes seemingly out of the world of Ralph Kramden, such as purchasing a horse he dreams will win prestigious races only to find that the horse will do nothing of the sort. In trying to explain the builders to his wife, Jack appears powerless, and she appeases him by saying, "Builders are strange, unaccountable creatures" (6). Unlike members of his crew, these men cannot be "disciplined."

In essence, all the seeming power and control that Aubrey has as a captain aboard a navy vessel simply cannot be brought to bear on the world outside of that isolated and strictly ordered milieu, despite his employing sailors as servants who keep his home "as trim as a royal yacht" (7). He hires current and former members of the Navy as his servants, and he encourages them to make over his house in the image of one of the King's ships, but he simply cannot control, order, and discipline that space in the same way he can a ship out at sea.

Of course, the somewhat unspoken complication in Jack's time on shore is the fact that he must live with his wife Sophie. In other words, while he appears to be the titular head of the household—the King's body at home as well as on the ship—the reality of the situation stands in contrast to that ideal. In many ways it is much more her domain than his. A passage from late in the series (*Yellow Admiral*, in fact) regarding both Stephen's and Jack's desires to be aboard ship underscores the nature of this recurring pattern:

> And although neither had more than a nine-inch plank between him and eternity (indeed not so much) while at the same time both were exposed to the perils of sea and the violence of the enemy, a kind of blessed relief came over them, as though the intricacies of conducting first a tender and then a large and crowded man-of-war to a rock-strewn and hostile coast, notorious for its foul weather, perpetual south-western gales and wicked tides, were little or nothing compared with those of life on the shore, of domestic life on the shore [87].

While I always tend to think of this passage in light of my own fear of flying—a fellow O'Brian fan once quoted this as I boarded a plane with him—it certainly makes the point that the dangers at sea hold nothing to those of the domestic sphere on land.

In *Desolation Island* these dangers appear both from Sophie and Jack's seeming gullibility to all comers. As his schemes build and grow seemingly more absurd, even Sophie recognizes the discord created by his presence at Ashgrove Cottage. She resorts to some scheming of her own. While more or less deceiving Jack so that he will accept a commission, Sophie tells Stephen, "I have an even more terrifying thought: that he is not really happy on shore, and that he plunges into one extravagant venture after another to escape from a dull life in the country; and from a dull wife too, perhaps" (67). Although Jack and Sophie's sexual incompatibility is explored and described elsewhere in the series (and in the previous chapter of this book), and may be a factor here, I would emphasize that Jack finds this world uncomfortable because he cannot bend it to his will. And because of various social conventions and his own views of women, he most certainly has difficulty imposing control over a space seemingly beyond a strictly male domain. They are not exactly bodies in his own image; despite conventions of propriety that suggest a wife

5. The Captain's Bodies

as a kind of sign for her husband, Sophie does not become an extension of Jack in, say, the manner of a handpicked first lieutenant aboard a ship.

We see something of this situation played out in the very opening sequence of the novel. As the book opens, we find Sophie waiting for Jack, a situation that recalls the clichéd plight of the sailor's wife. Upon his return, "The anxiety changed to unmixed pleasure as she heard his step" (5). Thus, his arrival on the scene appears triumphant; his wife reflects the joy on his face, and we see the gender stereotypes of the passive woman in the domestic space and the active man possessing the agency to come and go as he needs. He has also, we soon learn, purchased the horse he wanted (so we witness him in part expressing his economic power in the relationship as well). This dynamic soon alters considerably. We learn that Jack had failed to get the workmen to commit to finishing construction at Ashgrove Cottage. The purchase of the horse, it turns out, is not primarily an act of financial power or an expression of class luxury, but instead a compensation for his failure with the workers and the needs of his body: "I was a little put out, I must confess: and on an empty belly, too. But, however, seeing I was there, I stepped into Carroll's yard, and bought the filly" (6). In a short time, Sophie's mother and Jack's twin girls, as well as Jack's infant son, enter the "breakfast parlour." Rather quickly, Jack's position and power seem to shrink. After first seemingly inflating Jack's power by calling him "Commodore," Sophie's mother, Mrs. Williams, reprimands him for talking too loudly and directs a "reproachful look" in his direction. Then, "Jack felt a momentary and quite ignoble pang of jealousy at the sight of the women—particularly Sophie—concentrating their idiot love and devotion upon the little creature [his son George]" (8). As Jack mutters many times in the novels, he finds himself "laid by the lee again."

One last component of this opening scene also speaks to both the way in which Jack relates to his crew and this particular novel's interest in gender. After Jack mistakes one of his twin daughters for the other—Fanny is not wearing the properly colored-coded pinafore—two of Jack's most loyal followers, Bonden and Killick, arrive at the house. In a kind of brief parody of the opening sequence of Hardy's *The Mayor of Casterbridge*, we learn that Killick, Jack's steward, has bought a wife. Perhaps unconsciously expressing some of his own feelings, Jack reacts by declaring, "What in God's name does he want with a wife?" (9). However, when Sophie asks him to interfere because no one should "treat women like cattle," Jack demurs: "I should not like to go against custom.... Where would the Navy be without we followed customs?" (10). We learn that Killick weighed this decision for "the best part of twenty minutes," and Jack will accept her presence in "the establishment" if she and Killick "cut along to the rectory" (10–11). The dynamics here are rather Shakespearean, with Killick and, to a lesser extent, Bonden playing the clowns to the dramatic lead figure; but in much the same ways those foils work in Shakespeare, we can see a kind of parody of marriage and on-shore life in this sequence. As the section starts, Jack actually thinks that they have bought a horse—just as he has—but Killick has made nearly the same kind of impulse purchase. Marriage and the Navy align in that they are run and sanctioned by custom, rules, and law. However, the degree to which these laws and customs enhance or limit Jack's power and agency seems a bit muddled. The benefits do not consistently outweigh the detriments. There is custom, and then there is lived experience.

The "Terrible Old Leopard"

There simply seems to be too much grey area on shore and too many obstacles to the expression and fulfillment of Jack's desires. Typically, then, Jack views—even if he does not always fully articulate it—his life at sea, in contrast to this life onshore, as a world that, in its potential, can reflect himself and in which he, with the ship and crew as figurative extensions of himself, finds a control and wholeness lacking onshore. However, as the constant process—and sometimes failure in this regard—of remaking both the ship and the crew in his own image or ideal reveal, this notion of the ship and the crew becoming another body of Aubrey is not a natural occurrence. It is a labored process of disciplining men as Foucault describes—of giving them a greater power as a whole, but limiting and subjecting them so that they become docile under Jack's commands.

Early in *Desolation Island*, however, we can see that this relationship between an idealized extension of Jack, in the form of the ship and the crew, and the reality of that relationship will be dramatized and explored. When Jack and Stephen first discuss the prospect of taking the commis-

5. The Captain's Bodies

sion offered to Jack, Stephen, who is almost uniformly ignorant of naval matters, asks Jack if he means "the horrible old *Leopard*?" Jack, however, has already begun the process of imagining the potential of this ship, although he concedes that it "was something of a slug, and a ramshackle old slug" in its previous incarnations (19). He then launches into a kind of refashioning of the ship itself, which he has undertaken before, such as with the *Boadica* in the previous novel, *The Mauritius Command*. Defending his new prospect, however, Jack declares the ship the "finest fourth-rate in the service," which has had "a most thoroughgoing overhaul" (19). Despite this bravado, the narrator reveals the sorry state of the fourth-rated ships, which "had been excluded from the line of battle this last half-century and more" (20). Perhaps one significant weakness in Jack's assessment is that "he wanted her not for herself but for her destination: he longed for unknown seas, and the Spice Islands" (20). This is not love.

While Jack may have allowed himself to be charmed by the prospects of the *Leopard* because it was a means to get away and because he had "watched her overhaul with a very attentive, professional eye," O'Brian has already put us in a position to be skeptical: Jack makes these prognostications and assessments on shore, so they line up with his ventures with the horses, gambling, and mining schemes. The full corrective of Jack's over-idealized conception of his ship does not come until more than half-way through the novel, and it comes from one of Jack's most loyal followers, his coxswain, Bonden, who disillusions Stephen and not Jack, telling Stephen that others consider the *Leopard* a "floating coffin, and unlucky at that" (169). In fact, Bonden's explanation conflates Jack's various onshore follies, explaining that "being straight as a die, we sometimes believe them quick-talking coves are dead honest too, with their patent knees and braces [the supposed improvements to the *Leopard*] and goddamn silver-mines" (170). Bonden's reasoning suggests that men who live primarily outside the larger society have a greater but naive morality that leaves them susceptible to the corrupting figures on shore. In Bonden's explanation, these corrupting figures do not overtly include women, but we as readers must wonder. While Bonden's explanation reveals a kind of inherent weakness in men like Jack, it is a weakness that we are meant to forgive because it only appears because he lives by a higher standard than most humans.

However, as Bonden implies, this weakness on shore does have consequences for the life at sea. Essentially, the *Leopard* continues to rot in the manner Jack had once witnessed, and the Jack at sea must answer for the faults of the Jack on shore. Within the first few pages of the first chapter set at sea, we see Killick, Jack's steward, complaining about "those bleeding caulkers at the Yard" who "don't know their fucking business," as evidenced by the leak soaking the Captain's cabin (72). Later, a crewman says, "Would you ever of believed that even the Dockyard could pass such a rotten bit of wood? And the whole bleeding stern-post is the same. Punk. Incest is nothing to them, nor Sunday travel, so they get us to sea in an ancient sieve, the fucking bastards" (157–158). As a basis for this other body, then, the *Leopard,* from the start, speaks to an interior weakness masked by superficial covering and extensions, and we need take note of the bodily images evoked in the devices—the knees, used to secure and reinforce the structure of the ship. We might also wonder about the fact that members of the crew—members, in fact, of the lower deck— are the first to become aware of the weaknesses of the ship, as if these bodies cannot help but recognize the failings in a body with which they have such a close connection. As the problems of the *Leopard* continue to be revealed, we can hardly help recalling the famous lines of *Hamlet* involving rotting and the state of Denmark. The *Leopard* is rotting too.

A Mixed Crew

Although the ship Jack must sail to the Spice Islands is clearly problematic, its faults will ultimately seem minor compared to the conundrums Jack must face on the human front—namely, in terms of the crew and the passengers he must carry with him. The problems that emerge in terms of the humans on board the ship both help illustrate the complexities involved in the contrasting lives of Jack Aubrey, and point towards the problems involved in his attempts to master his ship. These problems, though, represent not so much an exception in the series but a spectacular example of a pattern—the problems that arise as Jack seeks to master or discipline his fellow humans on ship, to make them a positive extension rather than a site of resistance or weakness. Before looking at a few such examples, we might consider an important passage from *Treason's Harbor* in which Jack celebrates an ideal crew by way of comparison to the more typical situation he faces:

5. The Captain's Bodies

a crew of hand-picked seamen, every one of which could hand, reef and steer, and practically every one of whom he knew and liked. He knew exactly where he was with the Surprises and they knew exactly where they were with him and his officers; the Surprises could be allowed liberties unheard-of in a ship with a mixed set of people, including landsman and thieves as well as a large proportion of sullen, understandably resentful pressed men, a ship's company that needed the perpetual tight discipline usual in the service [231].

In this almost utopian vision, Jack need not hold fast to the tight line of discipline, for all involved work almost in concert—are almost of one body. Consider, by way of contrast, more typical scenarios. Earlier in the series, in the second novel, *Post-Captain*, Jack faces a similar situation in terms of his crew when his commission places him aboard the *Polychrest*—a ship of experimental design that Jack struggles to pilot—with a nearly mutinous crew (and here again, destruction of the ship actually prevents mutiny). The problem of women passengers aboard ship also gets picked up several more times over the course of the series. In *The Far Side of the World*, the gunner's wife (we learn of the naval practice of shipping the gunner's wife, which makes her presence only an anomaly in the series rather than the navy), Mrs. Horner, plays a central role in a destructive love triangle wherein three men, whose names all coincidently begin with the letter "h," die. One of those, Hallum, is considered a Jonah, like Larkin of *Desolation Island*. Other passengers feature prominently in later novels. In *The Thirteen Gun Salute*, Jack must carry Envoy Fox, a man who behaves badly aboard ship, cramps Jack's space, and eventually perishes, due in part to mishandled sailing. This novel, while not a direct parallel to *Desolation Island*, certainly reiterates some of its patterns.

The novel, however, that comes to closely resemble *Desolation Island*—so much so that it almost feels as if O'Brian, late in his career, wished to return to familiar ground in the way that Howard Hawks and John Wayne did when they essentially remade *Rio Bravo* together (well, actually remade it twice)—is *The Truelove*, the fifteenth in the series. In this novel the crew discovers that Clarissa Oakes, a former prisoner, has been smuggled aboard ship by one of the midshipmen. Like Mrs. Wogan, as I will discuss shortly, Clarissa Oakes disrupts life aboard ship, provoking severe jealousies among the crew, including Jack's primary officers, Davidge and West. Jack, too, will experience longings, as this novel begins with Jack experiencing a great deal of sexual frustration (and ultimately culminates with his sleeping with a queen of island natives). In short, these issues of problematic ships, crews, and passengers surface multiple times. *Desolation Island,* however, places these discussions most clearly into this broader canvas of the trope of the two bodies while also examining O'Brian's frequent theme, which I have explored throughout this book, of the desires of the mind in relation to the desires of the body—both literal and metaphorical. We may divide these problems—as they are explored in this particular text—into two main groups, the actual crew and the passengers on board the ship.

Below the Waterline

Let's begin first with the problem of the passengers in this particular text. We learn that the prisoners have been included, in part, as something of a ruse to disguise the transportation of a single prisoner, an American spy by the name of Louisa Wogan. Jack, however, has not been made aware of this situation and is simply aghast at the prospect of carrying prisoners with him to Australia. As Jack declares to Stephen, "to expect an officer of my seniority to turn his ship into a transport [a prison ship], and to play the turnkey!" (60–61). The nuances here seem to escape Stephen, who cannot quite see the difference between transporting these prisoners and transporting prisoners taken in battle. Jack never quite gets around to a full disclosure of what troubles him about the very concept, but we might contemplate how this is one of the folds in the trope of seeing the ship and its contents as extensions of himself. Consider that while prisoners of war, such as captured French, represent England's—and hence Jack's—enemies, they also reflect positively upon the captain. If there are French prisoners captured in battle in the ship's hold, then the ship—in its ability to outlast that of the enemy—and the captain are likely literarily and figuratively thriving. In fact, Foucault argues that in the trope of the King's Body as described by Kantorowitz, the "body of the condemned" is quite "at the opposite pole" of the king, for "he, too, has his legal status; he gives rise to the ceremonial and he calls forth a whole theoretical discourse, not in order to ground the 'surplus power' possessed by the person of the sovereign, but in order to code the 'lack of power' with which those subjected to punishment are

5. The Captain's Bodies

marked" (29). Foucault continues by suggesting that "in the darkest region of the political field the condemned man represents the symmetrical, inverted figure of the king" (29). Thus, following this line of reasoning, Jack has a kind of symbol in the "darkest region" of his ship, one that represents his opposite, a body that signifies powerlessness. In contrast to prisoners taken in battle, these prisoners reflect no esteem on the ship or any other element of the crew, but rather lower the esteem, suggesting the ship and its crew are engaged in work below their dignity. Perhaps, too, the prisoners signify a subject position that Jack would prefer his own crew not be fully conscious of, but which they cannot help but reflect on in the bodies of those condemned and imprisoned in the dark, airless hold of the ship. In short, that the crew members, some of whom have at least at some time likely been impressed, may see a stronger connection between themselves and these prisoners than Jack would like them to see. While both sets of prisoners could represent a danger, something that must be contained, the risk and rewards involved here are simply not equivalent. In addition, these prisoners have been taken on land and hence are a part of the system and space that, as we have seen, typically stands outside of Jack's control.

As to the effect of the prisoners on Jack, the narrator, perhaps through a certain degree of indirect discourse, make the matter quite plain: "Although he was sole captain, under God, aboard the *Leopard*, this [the prison hold] was another world, a living-space inconveniently cut out of his kingdom, and one that was to be transported to New Holland with the utmost dispatch, there to be emptied and restored to its true function as part of the man-of-war" (79). Thus, initially, he lacks even the position of authority in this dynamic; instead, the prison space represents a lessoning of his area of autonomy. The following description of where Jack located this prison hold makes even more distinct his attempts to repress their presence: "And all these people, the convicted and the unconvicted [the guards and attendants], inhabited the forward part of the orlop and the forepeak, under the waterline, where they would not get in the way of the working of the ship, and where, he had hoped, they could be forgotten" (79). It is hard not to see this space in terms of what Foucault called the "darkest region" to describe the location of the condemned in opposition to the king.

These passages are striking on several levels, as they speak to Jack's view of his place aboard the ship—it is "his kingdom" and one that is "under God"—as well as the way in which the ship can reflect both Jack's body and his mind, so that the prison had been something he had hoped to keep "under the waterline" in several ways. However, almost immediately we see this will not be the case. O'Brian begins the section at sea, Chapter 3, essentially in media res, as the ship has already begun passing by the Spanish coast. As we readers then enter the shipboard world, we find that world already disturbed by the prison, for "the convicts have scragged their superintendent; and their surgeon, he pitched down into the hold and broke his neck" (74). When Stephen and Jack must enter into this space Jack had hoped to forget, he finds it abominable. As his Lieutenant Pullings notes, "The filth down there, you would not credit" (74). Shortly thereafter, the narrator informs us that "the stench was appalling, and the air so foul that when Jack lowered his lantern the flame guttered, burning faint and blue" (80). With the death of the superintendent, then, the repressed return, and in this death we may see a symbol of the threat to Aubrey's control and authority. Essentially, then, Aubrey must struggle to contain and control this space now that its presence cannot simply be forgotten. He is now King of both his ship and this "darkest region."

While I have been describing this dimension of O'Brian's novel largely in terms of the language of Foucault, we must also note how close that language is to that of psychoanalysis. We need not be totally wedded to Freud's conceptions to feel that O'Brian himself seems to be evoking a kind of Freudian spacial model of the mind here—with the below decks recalling the unconscious and a place that Jack has tried to keep contained, even repressed. However, the storms seem to have destroyed the gatekeeper—the figurative entity that stands between the unconscious and conscious in Freud's original, hydraulic understanding of the mind. Thus, with the passing of the turnkey—"scragged" by the repressed fears, the prisoners—Jack has no way to mediate between those spaces. He literally must enter into that space, and he must own it now. As the narrator says, "Now the unfortunate, pompous, brutal, pretentious fellow was dead, and that means that Jack would either have to shuffle the responsibility for the convicts off on to the useless half-witted illiterate turnkeys or assume it himself" (84). Although the narrator goes on to discuss how many bureaucratic entanglements Jack could get into if he had more trouble with the prisoners, the real problem here seems to be psychological. In fact, the consequences of his failed attempts to repress the existence of this prison space—to essentially have no part of it—has been to his mind:

> He was extremely depressed; he was conscious of having failed in his duty as far as the forepeak was concerned. He should never have allowed the cage to be so built that it would flood: the deep bottom bar, upon the uprights rested, had acted as a dam—that was obvious to him now, as obvious as the simple remedy. And he should have sent for a report from the superintendent [84].

There seems to be some real guilt here. Although Jack does make mistakes in the managing of his ship, I cannot help but wonder if this passage implies that we read Jack's actions—or inactions—as part of the unconscious desire to repress the presence of the condemned, and if the "depression" and guilt that come through in this section speak to the ways in which he had perhaps unconsciously desired that a flood would wipe out the entire lot of the condemned (after all, now facing the actual situation and his choices, it all seems quite "obvious" to him).

It almost seems a rule of literature that the repressed must return. At first, it seems as if this will not be the case. Stephen begins to take a forceful hand in supervising the prisoners and in seeing that they are treated more humanely, and that the space itself is no longer as fetid and wretched as it had been. However, we soon learn that it is too late; the attempts to ward off and repress the existence of the prisoners come back upon the ship in spectacular ways. I will discuss in particular the role of the women in this return shortly; however, the most obvious expression of this failure of containment is "gaol-fever, and gaol-fever of the most virulent kind" (144). Just prior to this revelation of the disease, we have read one of those rhapsodic passages of the ship sailing at its ease: "The *Leopard* had just run one of her finest distances in this or any other of her voyages, tearing along, top-gallants just holding in the splendid breeze on her quarter, the log racing astern glass after glass, reeling off ten and eleven knots at every cast, and filling all hands with pleasurable excitement" (143). However, after Stephen's first victims of the gaol-fever die, "Stephen noticed that the way had come off the ship: the innumerable sounds that spoke of movement had fallen silent, and the voice of the water, usually slipping by just above the head, had died away" (145).

The spread of this disease has fairly disastrous consequences for the ship. First, it has a great impact on the morale of the crew, for the *Leopard* had become "a gloomy ship now, oppressed by heat, and disease, and dread of the future" (147). At first, the disease primarily decimated the prisoners, but "when the disease struck the lower-deck it killed men faster than the plague" (148). We should not simply pass over the repeated use of metonymy in the descriptions of the crew and the ways in which the crew and the ship are inextricably tied throughout most of these descriptions. After all, as the disease first appears—signaling in very real ways the failure to contain that which was below the waterline that Jack wished to keep hidden so as to maintain his sovereignty—the ship itself simultaneously stops moving and the crew's morale sinks, for "excessive dread and general despondence ... had come over all the crew" (148). We might say that the rot—a kind of disease—that has spread through the material ship (one figurative extension of Jack's body) has also spread through another, namely his crew.

Not only does this disease severely damage the crew, it also rather significantly isolates and damages Jack. First, for much of the disease's outbreak, Stephen remains below deck with his patients, "forbidden territory from which he never emerged except for the daily burials" (147). By the end, the ship loses one-hundred-and-sixteen men, and, as Jack observes, "One of the saddest things about this tally ... is that it hits our volunteers so much harder than the rest. Once I knew a good third of the men aboard. Now it is nothing like" (155). Essentially Jack faces the fact that the disease has decimated the section of his crew who chose to sail with him and who most fully responded to his desires—the most obviously disciplined bodies of the crew—and now, after the disease has spread, that ratio has greatly altered. Thus, the spread of the disease has an impact on many aspects of the literal and figurative bodies of the ship. Most significantly, Jack loses his First Lieutenant, Thomas Pullings, who he had trained and sailed with from his first command onward (Pullings does not die but is so damaged by the disease that he must be left ashore to convalesce). With the removal of Pullings, the make-up of the officers changes significantly, and the most recalcitrant of all of Jack's officers rises to the position of first officer.

In his essay "A Difficulty in Psycho-Analysis," Sigmund Freud describes the goal of the "psycho-analytic method of treatment" as to "subject this process of repression to revision and to bring about a better solution of the conflict" (138). Although the opening up of the repressed space in Jack's ship is not necessarily a process of cure—in fact, its initial impact is, as I have discussed, to spread illness through the ship—it is

5. The Captain's Bodies

the first step in a necessary process that moves toward remedying the problems of the ship and of Jack. Thus, we can begin to wonder whether this exposure is part of the ultimate process by which the ship and Jack can eventually be healed. In this essay Freud goes on to describe the place and impact he sees for psychoanalysis. Never one to be too modest, Freud sees the field that he has pioneered as the third step in forcing humanity from its narcissism after the discoveries of Copernicus and then Charles Darwin. He argues that the discoveries of psychoanalysis have been "probably the most wounding" (141). Freud's discussion of this breakdown speaks very directly to the ways in which O'Brian depicts the crises of Jack Aubrey in *Desolation Island*.

Freud begins by suggesting that "man feels himself to be supreme in his own mind" (141). Essentially Freud is building the case that if humanity's centrality has been undermined by these previous discoveries, humans still hope that they can control themselves—that they are the masters of their own minds. Typically, a ship's captain would seem to most fully resemble Freud's conception of humanity, for they seem to hold the utmost positions of authority. In *Fortune of War*, for instance, Captain Broke says, "The captain of a King's ship can do close to anything for a man except hang him without a court-martial" (300). Jack, as this passage from *Surgeon's Mate* underscores, can often be seen as a prototypical figure of power: "He was a formidable figure, standing there silent, larger than life in the twilight, by the nervous Mr. Hyde: a figure that did not seem in the best of tempers either, one that obviously had the habit of command, a figure that emanated authority" (187). In *Desolation Island*, though, holes begin to appear in this portrait. Let us note how Freud continues: "Somewhere in the core of his ego he has developed an organ of observation to keep watch on his impulses and actions and see whether they harmonize with his demands" (141). Thus, Freud describes the process of repression. The mind seeks order and tries to exclude that which would disturb or interrupt that order. It takes very little to see how Jack plays out this process writ large in his desire to keep the prisoners below the waterline.

Freud's trope in expanding upon how neuroses work is particularly telling:

> In certain diseases—including the very neuroses of which we have made special study—things are different. The ego feels uneasy; it comes up against the limits to its power in its own house, the mind. Thoughts emerge suddenly

without one's knowing where they come from, nor can one do anything to drive them away. These alien guests even seem to be more powerful than those which are at the ego's command [141].

Freud ultimately concludes that psychoanalysis reveals that *"the ego is not master of his own house"* (143). Freud's trope, the mind as house, can easily be shifted to the mind as ship. In fact, as we have discussed, it is precisely the unconscious knowledge that Jack is not the master of his own house (namely, Ashgrove Cottage)—that he cannot create the order in that space that he wishes—that, in part, drives him again and again to seek that power onboard ship. However, it seems like the inevitable movement of the novel is to reveal the very limits of Jack's ability to "master" his own ship, his own house, and this is demonstrated in the spectacular fashion of the prisoners and the epidemic of gaol-fever that severely weakens his crew, most notably through the loss of Pullings. Before we can discuss the full weight of this breakdown in Jack's control, we need to look at the other major component of what undermines Jack's autonomy—namely, the presence of women aboard his ship.

Why Jack Hates Women and Priests on His Ship

Throughout the series we repeatedly learn that, besides prisoners, Aubrey most dislikes having religious figures and women aboard ship. His reasons for disliking ministers onboard lies in what he views as hypocrisy; as he explains to Stephen, "It seems to me uncommon odd, and precious near to cant, to tell the ship's company of a man-of-war with loaded guns to love your enemy and turn the other cheek, when you know damned well that the ship and every man aboard her is there to blow the enemy out of the water if he possibly can" (86). Instead of having a parson then conduct a Sunday service when the ship "rigs church," Jack favors "reading them the Articles of War or giving them a piece about their duty: coming from me, with no bands or surplice on, why it has another effect" (86). Thus, while Jack does not necessarily see ministers as a direct threat to his authority, his explanation moves toward eliminating a religious authority on board ship and consolidating religious and legal authority in his person. After all, the Articles of War largely spell out the laws and regulations the sailors must abide by and also explains that breaking these laws will result in either execution or

5. The Captain's Bodies

another punishment decided upon by the captain, who holds ultimate power in such cases.

The problem of having women aboard ship is more complicated, however. We know that among the sins of Aubrey's youth was his having kept a woman aboard ship; and as punishment he was sent before the mast—demoted, if temporarily, from a midshipman to the rank of common sailor and hence forced to live among the men he had formerly commanded. Thus, from early in Jack's life he perhaps associated physical desire for women with a loss of control and authority. In *Desolation Island*, O'Brian seems intent on exploring the consequences of a woman's presence aboard ship by constructing several of the narrative strands around the key prisoner, Louisa Wogan. She has not, however, come on board the ship alone. There are three female prisoners in all. It seems each somehow poses a threat to the ship. The gypsy woman tells members of the crew that the ship contains a ghost, and the superstitious sailors thus become convinced that their journey is ill-fated. Stephen also discovers that Salubrity Boswell, "the Gipsy woman," is carrying her brother-in-law's child (as a means of avoiding execution and for following her husband to Australia). Stephen discovers that Wogan's servant, described as a half-wit, is spreading venereal diseases; or, as Stephen puts it, "A fireship is among us, and her unlucky name is Peggy Barnes" (178). Jack's response to this information exceeds that of Stephen's in its dramatic tone: "There is this Peggy of yours, that will reduce the whole ship's company to a parcel of noseless, toothless, bald paralytics unless she is headed up in a barrel with no bunghole" (179). Stephen appears to seriously consider having the armourer or sailmaker devise some kind of chastity belt in order to restrict her behavior. In this particular instance we see a clear connection to the particular issue of women and the larger issues raised by the presence of the prisoners more broadly—namely, they serve to infect the crew with disease. Again we see the ways in which this notion of disease often becomes tied to a kind of rot: Jack imagines the men crumbling, coming apart in much the manner that we know the *Leopard* is physically disintegrating. The cure again seems to be repression. Jack imagines, however tongue-in-cheek, imprisoning the woman in a barrel, and Stephen contemplates much the same thing in his vision of the chastity belt. These passages recall the discussion of my previous chapter in regards to how the series depicts the sexual needs of the body. Both approaches floated by the protagonists here suggest the ways in which women make men vulnerable, and since men cannot be disciplined or made so docile so as to contain these desires, something must be done to contain the women instead.

The problems posed by the female presence, then, are not very subtle. Essentially, they pose a threat to the order of the ship by first posing a threat to the order of the male body. Despite Peggy's sexual relations with the crew, this process of disordering the ship is highlighted most directly in the novel by the effects of Louisa Wogan on other members of the ship. Not coincidently, I would argue, the emergence of the problems created by the presence of Wogan do not appear at the same time as Jack's venture into the hold merely by chance. As part of the measures Stephen prescribes for the health of the prisoners, he gets Jack's permission to escort Wogan on daily walks on deck. Thus, along with the other prisoners, what has been stowed below must be exposed to all. As Stephen brings Wogan on to the deck of the *Leopard* the first time, the narrator notes an immediate response: "The talk instantly stopped; the sextants drooped; Babbington [the officer of the watch renowned for his interest in sex] straightened to his full five foot six and darted an old clay pipe from his pocket; the *Leopard* came up half a point, her headsails gave a hint of shiver" (108). The conflation of these descriptions emphasizes the ship and the crew equally finding their focus disrupted.

Things quickly escalate from there. First Jack, completely naked from his daily swim, finds that he "caught Mrs. Wogan's astonished gaze full in the eye. He blushed like a boy, seized the fully-clothed Pullings as a shield and darted down the main hatchway" (122–123). A psychoanalytic reading of that incident seems almost too obvious to engage in, but I will just mention in passing the fact that the presence of a woman clearly disrupts the world of men, and her vision—in a kind of reversal—reduces Jack to immaturity (he hides behind his figurative extension in Pullings, his first officer). While this reduction in Jack's authority and control is relatively temporary, he comes to recognize that Wogan inspires greater problems with discipline aboard the ship. He soon finds himself reprimanding the Marine officer, Captain Moore, declaring, "I will not have my ship run like a bawdy-house: I will have a taut ship. I will have my orders obeyed. And if there is the least hint of recurrence, by God, I shall break them without mercy" (138). This episode leads directly to one of Jack's more extended misogynist diatribes: "I have

5. The Captain's Bodies

always loathed women, from clew to earing; hook, line, and sinker; root and branch. I always said this would happen you remember; I was against it from the start. Damn her for a flibbertigibbet, the hussy. With her we would be sailing along as sweet as—" (141). Jack picks up this theme later on in a moment the narrator describes as Jack "particularly inflamed against the sex": "They make a sorry heart, an heavy countenance, a wounded mind, weak hands, and feeble knees.... And that is in the Bible: I read it myself. Damn them all. There are only three women aboard, but they might as well be a troop of basilisks" (179). These rants clearly indicate Jack's sense that Wogan and her companions have disrupted his authority, and this gets figuratively played out in Jack's notion that somehow the ship itself has become disrupted by their presence; hence the ship appears not to be sailing as Jack would hope, and he somehow attaches this failing to the presence of the women. They also literally appear to damage and weaken the male body; thus, both the figurative and literal bodies at work here susceptible to the power and attraction of women's bodies.

These passages in which Jack appears to demonize women refer overtly to their effects on the crew, but he is not immune either. In fact, a fairly short time after his rant against women appears in the text, we learn that "Jack sprang from his cot at dawn, in answer to the rapping on the door, his mind, snatched from a dream of a soft, consenting Mrs. Wogan" (193). The next chapter in the novel begins in a similar fashion: "Dawn broke, and once again Jack was knocked up; once again he was torn from the arms of an ideal Mrs. Wogan" (206). As I have discussed in the previous chapter, O'Brian frequently alludes to Jack's more than healthy sexual appetite, so these dreams may not appear unusual. However, in the context of this particular novel, O'Brian clearly seeks to emphasize—through the repetition of basically the same sequence within such a short space—that Jack struggles to control himself; his body responds even as he knows that he should not. We see a clear indication of this situation earlier in the novel during one of Mrs. Wogan's early appearances on deck. Jack at first hears her laughing, and the language of this indirect discourse describing the laugh evokes the sea itself and perhaps a bit of Lawrentian sexual symbolism: "Again the laugh began, low but quite near, by the poop rail: it went on and on, swelling, rolling in pure amusement." In some ways the key moment of this passage, however, comes in Jack's response: "For the life of him he could not resist: disagreeable though his situation was, and heavy in his mind, he felt an answering catch in the region of his stomach" (160). Throughout the series we see O'Brian's interest in depicting this struggle between the desires of the mind and the desires of the body, and again and again we see how the body cannot fully be denied.

Although my main focus in this section is on Jack and the crew, I also want to note that Jack's primary foil, Stephen, also finds himself fighting his desires for Wogan. In Jack, such desires come as expected—even by only the fifth novel in the series—but from Stephen this appears fairly extraordinary. Stephen confesses to this situation in his journal, noting first that "I have been aware that an advance on my part would not be cruelly resented," and then more to the point: "Furthermore, deep stirrings within my own person are by no means absent: a consequence of my abstention, opium in all its forms being an antaphrodesiac, counteracting venereal desire" (132). Stephen here contemplates whether "does duty require that I should resume [opium use]?" because in his work spying on Mrs. Wogan, a "chaste mind is essential" (132). Later on he will have an extended discussion with Michael Herapath, a young American who has stowed on the ship because of his love for Mrs. Wogan. In the course of his long interview with Herepath, the young stowaway describes how he has used opium and how one can avoid becoming addicted. Stephen sees his attraction to Mrs. Wogan again as a firm rationale for the need to begin taking opium again: "Mrs. Wogan's beauty, her pretty ways, and above all that infinitely diverting laugh, have stirred my amorous propensities these last many days. I have caught myself peering at her bosom, her ear, the nape of her neck, too frequently by far.... There is no doubt that duty directs me to my laudanum and thus to chastity" (192). Now, quite obviously, we can read this passage as the logical maneuverings of a self-serving opium addict, and that certainly is true. Nevertheless, one way or another Wogan becomes a triggering mechanism for the desires of the body. Stephen either gives in to his sexual desires—which the novels frequently suggest become relatively dormant due to his addiction—or to his body's craving for opium.

Ironically, in his rationalizing his need to return to opium, it is not so much the mind dictating what the body will do, but the body seemingly driving the mind to find motivations that will allow it to be satisfied—whether that satisfaction is sexual or not. In a way, this passage reflects in miniature the larger patterns of the novels—both in terms of

5. The Captain's Bodies

sexual attraction and in terms of its attitudes towards Stephen's addictions. Later in the novel, when Stephen detects the outbreak of scurvy aboard ship, the split between mind and body comes to the fore in Stephen's observations to Herapath: "Nothing grieves me more than the dependence of the mind upon the body's nutriment. It points to a base necessitarianism that I rebel against with all the vehemence my spirit can engender" (271). In short, Stephen would like to hold fast to a kind of enlightenment view of the mind's preeminence, but he can also not deny the evidence of the case of scurvy that the body needs the nutrients of "sovereign lime-juice" (271). (In fact, as it turns out, these men who have succumbed to scurvy have done so by trading away their grog, which contains the scurvy-preventing juice.)

Mixed No More: The Division of The Leopard, *Its Crew and Its Captain*

For a time, Jack and his ship appear to be able to move past the prisoners, the gaol-fever, and the presence of women aboard ship; however, the crisis in the captain's bodies appears eventually through two fairly spectacular incidents—the sinking of the *Waakzaamheid,* a much more powerful Dutch ship, and the *Leopard*'s unfortunate encounter with an iceberg. The divisions among the crew, however, have been there more or less from the start. After we join the *Leopard* at sea, we learn that Jack has obtained an officer like Babbington, "a young man he had formed himself" (71-72)—a character from earlier in the series (in fact, when we first see Babbington, Jack contemplates how best to invest his authority into the young lieutenant). It seems like a similar situation will hold true for the majority of his crew, but we find out that he lost one hundred good crewmembers just prior to setting sail and had them replaced by a motley assortment of unskilled men and folks who chose "the sea to a country gaol" (77)—the echoes of the prisoners in the crew seems rightly ominous. In essence, then, Jack will have a divided crew—divided between men with experience and men without, men who have sailed with Jack and Stephen and men who have not. For a time, these divisions, like the prisoners and the disease they carry, will either remain hidden or will be suitably repressed. Similar divisions appear among the officers—with Pullings and Babbington being followers of Jack, and the other officers being potential problems (for example, the Master, Larkin, will prove both a murderer and a Jonah to the crew).

The cracks that rend the body—both literal and figurative—begin to appear in the aftermath of the gaol-fever and the loss of Pullings. The loss of Pullings has two equally detrimental effects. First, Jack loses a first officer whom he has trained and sailed with for years, one who can fully extend Jack's figurative control onto the crew and the officers in the gunroom. Before Pullings succumbs to the fever, he is so nearly a perfect extension of Jack that Jack muses that Pullings "relieves me of almost all my work" (124). Second, the removal of Pullings means the promotion of Grant, a former captain who was assigned to the ship because of his knowledge of the waters they are to sail on the way to Australia. However, Grant, despite his age and experience, has almost no history of combat and is quite beyond Jack's influence at this point. He cannot be "disciplined" to conform to Jack's expectations. Jack confides to Stephen that he had recognized the problem from the start, because "you cannot have two captains in a ship," and Grant's experiences had "set him above subordination" (126). Even before Pullings leaves, Jack indicates his fear of the consequence: "How I hope to God that Stephen will let Pullings stay.... A year or so with that fellow Grant as my first would be..." (161). The thought remains unformed. In essence, Pullings served as a mediating force, repressing Grant's influence—both in the gunroom and in overseeing the affairs of the ship. Although Jack never finishes expressing his sentiment, his fears will be realized soon enough.

Later, in the midst of the chase with the Dutch ship, Jack will make the effects of Pullings absence more clear: "How often I think of Tom Pullings. It is not only that I could leave everything to him, action or no action, knowing he would what we have always thought right, but I so often wonder how he does" (197–198). This passage has an intriguing shift in its pronouns, as Jack suggests that the proper mode of behavior is one that "we have always thought right"; however, what he actually means is that Tom has come to see what proper behavior is as something dictated by what Jack thinks proper to do. In other words, Pullings so corresponds to his desires that Jack conflates the two of them in his thoughts. They are one body, a royal we.

Among the most immediate indications of the loss of Pullings is the effect his absence has among the officers. Stephen observes "the curi-

5. The Captain's Bodies

ous division of wardroom into two parties," a division that pits Grant and those he has befriended against the new second officer, Babbington, another longtime follower of Jack's (168). Later we are told that "Grant began to assert his authority as president of the mess" (178). As Jack begins the process of trying to rebuild his crew, a process he often attempts throughout the series by practicing gunnery—an activity Jack believes teaches teamwork and pride, and integrates the men of the crew—he again feels Pullings absence. "Grant was dead weight," since Grant "could not know the inward nature of a fight at sea: nor did he seem willing to learn" (174). This failure would not be so problematic except for the fact that "his tolerably obvious attitude, infected many of those whose idea of battle was as hazy as his own" (175). Thus we again have the language of disease. Like the outbreak of gaol-fever, Grant represents a danger, as he can spread his harm to the larger body of the crew in much the same manner. He can cause further rot. Or in his desire to be captain, we have the danger of a kind of deformed body, one with two heads. Nevertheless, in these moments Jack persists in hoping that he can continue "with the task of turning the *Leopard* into a fighting-machine as efficient as his means would allow," even if it means adjusting his methods (175). Again the metaphor, while somewhat clichéd, is telling in its suggestion of the need to transform men and individuals into a machine with interchangeable parts that he can control.

However, as the two aforementioned incidents of the plot suggest, Jack will struggle in this endeavor. As the novel has prefigured through the attempts to repress the prisoners and the women, the figurative body of the captain has been weakened, and Grant becomes an integral part of the division within the body. It is perhaps no coincidence that after Jack chastises Grant for a failure of seamanship—"For God's sake, Mr. Grant, don't you know enough to take in your topgallants in such a case?"—he calls him a "cursed old woman" (194). When gunfire is exchanged between the Dutch ship and the *Leopard*, O'Brian makes the connections between feminizing Grant and the divisions and weakness in the hold of the captain explicit through Stephen's observations. Stephen compares Grant's complaining to that of his "maternal grandmother in her last years," and wonders "whether [his] manliness would reassert itself in an obvious crisis" (213). We are told that Grant has taken to complaining, and among his subjects are "the ill conduct of the government, of political parties, and of those about the King: a general denigration, a frequent imputation of motives, always discernible" (213). Later, in a similar fashion, Grant will repeatedly raise questions about Jack's decisions. In response to some of Jack's orders, Grant responds by criticizing his course: "I speak with thirty-five years' experience, a prudent commander will never go south of thirty-nine degrees [as Jack has ordered the ship to do]" (241). Some old saw about chefs and a single kitchen creeps into the mind at such moments.

Seemingly, Grant finds his opportunity to fully assert his authority in the aftermath of the battle with the Dutch ship. The situation and setting of this battle for authority seems a confusing one in that we might suspect Grant's limited role in the great victory would have weakened his position. However, in firing off the cannon shot that ultimately destroyed the enemy ship and killed over six hundred men, Jack had been severely injured. He sustains both a head injury—one that gives him a concussion and also severely bloodies his face—and an injury to his leg, leaving him without feeling in it (he only realizes this loss of feeling once Stephen mentions the leg) and the chance that the leg itself will need to be removed. While Stephen suggests the head injury gives Jack the appearance of Nelson—who had lost his eye—it creates a physical echo of the ship's fragility. After all, in a sense, his body is a figure for the ship itself.

Jack's position becomes compromised in other ways as well. Because Jack was not triumphant at the thought of so many men dying, rumors had begun to surface "about the Captain's intellects being disturbed" (239). One of his officers, a marine named Moore, while defending Jack to others, makes the case based solely on Jack's failure to take joy in the victory. In essence, Jack becomes horrified in the moment of victory at the fact that the battle cost the lives of over six hundred men on the Dutch ship, after the Dutch captain transformed the ground rules of the battle from capture to destruction. Moore sees only the remarkable victory of a smaller and undermanned ship (undermanned since so many men were lost to disease). Grant, however, seems anxious to read the captain's response as an indication of larger problems. What Jack actually mutters at the moment of victory may be telling. Upon seeing the Dutch ship go down, he says, "My God, oh my God.... Six hundred men" (236). In essence, Jack's response may be read as a slip in his position, since throughout the novel—and the series more broadly—the ways in which the captain of the ship has his authority equated with God's (and

5. The Captain's Bodies

with the King's, who also has his authority as God given). Here, however, he clearly wishes to abandon that authority; he did not wish the power to destroy so many men's lives (and especially when, as he indicates earlier in the chase when he comes to realize that the Dutch captain is intent on making it a mortal affair on a grand scale, he does not view death as a necessity).

In other words, Grant sees Jack's injury as his chance, but there may be some level on which Jack also wishes to turn over the authority, for the burden has become too great. Jack later confides to Stephen that this post-battle despair is common to Jack's experience—he often deflates after the violence of war—but the scale here of the battle and the depression is perhaps greater than in any other such moment in the series. Thus, a very real opening emerges, however briefly, for Grant—an opening he suspects. When Stephen tells Grant that Jack "must not be disturbed; disturbance might agitate his mind," Grant anxiously asks, "Do you mean he is not right in the head?" For if that were the case, Grant could take over the ship. Thus, in the aftermath of the battle, a crew that had already been divided and fractured becomes mirrored in the physical disability of the captain's body. With his injuries and absence, rumors spread throughout the ship and seem to escalate the disintegration of the crew and the situation—at one point the chaplain asks Stephen if Jack is about to expire. In response to these rumors and the anxiety among the crew, Jack makes an effort to finally leave his cabin and appear on deck—and to ultimately regain the authority he has begun to lose; however, shortly after his emergence on deck, "He clapped his hand to his forehead, turned, stumbled on his game leg, and fell flat on the deck," leading Grant to notice that Jack's "wound had opened, and the bandage was soaked already, the red blood dripping down his face" (246). Jack tries to make the best of it because "he was fully aware of the importance of the invulnerable, infallible commander, superior to all mortal ills, particularly with a crew like the Leopard's"; but it is clear Jack can no longer present that infallibility, a body untouched, stable and "invulnerable" (246).

I began this chapter with some discussion of the kind of readerly frustration this novel builds, and I would read this sequence as a part of it. O'Brian's use of Freytag's pyramid—the basic plot structure of rising action, climax, falling action, and resolution—has always been a somewhat uncertain one. Almost as if he seeks to work against the conventions of a typical adventure story, which would feature a good deal of rising action, culminating in adventures set at sea, with a great sea battle, O'Brian tends to upend this formula. If we are looking for a climax to this story, then, it would have to be the defeat of the Dutch ship. That happens, in the Norton paperback edition, on page 236, almost a hundred pages before the novel ends. With over a quarter of the novel left to go, the shift from climax to falling action here is precipitous; it's as if the reader collapses down onto the deck next to our fallen, bloody, and, frankly, largely impotent hero. As I have contended from the outset of this project, O'Brian has always, from the very start of the series, undercut or deflated Jack's position as a hero, and nothing could more dramatically exemplify that undercutting than literally dropping Jack to his own deck. The novels often seem constructed upon a tension between what we might call—and I apologize for the cliché and metaphor (that is not really a metaphor)—smooth sailing and crisis. We, along with Jack, take joy in smooth sailing, but smooth sailing is akin to "happy families" for Tolstoy. They provide no sustainable interest. Readers and novels—well, almost all narratives—need conflict. Conflict works like tension, though; we want it because it provides interest, but we also come to seek release from it (this process resembles Freud's hydraulic model of the mind—the pressures build and must be released in order to return to stasis once more).

The challenging nature of this particular novel for the reader is that it offers little smooth sailing—and I would say that the odd part of being a reader of these novels lies in the fact that these moments do bespeak of a kind of harmony which, however impossible to sustain, does give joy (to the characters and, I daresay, to us readers)—little in the way of climactic or even rising action, but a lot of sustained, low-level conflict and tension. The parallel plot of the novel, Stephen's attempts to upend the French spy network by way of "poisoning" the body of spies seems to be similarly collapsed by the novel's main climax, since the chase with the Dutch ship had taken the ship too far beyond the Cape, where Stephen had hoped to provide the necessary dispatches. Jack's fall leads rather directly into the novel's next crisis, the possible capsizing of the *Leopard* after it hits an iceberg—but it is a crisis derived from crisis. The situation arises from both the vacuum of power left by Jack's absence (and Grant's desire to fill that vacuum) and the divide among the crew, particularly its officers. Stephen overhears an argument between Babbington, who

5. The Captain's Bodies

wishes to discuss matters with the captain, and Grant, who believes that the captain simply is too infirm to be consulted at this time (obviously, those beliefs have been shaped by his own desires). Though with Babbington's assistance, Jack manages to get out on the deck, the course that will lead them into the iceberg has already been set; seemingly moments later the ship hits the iceberg, leading to "an appearance of complete disorder" (251).

The *Leopard*'s collision with the iceberg provides a climax for the novel's metaphoric play of bodies, if not the plot. As I have sketched out here, O'Brian seems to draw direct connections between the body of Jack, the captain and a stand-in for the King and perhaps God (or both) aboard ship, and both the ship itself and the crew—as each in a way comes to represent a kind of metonymic extension of the king, and vice versa. However, the novel also suggests—both in the kind of political metaphor and the Freudian psychic metaphor—that what appears to be whole or has been made whole (that is, the revamping of the ship itself, the creating of unity, eventually, in and among the crew) has been an illusion, perhaps much in the way that Freud suggests that our control over ourselves is a self-delusion (Stephen's confessions about our powerlessness in the face of scurvy without attending to the body's needs serves as yet another echo of this issue). In the aftermath of the battle, Jack appears on the verge of literally coming apart—he may lose his leg—and he cannot muster the physical power to stand unassisted on the deck. Meanwhile, the wardroom, already fissured, divides even further. In the midst of these fractures, the *Leopard* crashes into an iceberg, ultimately sustaining a leak that the crew cannot locate. This helpless search for the leak brings the problems of what has been hidden beneath, in the lower decks, back around once more. In other words, in the leak—the rending of the ship itself—disguised, hidden, and now inaccessible as the water pours in, we have a kind of duplication of the scenario from the novel's opening where the prisoners had been hidden and out of Jack's control.

Careful readers will note that O'Brian had foreshadowed these events earlier in the novel when Pullings describes how crews typically respond to ships running "aground": Pullings tells Stephen that the "old belief" of sailors is that "once a ship's aground, or once she can't steer, then the captain's authority is gone: that's the law they say, and nothing will get it out of their stupid heads" (104). When the *Leopard* struck the iceberg it lost its rudder. The ship could not be steered. Pullings' lament of this behavior suggests the limits of "discipline" and "disciplining" (the many times throughout the series that the superstitions of the sailors must be dealt with—such as the faux exorcism Stephen performs in this novel—offers yet another example of these limits). For a series, then, which often seems to celebrate naval discipline, these novels regularly suggest its limits, the ways in which it appears to be tenuously holding on. In other words, it seems that the novels, while celebrating the comforts of order, realize that the natural state appears to be chaos; it takes but one mishap, one rumor, one sailor coming to resemble a Jonah, for the cracks in that sheen of order to begin to be revealed.

Perhaps what makes Jack such a good commander is his ability to plug these leaks. In some respects, the crisis of the iceberg can be read as something of a narrative tease. What I mean by that is the desperate attempts to salvage the ship immediately afterward suggest the idea that crisis will restore rather than destroy the ship, the crew, the literal and figurative bodies. And in some ways it does, but not in the expected ways. Jack begins to become active in trying to find the leak and pump the ship; thus, the new crisis begins to see a reviving of the captain's body, while Grant "had behaved extremely well" as they fought against the leak (255). O'Brian, though, does not clearly take us in one direction or another; in other words, the bodies do not either fully recover wholeness nor fully come apart. Since the crisis seemingly cannot be averted—they have pumped and pumped without much success—the renewed spirit of cooperation seemingly cannot last. Bonden, so frequently the voice of the lower decks, tries to explain the situation to Stephen. Referring to the crew, he says, "I doubt that they'll last out today.... I mean the hands that don't know the captain" (257). If part of Jack's mission had been to bring the crew together, to make it one body that acted as an extension of his will, the clear indication here is that Jack failed. In short, the crew divides—not exactly upon the lines Bonden draws, but close to them—Grant sails off, and Larkin, the "Jonah," is dispatched in the chaos.

In some ways the denouement, with its conclusion that does not fully stamp a closure on events, seems typical of the series, but it nevertheless reads somewhat strangely. The crisis of repairing the ship, and the growing discord and division of the crew, does see Jack experience something of a rebirth. After allowing Grant to leave—and thus in some

5. The Captain's Bodies

ways avoiding the situation resulting in a mutiny in official terms—Jack feels that the "shift between himself and the present broke down, vanished entirely." In essence, the narrator suggests that Jack has never quite been a part of things since the day he sank the Dutch ship, and "the moment of its breaking, of his coming wholly to life, was exquisitely painful" (260). This passage and what it describes can be read in a number of ways. On the one hand, it suggests a kind of common description of birth/rebirth, with its struggle and pain (and clearly coming back into contact with actual life means coming back into contact with actual pain). On the other hand, we can also locate the somewhat paradoxical element of the division of the crew—and with it the eventual excise of those elements of the crew that Jack could never fully "discipline"—leading to a kind of unification of Jack. He both psychically and physically seems to be reuniting. As with much in O'Brian's Aubrey-Maturin novels, though, this matter gets complicated, as Stephen reflects on "the general health of the crew"—that is, the crew that remains on the *Leopard*—as they continue to deal with the crisis of the missing rudder and the leak. After postulating first that this might be the result of the greater room in the sleeping cabin and thus promoting better sleep—in other words, a scientific explanation based on the notion that the body dictates the states of the mind—another crew member, a Turkish eunuch, explains Stephen's "singular harmony" quite differently: "We got rid of the Jonah, is all that matters" (267). Thus, in contrast to Stephen's theory, and from the mouth of a man who has been physically altered in order to curb his bodily desires, we get an entirely psychological (that is, one rooted in belief rather than physical phenomena) argument for what has brought the crew back together. We are left to choose.

In fact, as Stephen finds himself about to concede the point, cries of "land ho" break out, signaling the start of the very end sequence of the novel (268). In some ways this ending sequence stands apart from much of what I have discussed, in part because Jack's role in this ending becomes largely marginalized. Jack manages to steer the ship into the bay of Desolation Island, where they feed on the animal life of the island and the cabbages planted by American whalers, as Jack seeks to repair his ship. However, much of the narrative focus centers on Stephen here and his attempts to use Wogan and Herapath to undermine the French spy network. History, in a sense, also returns as a limit and motivator for plot in this closing section, as an American whaler soon follows the crippled *Leopard* into the bay. In essence, tension arises both because of the previous role played by the *Leopard*—under a different command, of course—in an ugly and historically real incident with an American ship, and the fact that the novels have chronologically reached the precipice of the War of 1812. While Jack continues to work on repairing the ship and hopes to be able to negotiate some kind of exchange with the American ship in order to use their forge to repair the *Leopard*'s rudder, the tension over his position aboard ship, his ability to maintain control, to have his way, seems to largely fade from the narrator's attentions. Instead, we move about with Stephen as he explores, provides medical services to the desperate American ship, and not all that subtly—at least from my non-professional spy point of view—encourages Herapath and Wogan to escape on the American ship ... along with the poison information he has made available to the couple.

On some level the ending reads like a moment of some exhaustion. Everything has been spent on holding the ship together, Jack's recovery, and the saving of what crew they have left. The very ending of the novel finds us on what has becomes Stephen's island in the bay, sitting next to Bondon. It reads quite cinematically, as if we gaze from their point of view upon a setting sun as the two strands of the novel's plots find their ultimate conclusion. On the one side of the imaginary film screen of our minds we can see the marines struggling with the rudder, as Bonden mocks their progress, whereas Stephen intensely watches to see if Wogan has convinced Herapath to assist her in escaping to the American ship (they are both American citizens, after all). Eventually, Bonden spots the couple, but Stephen tells him to let them go. The novel ultimately ends on a bit of irony, as they both hear Wogan's infectious laugh—the one that caught Jack's stomach—with a "fine triumphant ring," she being unaware that the triumph had instead been achieved by Stephen. We might read this conclusion in a few different ways. On the one hand, it seems as if Humpty Dumpty was put back together: the Leopard has been repaired, Jack now has a relatively healthy crew he can work with, and Jack seems to be returning to health. However, Jack has received injuries that will, as Stephen surmises, erase much of the youth remaining in his countenance; he has lost all of the prisoners and hence failed in that part of his mission; and he has lost a large portion of his crew, not to mention most of his weapons (thrown overboard in the desperate flight or desperate attempts to keep the ship afloat). Only Stephen suc-

5. The Captain's Bodies

ceeds in his mission—though he largely orchestrated the parameters of his mission—and his story has largely been in the background for most of the novel. Has Jack learned a lesson about the limits of his real and symbolic self, about his ability to create or establish order? If so, what can he or any of us do with that information? For Jack, I would say it is something of a paradox: in other words, knowing those limits cannot prevent him from trying to exceed them or at least get to their very edge. The novel began with Jack going on and on about custom, something he likes to prattle on about (in *H.M.S. Surprise* we learn that "Naval custom is holy at sea" [104]); and custom insists that the captain must be himself and something other—larger, symbolic and impossible. For instance, a passage from the later novel *Yellow Admiral,* in which Jack laments Stephen's absence, underscores the way custom defines the captain. Jack misses Stephen when he's away—as a voice of dissent:

> For a great while Jack Aubrey had sailed with Stephen Maturin, and now missed his companion quite severely—a wholly human and often contradictory companion, essentially different from the only other guests he would invite, lieutenants, master's mates or midshipmen, who were all debarred by custom, and by common prudence, from disagreeing with the skipper on any point whatsoever: and who in any case were not to speak until they were spoken to [142].

As this novel illustrates, however, even knowing the illusion of that elevation—should he be willing to accept it—cannot allow him to transform or transcend that custom.

Conclusion: Weighing Anchor

"May I too congratulate you, Admiral dear?" These words come oh so very late in the Aubrey-Maturin series, a mere few paragraphs before the end of the final novel, *Blue at the Mizzen*. They follow the announcement that Jack will be "hoisting [his] flag, blue at the Mizzen"—that, in short, he has crossed the line which divides post-captains from admirals. You could be excused for guessing that these words come from Jack's wife Sophie, but they come instead from Stephen, to whom Jack had said, "By God, Stephen, I am so glad it was you brought me this news" (261).

We could say that at long last O'Brian settled for a conclusion rather than a stopping, since the long journey of Jack's career seems to have climaxed in the aftermath of Napoleon's defeat at Waterloo. The novel appeared in 1999, shortly before O'Brian passed away, in January 2000, at the age of 85 while working on yet another Aubrey-Maturin novel. In the Norton paperback edition we can find snippets and blurbs which suggest a mixture of valedictory and eulogy. From the gifted historian Amanda Foreman's review in *The New York Times* we hear that "There is nothing that rivals Patrick O'Brian's achievement in his chosen genre." John Casey, in the *Washington Post*, compares his passion for the novels to his daughter's love of Harry Potter. Like a boy resisting bedtime, Rob Layman says, "I want Stephen and Jack to go on and on..." in the *Philadelphia Inquirer*. These reviews remind us in many ways of the issues with which this project began and the issues I have tried to address. Foreman's review seems to both take for granted the issue of genre and, by reference to genre, dampen the achievement she wishes to salute. Casey compares the novels to fantasy fiction—but for adults rather than young adults. Yet I also share, like most fans of the series, Layman's seemingly adolescent wish.

Conclusion: Weighing Anchor

At various times in this book I have talked of the pleasure the characters have in setting out to sea, of weighing anchor, and of the joys when captain, crew, ship, and seas find harmony. The very end of O'Brian's last completed novel speaks quite plainly to these notions, for, "after a last salute Jack glanced aloft—still the sweet west wind—and then he looked fore and aft: a fine clear deck, hands all at their stations and all beaming with pleasure," before Jack gives the order to depart (262). Ever resistant to dramatic conclusion, even here—at what turned out to be the end—we get a departure but also a new beginning. And I do so love that O'Brian worked one last colon into the novels.

I want to conclude my discussion of these novels by returning to some of the questions with which I started: namely, I would like to contemplate more fully on why I share Layman's desire for the series to never end, what brings me back again and again (and perhaps, if you are a fan of the series, answering that question for you as well), while also considering the implications of the discussions of the relationship between bodies and the novels with which I have been so preoccupied. The reasons for deriving pleasure from these texts, to borrow a famous phrase of the French theorist Roland Barthes, may be seemingly as numerous as O'Brian's many fans. Consider, for instance, the rationale offered by Richard Snow's blurb for *Blue at the Mizzen:* "In an era that likes adventure yarns, no books offer better adventure than these." I don't know that I have ever thought of the last forty years or so as such an era, and, as I have discussed elsewhere in this book, I am not sure that O'Brian's over-riding mission was to deliver "adventure yarns"; nevertheless, I will concede that action can be found. And I am not immune to it. I am sure that when the *Waakzaamheid* chased the *Leopard*, seemingly on the verge of dispatching Jack and Stephen to eternity, my breathing became more uneven and my heart raced—and I kept reading until Jack sunk the enemy while sustaining (to no experienced reader's surprise) major injuries. But adventure gets us through once. If adventure alone drove the readerly passions for these novels, then these texts would be much more disposable than they have proven to be.

What else might drive our passions for these novels? The blurbs again prove remarkably helpful. Foreman declares that O'Brian's "novels embrace with loving clarity the full richness of the 18-century world." This assertion emphasizes the attraction of historical fiction more broadly—a chance to explore, learn about, and simply, through the illu-

Conclusion: Weighing Anchor

sory magic of storytelling, bring back to life a world that has departed. Such reading journeys speak to our desire to learn our origins, perhaps our nostalgia for what we consider—and the reasons can be many—better times (for better can be measured even in times of great pain and danger, because those times require heroism, action, commitment: you get the idea). And Foreman highlights the particularities of O'Brian's chosen past—namely, the late eighteenth century, a time where powerful movements like the Enlightenment and Romanticism emerged, a time of great social and political upheaval and strife. As someone who loves history and has found this period greatly fascinating, I will concede that Foreman may, at least in part, have struck a chord with me. Other reviewers mention O'Brian's humor, and I would also contend that O'Brian's wit—as my liberal quoting has hoped to elucidate—rewards us again and again. The books make me laugh out loud. And very few things do.

I want, however, to offer two other possibilities—friendship and bodies. Let us start with the former. The passage from *Blue at the Mizzen*, with which we began, underscores the extraordinary closeness of Jack and Stephen. Stephen's affection comes through with his frequent addresses of "dear" and "brother," whereas Jack can think of no other person who he would rather give him the greatest news of his professional life. In short, I would contend that no sustained literary work surpasses these novels in their portrait of friendship. In the previous chapter I quoted *Desolation Island* at length as part of my extended analysis of that novel, but I have omitted what may be my favorite passage from the entire series. It occurs early in the novel when, after Stephen asks Jack for a loan, Jack says to Stephen: "I beg you will not speak of obligation. Between you and me, it would be precious strange to speak of obligation" (27). In other words, with true friendship you do not act out of duty, of a sense of fulfilling some legal arrangement or piece of the social contract; you assist the other person because you love the other person. The novels begin with the birth of this friendship; we see it strained almost immediately to breaking, but ultimately we come to see it both grow and sustain itself. In many ways the novels become an ode to that friendship, and we, as readers, come to share in it. How can we give it up?

Friendship speaks on some level to the comfort level readers come to find in these novels. When people ask about why they re-read books, they often use some cliché along the lines of, "It's like returning to an

Conclusion: Weighing Anchor

old friend." No doubt, after we have read even a few of these novels, we get to know Jack and Stephen—and many of the other characters, like the loveable Bonden—as we do very few people in real life. If we re-read the novels, then, yes, we can ease back into those familiar patterns, akin to reuniting with such a good friend that, even after long silences, conversation comes easy, steady, and full. No doubt, too, re-reading these novels provides a return to texts where we know the plot, the outcomes, and where most characters end up remarkably safe. (Let's note the exceptions: I can forgive O'Brian for Diana's dramatic demise, but Bonden! How could you?) Humans seem to enjoy re-experiencing familiar patterns, familiar rhythms, as writers as dissimilar as Aristotle and J. Hillis Miller have suggested.

Friendship, thus, offers one explanation. As I write this section, I cannot help but think of a line from Christopher Nolan's postmodern film *noir Memento:* "I always thought the joy of reading was not knowing what happens next." In a flashback, the film's main character sees himself saying this to his wife as she begins to thumb through a fraying, much-handled novel. The irony is that *Memento* is a film I have re-watched numerous times and which starts at its chronological ending. Nolan's film, like many Modernist novels, such as Joyce's *Ulysses,* practically requires the reader or viewer to return; they ask to be re-read, not read. However, O'Brian's work does not call out for this kind of re-reading exactly. His work is not so intentionally fraught with difficulty that a reader can only hope to grasp its means after first experiencing a near crippling incapacity (and this from someone who loves and teaches *Ulysses!*). I once heard the French novelist Alain Robbe-Grillet refer to writing by Joyce and Kafka as a bad choice for bedtime reading. One cannot say the same for O'Brian.

Nevertheless, I hope this volume has made the case that O'Brian's work not only bears but rewards close attention. And this is where I would, in part, make the case for the significance of bodies in encouraging readers to return so frequently to the series. O'Brian's complicated use of, and remarkable attention to, the body both as a figure—that is, as something that suggests meaning by way of comparison or association (metonymy or metaphor)—and as real, material, biological systems helps provide depth and complexity; it provides another way back and through the series besides comfort and friendship. Perhaps friendship can also be thought of as a need for the body as well—for readers as well as the

Conclusion: Weighing Anchor

characters. While I would not go so far as to say that this attention to the body needs to be seen as either the transcendent factor for the novels' depth or the primary argument for the novels' hold on its readership, I would, however, argue that it clearly provides a remarkable breadth to the works; it is part of the ways in which characters gain depth, where issues gain traction, and where O'Brian's ambiguous relationship to questions of genre come to the fore.

This attention also lends itself to the exploration of philosophical underpinnings to O'Brian's vast and lengthy project. The novels use this attention to question our assumptions—about ourselves, about our culture, about how we interact with our worlds and experience historical force, and how we seek to cope with our own physical selves. The world becomes written upon the body, and the body can be read. But interpretation of the body is as problematic as any other kind of interpretation—perhaps more so. Of course, bodies also become quite clearly interlaced with both O'Brian's and our own sense of mortality. Throughout the series, then, O'Brian explores the mind and body split in compelling and, most preciously, sympathetic ways, perhaps suggesting, in fact, that the split is, after all, a false dichotomy, that perhaps the greatest deception the mind plays upon itself is to see itself as divorced, as independent, from the body which houses it.

Here I find myself returning, at least partially, to where I began. The reviewers I have cited at the outset of this concluding section seem to wrestle continuously with problems of genre. I have contended that this problem—namely, that O'Brian's work falls into a particular kind of genre that sits below the "literary"—is a false one because an investigation into the texts suggests the ways in which these novels resist easy categorization. In fact, O'Brian shows a keen awareness of this apparent problem and frequently subverts our attempts to read the text based on preconceived notions of what a given text ought to do. This problem, though, may be a false one in other ways. My use of scare quotes around literary suggest part of the problem. Although I will not here fully rehearse those arguments, there have been many debates about how we arrive at the notion of the literary or how we ascribe value to texts—and whether literary value is intrinsic or contingent. Clearly, part of this problem that O'Brian's work creates derives not from the content but his prodigious output. The Romantic cult of the artist has lasted a long time now, and it has little polite to say about the kind of workmanlike

Conclusion: Weighing Anchor

commitment needed to produce twenty novels in the same series (or, as I would rather have it, one novel in twenty parts). Unintentionally, J. R. R. Tolkien, for example, has helped establish the notion that no fantasy story can be told in anything less than three volumes. In other words, output for commercial reasons rather than artistic ones then becomes one of the indictments against "genre fiction." I will not go so far as to suggest that all writers of "genre fiction" have artistic ambitions, but I would also not go so far as to say that literary writers have no commercial ambition. Instead, I would contend that we can view all literature as existing on a spectrum, and that O'Brian's work, however much it may partake of or resemble more commercial enterprises, has been written in a way that certainly suggests it is much more than that. And genre, in any case, cannot be seen as acid to art. What happens, for instance, when so-called "literary writers" like Thomas Pynchon, Michael Chabon, or David Mitchell write "genre-fiction?" All these scare quotes can get dizzying.

Perhaps the oddest phrase in any of the reviews blurbed in *Blue at the Mizzen* comes from the unnamed reviewer from the *Cleveland Plain Dealer* who declares that the novels "show, not for the first time, that storytelling can sometimes rise to the level of art." The strangest part of this quote, for me at least, is the implication that usually storytelling and art fail to go hand in hand. I hope that over the course of this volume, through showing rather than telling, I have made a strong case for the ways in which O'Brian's Aubrey-Maturin saga ultimately transcends the kind of backward compliments and apologies for his work. Let us then separate as the two ships at the end of Patrick O'Brian's final completed Aubrey-Maturin novel—"with hearty ... cheering" for the gift O'Brian has bestowed upon us (261).

Chapter Notes

Chapter 1

1. To be fair, there is a corresponding scene later in the film in which the Captain puts off pursuit of the enemy ship so that the injured Stephen may be operated upon while on land.

2. The "Author's Note" is not paginated.

3. In her essay "Patrick O'Brian: (Dis-)United Irishman at Sea," Kristin Morrison argues that "by undermining orthodox and facile opinions about various matters—race, gender, and sexual behavior, for example—O'Brian subtly calls into question stereotypes of all kinds" (339–340). Although Morrison's primary focus is on how O'Brian seeks to complicate stereotypes of national identity, I am in agreement with her notion that O'Brian never allows stereotypes of any kind—and here I am thinking about those related to bodies—to remain unexamined.

4. This amounts to approximately 224–238 pounds for Jack and 126 for Stephen. Stephen's weight is consistently identified at nine stone while Jack's fluctuates as I have discussed.

Chapter 3

1. The remarkable list recorded by Boon includes Pope Leo XIII, Henrik Ibsen, Thomas Edison and William McKinley, among others (179).

Chapter 4

1. What language to use here, and throughout the chapter, is complicated by the fact that the term "homosexual" is anachronistic to the time in which the novels are set, but not when the novels are written. In addition, most discussions of homosexuality tend to suggest that it was seen more in terms of practice at the times the novels were set than a sexual orientation. Nevertheless, the use of the stand-in terms—sodomite, for instance, and the even more complicating use of pederast—can be difficult to always pin down (in other words, I don't know that the novels use these terms consistently in terms of theories of their use). A good discussion of this problem more generally can be found in Christopher Looby's "'Innocent Homosexuality': The Fiedler Thesis in Retrospect," which discusses shifting understandings of sexuality in the 19th century and the shift to our more modern conception of homosexuality. I have done my best to navigate these challenges, and some inconsistencies in usage conform to inconsistencies I see in the texts themselves. I have tended to use modern terminology when the appropriate term is ambiguous.

2. In *Sexual Visions*, L. J. Jordanova asserts that "during the eighteenth and nineteenth centuries it was taken for

Chapter Notes

granted that the human body was legible, even if there was no consensus on exactly how it could and should be 'read'" (51).

3. Jack's views align with Gilbert's description of how "the ambiguity of homosexual relations probably challenged naval order in a special way" (87). Gilbert asserts that homosexual behavior "was somehow symptomatic of lack of discipline and control in all areas of life" from the point of view of the naval authorities (87).

4. It is possible that the scenario involving Duff was inspired by an actual incident aboard the *Africaine*, the most notable case of apparently fairly widespread homosexual behavior aboard a ship. Extended discussions of this case can be found in Gilbert's "The *Africaine* Court Martial" and in B. R. Burg's "The HMS African Revisited: The Royal Navy and the Homosexual Community."

5. This evidence was found among O'Brian's papers held at the Lilly Library at Indiana University.

6. While in some ways this division of types may appear almost clichéd, Roy Porter underscores the difficulty women of the Enlightenment faced in reconciling both a notion of women as sexual and as rationale (*Facts of Life* 29).

7. I began this section by mentioning the photocopies of Vennette I found among O'Brian's papers. Roy Porter, in *Facts of Life*, has an extensive discussion of Vennette's work, and his description lines up in many ways with how women's sexuality is presented in the novels. Porter notes that "Vennette operated within sexual stereotypes, yet these were quite complex." Vennette finds that "men and women share a common lasciviousness. In both, libidinous fires blaze to engender transports of delight" (76).

8. Later in the series, Stephen will come to more and more agree with McAdam's position and turn his focus more squarely towards humanity.

Works Cited

Bakhtin, Mikhail. "Epic and Novel." In *The Dialogic Imagination*, ed. Michael Holquist. Trans. Caryl Emerson and Michael Holquist. Austin: University of Texas Press, 1981.

───. *Rabelais and His World*. Trans. Hélène Iswolsky. Bloomington: Indiana University Press, 1965.

Battersby, James L. *Reason and the Nature of Texts*. Philadelphia: University of Pennsylvania Press, 1996.

Baudrillard, Jean. "Simulations and Simulacra." In *Selected Writings*, ed. Mark Poster. Trans. Paul Foss, Paul Patton and Philip Beitchman. Stanford, CA: Stanford University Press, 1988.

Berridge, Virginia. *Opium and the People*. New York: Free Association Books, 1999.

Blanning, Tim. *The Pursuit of Glory: Europe 1648–1815*. New York: Viking, 2007.

Boon, Marcus. *The Road of Excess: A History of Writers on Drugs*. Cambridge, MA: Harvard University Press, 2002.

Booth, Martin. *Opium: A History*. New York: Simon & Schuster, 1996.

Booth, Wayne C. *The Rhetoric of Fiction*, 2nd ed. Chicago: University of Chicago Press, 1983.

Bourdieu, Pierre. *Distinction: A Social Critique of the Judgement of Taste*. Transl. Richard Nice. Cambridge, MA: Harvard University Press, 1984.

Brooks, Peter. *Body Work: Objects of Desire in Modern Narrative*. Cambridge, MA: Harvard University Press, 1993.

Burg, B. R. "The HMS Revisited: The Royal Navy and the Homosexual Community." *Journal of Homosexuality* 56, no. 2 (2009): 173–94.

Cook, Matt, Robert Mills, Randolph Trumbach, and H. G. Cocks. *A Gay History of Britain: Love and Sex Between Men Since the Middle Ages*. Oxford: Greenwood World Publishing, 2007.

Dasenbrock, Reed Way. "Do We Write the Text We Read?" *College English* 53, no. 1 (1991): 7–18.

De Certeau, Michel. *The Practice of Everyday Life*. Transl. Steven Rendall. Berkeley: University of California Press, 1984.

Diderot, Denis. *Rameau's Nephew and D'Alembert's Dream*. Trans. Leonard Tancock. New York: Penguin, 1976.

Ellis, Joseph J. *Founding Brothers: The Revolutionary Generation*. New York: Vintage, 2002.

Farrell, Thomas J. "The Diegetic Achievement of Patrick O'Brian." *Papers on Language and Literature* 45, no. 2 (2009): 150–179.

Fish, Stanley. "How to Recognize a Poem When You See One." *Is There*

Works Cited

a Text in This Class? The Authority of Interpretive Communities, 322–337. Cambridge, MA: Harvard University Press, 1980.

Fleishman, Avrom. *The English Historical Novel*. Baltimore: Johns Hopkins University Press, 1971.

Forester, C. S. *Beat to Quarters*. Boston: Back Bay Books, 1966.

Foucault, Michel. *Discipline and Punish: The Birth of the Prison*. Trans. Alan Sheridan. New York: Vintage, 1979.

Freud, Sigmund. "A Difficulty in Psycho-Analysis." Trans. Lytton Strachey. *The Standard Edition of the Psychological Works of Sigmund Freud, Vol. XVII*. London: Hogarth Press, 1986.

Gilbert, Arthur N. "The Africaine Courts Martial: A Study of Buggery and the Royal Navy." *Journal of Homosexuality* vol. 1, no. 1 (1974): 111–122.

———. "Buggery and the British Navy, 1700–1861." *Journal of Social History*, vol. 10, no. 1 (1976): 72–98.

Glausser, Wayne. "Stephen Maturin in the Age of Lamarck: A Fictional Restoration of Cuvier." *Mosaic*, vol. 36, no. 1 (2003): 69–84. Print.

Hayter, Alethea. *Opium and the Romantic Imagination*. Berkeley: University of California Press, 1968.

Homer. *The Odyssey*. Trans. Robert Fagles. New York: Penguin, 1996.

Hutcheon, Linda. *A Poetics of Postmodernism: History, Theory, Fiction*. New York: Routledge, 1988.

———. *The Politics of Postmodernism*, 2nd ed. New York: Routledge, 1989, 2002.

Jameson, Fredric. "Postmodernism and Consumer Society" *The Cultural Turn: Selected Writings on the Postmodern, 1983–1998*. London: Verso, 1998.

Jay, Mike. *Emperors of Dreams: Drugs in the Nineteenth Century*. Sawtry, UK: Dedalus, 2000.

Jordanova, Ludmilla. *Sexual Visions: Images of Gender in Science and Medicine Between the Eighteenth and Twentieth Centuries*. Madison: University of Wisconsin Press, 1989.

King, Dean. *Patrick O'Brian: A Life*. New York: Henry Holt, 2000.

The Last Detail. Dir. Hal Ashbey. Perf. Jack Nicholson, Otis Young, and Randy Quaid. Sony Pictures Home Entertainment, 1999.

Looby, Christopher. "'Innocent Homosexuality': The Fiedler Thesis in Retrospect." In *Adventures in Huckleberry Finn: A Case Study in Contemporary Criticism*, edited by Gerald Graff and James Phelan. New York: Bedford/St. Martin's, 2004.

Lukács, Georg. *The Historical Novel*. Trans. Hannah Mitchell and Stanley Mitchell. Lincoln: University of Nebraska Press, 1983.

Mandelbaum, Maurice. "Family Resemblances and Generalizations Concerning the Arts." *American Philosophical Quarterly*, vol. 2, no. 3 (1965): 219–228.

Master and Commander: Far Side of the World. Dir. Peter Weir. Perf. Russell Crowe, Paul Bettany. 20th Century-Fox, 2008.

Matthee, Rudi. "Exotic Substances." In *Drugs and Narcotics in History*, edited by Roy Porter and Mikuláš Teich. Cambridge: Cambridge University Press, 1995.

McHale, Brian. *Postmodernist Fiction*. New York: Routledge, 1987.

Morrison, Kristen. "Patrick O'Brian: (Dis-)United Irishman at Sea." *Irish Studies Review*, vol. 8, no. 3 (2000): 339–351.

Nealon, Jeffrey, and Susan Searls

Works Cited

Giroux. *The Theory Toolbox: Critical Tools for the New Humanities.* Lanham, MD: Rowman and Littlefield, 2003.

O'Brian, Patrick. *Blue at the Mizzen.* New York: W. W. Norton, 1999.

———. *The Commodore.* New York: W. W. Norton, 1994.

———. *Desolation Island.* New York: W. W. Norton, 1978.

———. *The Far Side of the World.* New York: W. W. Norton, 1984.

———. *The Fortune of War.* New York: W. W. Norton, 1979.

———. *H.M.S. Surprise.* New York: W. W. Norton, 1973.

———. *The Hundred Days.* New York: W. W. Norton, 1998.

———. *The Ionian Mission.* New York: W. W. Norton, 1981.

———. *The Letter of Marque.* New York: W. W. Norton, 1988.

———. *Master and Commander.* New York: W. W. Norton, 1970.

———. *The Mauritius Command.* New York: W. W. Norton, 1977.

———. *The Nutmeg of Consolation.* New York: W. W. Norton, 1991.

———. *O'Brian mss., ca. 1970–1994.* Papers, ca. 1970–1994, of Patrick O'Brian, at the Lilly Library, Indiana University, Bloomington, IN.

———. *Post Captain.* New York: W. W. Norton, 1972.

———. *The Reverse of the Medal.* New York: W. W. Norton, 1986.

———. *The Surgeon's Mate.* New York: W. W. Norton, 1980.

———. *The Thirteen Gun Salute.* New York: W. W. Norton, 1989.

———. *Treason's Harbour.* New York: W. W. Norton, 1983.

———. *The Truelove.* New York: W. W. Norton, 1992.

———. *21: The Final Unfinished Voyage of Jack Aubrey.* New York: W. W. Norton, 2010.

———. *The Wine-Dark Sea.* New York: W. W. Norton, 1993.

———. *The Yellow Admiral.* New York: W. W. Norton, 1996.

Offray de la Mettrie, Julien. *Man a Machine and Man a Plant.* Trans. Richard A. Watson and Maya Rybalka. Indianapolis, IN: Hackett Publishing, 1994.

Palmeri, Frank. *Satire in Narrative.* Austin: University of Texas Press, 1990.

Parker, Patricia. *Literary Fat Ladies: Rhetoric, Gender, Property.* New York: Methuen, 1987.

Pope, Alexander. "Essay on Man." *Essay on Man & Other Poems.* New York: Dover Publications, 1994.

Porter, Roy. *Bodies Politic: Disease, Death, and Doctors in Britain, 1650–1900.* Ithaca, NY: Cornell University Press, 2001.

Porter, Roy, and Lesley Hall. *The Facts of Life: The Creation of Sexual Knowledge in Britain, 1650–1950.* New Haven, CT: Yale University Press, 1995.

Powers, Katherine A. "An Eighteenth-Century Voice." *The Atlantic Monthly*, July 1995.

Welleck, Rene, and Austin Warren. *Theory of Literature*, 3rd ed. Orlando, FL: Harcourt Brace, 1956.

White, Hayden. "The Historical Text as Literary Artifact." *Tropics of Discourse: Essays in Cultural Criticism.* Baltimore: Johns Hopkins University Press, 1978.

Index

addiction 92, 99, 104–8, 113–8
alcohol 6, 85–90, 103, 116, 117
Aristotle 187
Ashby, Hal 150–1
Aubrey, Jack: and genre 15–7; as naval captain 151–4, 160–83; sexuality 20, 120, 141–5, 171–2; weight 2, 17–21, 25, 28–32, 142, 191*ch*1*n*4
Aubrey, Sophie (Sophie Williams) 137–40, 143–4, 151–2, 156–8
Austen, Jane 20

Bakhtin, Mikhail 4, 21–4, 27
Barth, John 23, 57, 70, 72
Barthes, Roland 185
Battersby, James L. 13–4
Baudrillard, Jean 58–9
Berger, Thomas 70
Berridge, Virginia 91
Bettany, Paul 9
Blanning, Tim 61
Blue at the Mizzen 69, 72, 78, 79, 110, 116, 118, 184–6, 189
bodies: and genre 21–22, 45–6; and historical narrative 72–5; as signifiers 5, 11–2, 73, 125, 191*ch*4*n*2
Boon, Marcus 80, 83–4, 92, 96, 104, 107, 108–11, 113, 191*ch*3*n*1
Booth, Martin 94, 96
Booth, Wayne C. 4, 90, 91
Bourdieu, Pierre 11, 17–8, 20
Brooks, Peter 11, 18
Brown, John 92, 97
Burg, B.R. 192*ch*4*n*4
Burroughs, William 107
Byatt, A.S. 71

Casey, John 184
Chichester, Francis 48

cocaine (coca) 6, 84, 86, 99–100, 105, 110–6
Cochrane, Thomas (Lord) 100–1
coffee (caffeine) 6, 80–4, 103, 112, 113–4, 116
Coleridge, Samuel Taylor 91–2, 104, 109
Collingwood, RG 54
The Commodore 1, 112, 116, 117, 131, 138
Cook, Matt 126
Cowley, Abraham 110
Crowe, Russell 9

Darwin, Erasmus 92, 121
Dasenbrock, Reed Way 14
De Certeau, Michel 29, 74–5
De Quincey, Thomas 94, 104, 108–9
Derrida, Jacques 29
Desolation Island 6, 40–1, 73, 139, 147, 151–83, 186
Diderot, Denis 121–2
Doctorow, E.L. 58

Eco, Umberto 71
Eliot, George 7
Eliot, T.S. 13
Ellis, Joseph J. 59

The Far Side of the World 11, 15, 18, 22, 27, 31, 36, 37–8, 39, 76–7, 78, 84, 86, 88, 97–9, 110, 128, 136–7, 139, 140–1, 161
Farrell, Thomas J. 22, 24
Fish, Stanley 4, 14
Fleischman, Avrom 53–6, 59, 65–7
Foreman, Amanda 184–6
Forester, C.S. 25–6, 119; *see also* Hornblower, Horatio
The Fortune of War 29, 42, 64, 67–8, 76, 167
Foucault, Michel 4, 6, 153, 154, 158, 162–3, 164

197

Index

Fowles, John 70
Freud, Sigmund 4, 6, 86, 113, 148, 164, 166–8, 179

genre: and Aubrey-Maturin novels 4–5, 15, 22–4, 49–50, 141, 188–9; and historical novel 5, 23, 49–60; identification 12–5; and novel ideas 23, 35, 39, 45; and satire/epic 21–5, 45; and spy thriller 23, 39, 42; *see also* historical fiction
Gilbert, Arthur N. 124, 192*ch*4*n*3, 192*ch*4*n*4
Glausser, Wayne 64
Graff, Gerald 4
Grass, Gunter 70–1
Guillory, John 13

Hardy, Thomas 157
Hayter, Alethea 96–7
historical fiction: Aubrey-Martin novels as 5, 23, 49–53, 55–60, 65–70, 75–9, 185–6; definition 53–5, 57–8; *see also* postmodernism
Homer 12
homosexuality 6, 123–35, 191*ch*4*n*1, 192*ch*4*n*3, 192*ch*4*n*4
Hornblower, Horatio 15, 16, 25–6, 89, 119, 124
The Hundred Days 56–7, 131
Hunt, Geoff 48
Hutcheon, Linda 71–2

The Ionian Mission 96

Jameson, Fredric 15, 57–60
Jay, Mike 93, 96, 110–1
Johnson, Samuel 92
Jones, John 96
Jordanova, L.J. 191*ch*4*n*2
Joyce, James 22, 30, 188

Kantorowitz, Ernst 154, 162
King, Dean 15, 49–50, 79
King's two bodies 6, 154–83

La Mettrie, Julien Offray de 121, 122
The Last Detail 150–1
Layman, Rob 184–5
Leibniz, Gottfried 100, 103, 121–2
The Letter of Marque 16, 27, 73, 77, 88, 89–90, 95, 101–8, 111, 143

Looby, Christopher 191*ch*4*n*1
Lukács, Georg 56, 65–6

Mandelbaum, Maurice 14
Mariani, Angelo 112
Master and Commander (novel) 1, 17, 18–9, 31, 35, 70, 95, 124–5, 142
Master and Commander: Far Side of the World (film) 9, 48, 123, 191*ch*1*n*1
Matthee, Rudi 84, 92, 93
Maturin, Stephen: appearance 33–5, 44–5, 94–5; drug use 40, 81, 84, 86–7, 90–118, 145–8; love interest 32–3, 94–6; political views 63–4; sexuality 141–8; surgical activities 2, 35–7, 43
The Mauritius Command 23, 38, 63, 91, 95, 131, 136, 138, 144–6, 159
McHale, Brian 54–5, 67, 70
Menand, Louis 4
Miller, J. Hillis 187
Mitchell, David 7, 189
Monardes, Nicholas 110
Morrison, Kristin 191*ch*1*n*3
Morrison, Toni 72

Napoleon Bonaparte 54, 55, 60, 62–3, 66, 184
Napoleonic Wars 5, 32, 55–6, 60–3, 73, 76, 135
Nelson, Horatio (Admiral Lord) 32, 36, 55
Nicholson, Jack 150
Nolan, Christopher 187
The Nutmeg of Consolation 27, 41, 46, 78, 79, 107, 113–5

opium (laudanum) 81, 86, 90–110, 112–6, 117, 147, 172–3

Palmeri, Frank 21
Parker, Patricia 4, 29–32
pastiche 57–8
pederasty 126, 128, 134, 145
Pope, Alexander 122
Porter, Roy 121, 192*ch*4*n*6, 192*ch*4*n*7
Post-Captain 21, 28, 30, 35, 60, 73, 81, 91, 94–5, 137, 152, 161
postmodernism 57–60, 70–5, *see also* historical fiction
Powers, Katherine A. 48–50, 56–8, 60, 71, 76
Pynchon, Thomas 7, 57, 189

Index

Renault, Mary 71
The Reverse of the Medal 27, 77, 99–101, 130, 134, 142
Robbe-Grillet, Alain 187
Royal Navy 66–7, 123, 130–1, 135
Rushdie, Salman 70–1, 72

Scott, Walter 65, 69
sexuality 6, 119–49; and drug use 103, 121, 145–8, 172–3; and Enlightenment 121–3; and women 6, 123, 135–40, 169–73, 192*ch4n6*; *see also* homosexuality; pederasty
slavery 64–5
Smith, Barbara Hernstein 13
Snow, Richard 49, 185
The Surgeon's Mate 33, 44–5, 55, 98, 144, 145, 167
H.M.S. *Surprise* 16, 20, 37, 61, 74, 126, 138, 183

The Thirteen Gun Salute 27, 36, 39, 43, 77–8, 87, 90, 129, 134, 148, 161
tobacco 84, 85, 99–100, 103, 111, 116
Tolkien, J.R.R. 189

Treason's Harbor 18, 39, 55, 82, 95, 98–100, 128–30, 147, 152, 160–1
The Truelove 37, 74, 117, 126, 144–5, 161
21: The Final Unfinished Voyage of Jack Aubrey 3, 33

Vidal, Gore 70
Villiers, Diana 33, 44–6, 64, 94–110, 113, 136–40, 143, 145, 152, 187
Vinnette, Nicolas 136, 192*ch4n7*

War of 1812 68, 76, 144, 182
Warren, Austin 12–4
Weir, Peter 48; *see also Master and Commander: The Far Side of the World* (film)
Welleck, Rene 12–4
White, Hayden 53–4, 78–9
wine 87–9
The Wine Dark Sea 16, 19, 31, 35, 39, 115, 143
Wittgenstein, Ludwig 14

The Yellow Admiral 62–3, 78, 139–40, 143, 156, 183

www.ingramcontent.com/pod-product-compliance
Ingram Content Group UK Ltd.
Pitfield, Milton Keynes, MK11 3LW, UK
UKHW042008140426
5217IPUK00015B/1047